LIBERTY AND LEGISLATION

LIBERTY
AND
LEGISLATION

Edited by
RICHARD HOGGART

FRANK CASS

First published 1989 in Great Britain by
FRANK CASS AND COMPANY LIMITED
Gainsborough House, 11 Gainsborough Road,
London, E11 1RS, England

in association with the Centre for Contemporary Studies

and in the United States of America by
FRANK CASS
c/o 8705 Bollman Place
Savage, MD 20763

British Library Cataloguing in Publication Data

Liberty and legislation
1. Civil rights
I. Hoggart, Richard, *1918–*
323.4

ISBN 0-7146-3308-9

Library of Congress Cataloging-in-Publication Data

Liberty and legislation / edited by Richard Hoggart.
  p.   cm.
  ISBN 0-7146-3308-9
  1. Civil rights–Great Britain. 2. Social legislation–Great
Britain. 3. Legislation–Great Britain. 4. Civil rights.
5. Legislation. I. Hoggart, Richard, 1918– .
KD4080.A75L53 1989
323.4'0941–dc19   88-36430
                                                        CIP

Printed and bound in Great Britain by
BPCC Wheatons Ltd, Exeter

Contents

Preface

This book emerged from the feeling – suspicion, or fear – among a good many people that legislation may now be overreaching itself; that the increase in legislative instruments of many kinds, often promoted with good intentions, may be progressively limiting both our individual and our communal freedoms.

These essays show that these laws fall into several different but overlapping areas. There are those, now very common in the developed or Western world, which – in Jane Austen's phrase – aim to "screw us into virtue" by, especially, requiring us on pain of penalties to behave better towards particular groups who are felt to be at a disadvantage.

There are also those instruments which are designed to reduce the dangers, to individuals and to the community, which new scientific knowledge and technological ability may pose (information processing, genetic engineering, the growing power of economic forces, the legal status of the mentally ill).

Those are two types of legislation which, though not altogether new (how could they be?) have taken on particular force in the last two or three decades.

To the decision to enact such laws has to be added the emergence of a call for more legislation on issues (for instance, about the limits of public protest or the control of obscenity) which are always with us but in some periods lie almost dormant and sometimes are rekindled by an apparent change in attitudes among a majority or, more likely, among a vocal minority who claim to be able to assess and speak for the attitudes of the majority. That such up-and-down issues have come to the front so much and so strongly in recent years is thought by some of our authors to be a sign that the habitual social consensus and its tolerance-ensuring muscles or fibres are now under exceptional strain.

At such times there emerges also the call for a British Bill of Rights. So that call is increasingly heard today, and is fuelled by a growing feeling that in the absence of such a Bill more and more decisions which do affect the rights of us all are being taken

vii

centrally, executively by the government of the day. It has never been fashionable to praise Quangos, least of all their most publicly-responsible peaks, the Royal Commissions or Departmental Committees on this or that aspect of growing public concern (homosexuality, broadcasting, medical ethics). They had and have their cultural limitations. The present author, to take a minute example, was once described by a King-Chairman of Quangos as "not sound" because he had made a joke at a public seminar about the English Youth Service's deference towards the Established Church (now no longer much in evidence). But the increase in rapid executive decisions, the ignoring of the advice of Quangos, or the refusal even to set them up on matters where they seem clearly called for, has heightened one's sense of their value as rubber-bushes or temporary insulators between the people's rights and freedoms and the headlong tendencies of some governments. The United Kingdom's poor record at Strasbourg, where it has been so often summoned to defend itself against alleged denials of human rights and has so often been found wanting, has increased the interest in a possible Bill.

The question of human rights here, in Europe and across the world, points directly at the most difficult perspectives of all. This book is largely British in its approach to the issues in its brief, though many of them figure in other nations – similar in some ways to their features here and differing in other ways, according to the different national histories and cultures. But there is a larger and more fully international set of pressures and changes which we felt a book of this kind could not ignore. Hence we have an essay on the long debate, which has taken place chiefly within the agencies of the United Nations, on the role of the mass media and the rights and duties of journalists – a debate which threw into high and indeed gross relief the weakening in many countries throughout the globe of a commitment to the idea itself of free speech and of the search for objectivity in analysis and reporting; and which asserted the powers of governments to deny these principles.

The second of these international essays examines the decline of the sense of the importance of individual human rights in themselves, that single most important of all the ideas which Europe has, at her best, proposed to the world. Many, perhaps most, of us who would be classed as "liberal progressives" may have a rather simplified view of the universal applicability in all times and places of that key European idea. It is nevertheless chilling to recognise how much in some parts of the world the idea of individual human rights has been swept aside on the grounds that traditional "cultural integrity" must override it (so women must continue to suffer involuntary circumcision); or because the needs of new-nation-building must be paramount, however much individuals are denied rights in the process. It is a sad irony that some people in the West too have lost patience with the principle of individual rights, having decided that it is too often made the justification and exuse for unbridled commercial competition and its twin, consumerism.

There is another way of cutting this kind of cake which these essays bring out very clearly. At first the cut might seem to fall so as to distinguish between laws which have primarily an individual and those which have a community focus. More than one author, inevitably, quotes Mill on the need to keep laws to the minimum required to protect us from others and others from us. So we agree to be ordered to drive on a particular side of the road. Or we have rights against our neighbour incommoding us by blocking our drive, and he against us. But even this minimum-based kind of law often has a community basis, as with regulations against many kinds of pollution, from that of rivers by industrial firms to "noise pollution" of a neighbourhood at night. I put the fashionable phrase in inverted commas because it is a typical linguistic, abstract and polysyllabic distortion which reveals a distortion of thought – as does "nuclear-free zone" when what is meant is "a zone run by a Council which is opposed to nuclear weapons" – whose "freedom" will certainly not be recognised if the bomb is ever dropped; or like that appalling conflation "positive discrimination"; or like "direct action" to mean by-passing the processes of democratic discussion by the use of violence. To put it mildly, such solecisms cloud public debate on important matters.

The approach to broadcasting is the most illuminating recent example of "community legislation". This was the first medium of communication for which virtually all states made regulations in advance or at the time of setting-up. Channels were few, so how were they to be allotted? They could all be held by the state, as in some countries they still are. But if not by the state then by what criteria should their allotment be decided? By the power of the purse? This was called true democratic freedom in some countries though it is not a "freedom" which Mill would have recognised or welcomed, since it is a handling over to the tyranny and constrictions of the search for mass audiences. The final of the three main forms of broadcasting regulation is that which requires broadcasters to act "in the public service" – for example, to "inform, educate and entertain", as in Britain. Whatever the weaknesses of British broadcasting, that prescription has worn remarkably well, better than any other system's guidelines.

At the far end of this line is the assertion that there should be community legislation designed to ensure that no one falls below a certain level in the provision made for them in such matters as expendable income, housing and health; a moral assertion which others, especially in this decade, have increasingly challenged as an encroachment on their freedom because it decides that their taxes shall be spent on causes which to them are irrelevant to the duties of the taxing authority.

In this cutting of the cake, the second main stress is on laws designed to protect us from ourselves, from our own "weaknesses": for our sakes, for the sake of others, and for the health of the community as a whole. Most protections of this kind may arise from the commission of acts which do affect more than ourselves. We may insist that we wish to go to hell in our own way and at our own speed, but boozing too much or smoking too much or taking drugs, though they may damage us more than others, do affect others and cost the community a lot of money: we may kill a child when drunk and driving, occupy hospital beds because we would not wear a seat-belt or have smoked too much. But the total supporter of individual freedom will not accept that those considerations are grounds for restricting our own freedoms to choose the kind of life we want to lead. They might agree that the state has a right to intervene on behalf of the unborn child which the mother- or father-to-be are putting at risk; not much more. And the out-and-out anarchist will question the state's right to restrict the passing on of classified secret information. These are not irresponsible positions and can be valuable cautions even to those of us who have long accepted the state's interventions in matters such as those above. I remember Hugh Carleton-Greene, then Director General of the BBC, saying that the airwaves were open to virtually anyone – but not to those who preached Fascism; and a Communist who, hearing this, asked: "Why not?"

In Britain all such issues are bound up with puritanism, paternal-

ism and the moral urge to do good to others. The laws on drinking
and the taxation levels on that and on smoking are the most glaring
illustration. Booze and fags bring in huge revenues to the Exche-
quer, but there is a deep-seated and widespread feeling that laws
about and taxation on them are and should be partly designed to
discourage, on health and generally moral grounds. So the state
walks a delicate tightrope between these two imperatives.

This leads to that foggy area where care for others who are doing
themselves no good because of one or other bad habit, care for the
silent majority who (it is assumed) may be being harmed without
knowing it, and personal concern, or just plain disapproval – all
come together. The libertarian says: if shopping on Sundays does no
harm to anyone why should the Lord's Day Observance Society
have a right to intervene? if a person chooses euthanasia, what
business is that of the state or of other individuals? "Men must
endure / Their going hence, even as their coming hither" may be a
heroic and beautifully-phrased maxim. But it is not, such a person
would say, the business of the law to push such a moral position into
the realm of the legally-forbidden. And so on and so on.

The area most in play here concerns the British laws on obscenity
in films and videos. Why shouldn't I watch obscene films if I wish?
Because I might as a result of watching such films be led to hurt
others. But there is no compelling evidence to that effect; and much
of Western Europe has already removed those restrictions, with no
discernible increase in obscene public actions. In his essay here
James Ferman, who has the unenviable job of making sure that
present British law is obeyed (his Board is now called the Board of
film "classification" but he knows as well as we do that it is a
censorship body), distinguishes between what is (say, rape)
impermissible on moral grounds and what on manners. Moral
infringements would not, it is argued, be likely to be acceptable on
the screen at any time; manners are about what at any given period a
reasonable citizen would find unacceptable (bare breasts were not
acceptable a few years ago, but are now seen, even on television,
many a night).

For Mr. Ferman this is, understandably, a useful and workable
distinction. Yet no other area in this whole business of legislation so
well illustrates the British habit of mixing morals with manners, a
concern for the freedom of individuals to do what they will so long as
they harm no one else and the use of the law to bring us all nearer to

conforming to a common morals-and-manners practice, one in which the claim of "offensiveness caused" moves over to the justification of censorship. One thing we can be sure of, given the present speed of change: that particular kind of regulation will disappear slowly; but it will disappear.

These essays have been written for non-specialists, for lay readers. And edited by a lay reader. In that reader at least they stirred a range of overlapping thoughts; for which he is grateful.

Richard Hoggart

SCREWING US INTO VIRTUE?

Can we Legislate against Discrimination?

BERNARD CRICK

The general grounds on which legislation and the law can extend our liberties as well as protect established ones need to be considered more carefully than has sometimes been the case – especially among fellow socialists. The old cautionary chestnut is apt. Harry Pollit is at Hyde Park orating about the shape of things to come. The rich ride by on their horses. "None of that after the Revolution, eh Harry?" "You've got it wrong, comrade. After the Revolution you'll all ride horses!" "But I don't like bloody horses." "After the revolution you'll ride bloody horses whether you bloody well like it or not!"

Bagehot said that "one cannot make men good by Act of Parliament". But then he would, wouldn't he? We all know what sort of liberal he was. He was only in favour of the Reform Bill of 1867 because he thought that it would prevent mass democracy and that moderate democracy could be managed by those of us who know best what is good for others. But Harold Laski, who was *almost* a revolutionary, was forever saying that "the state cannot make me happy, but it can prevent me from being happy". We are on sounder ground when we legislate to remove obvious obstacles to human happiness than when legislating to make people happy or good. We legislate draconially to improve road safety marginally, and it took Enoch Powell to put the case powerfully against seatbelts in the name of liberty (without any illusion that the statistical case in favour was other than strong: he argued that accidental death was terrible, but that loss of liberty was worse). But is legislation meant to benefit minorities directly and specially, to discriminate in their favour (oddly called anti-discrimination legislation), analogous? Any answer depends on defining both the problem and the key concepts carefully.

3

There used to be an American comic strip called "There Ought to be a Law" in which a small town busybody demands a law whenever anything shocks, worries or irritates him. He probably invented "Curb Thy Dog", "Don't Litter" and "Report Obscene Matters to Your Postmaster". He was invented to parody the spirit behind the old "blue laws" of which the Prohibition Amendment was only the most famous. Now, of course, he was a right-winger in any context. He first voted for Hoover. His politics would be Reaganite or Thatcherite today, anti-state, all for private action, but he is also famously quick – without showing the least awareness of the contradiction – to demand legislation against anything detestable. Left-wingers want laws of a different kind, but often with equal unhesitating frequency; and no censorship whatever, of course.

Law is, it is worth recalling, not the only form of social control. Banalities are sometimes hard to take seriously, but we should try. The rule of law is preferable to individual or group violence, but there is also tradition, education, example, public opinion, social pressure, enlightened self-interest, and even satire and ridicule. Satire can be extremely important, even in the minimal sense of mouth to mouth jokes in regimes where the law sets out to deny any freedom of speech, publication and assembly to criticise the government – sometimes even prohibiting anything that is not officially blessed. That Orwell in *Animal Farm* and in *Nineteen Eighty-Four* chose the form of satire to argue that liberty and equality can and must be reconciled was not merely a literary strategy; it came from a profound belief that the laughter of free men deflates the pompous and the proud, shows Emperors that they have no clothes other than those we make for them.

Laws need the support of public opinion; but public opinion can, of course, be intolerant, even oppressive, psychologically and physically; good laws and honest judges are needed to protect individual rights against some forms of public opinion and behaviour almost as much as against the state. But such laws are essentially a protection of liberties, constitutional law or protection of the procedures of public debate, not a prescription of substantive outcomes. Laws too far in advance of public opinion can stir resentment and prove self-defeating. Under what conditions can law go further than protection and be a positive enhancement of liberty as an instrument of public policy? Benevolent autocrats or old-fashioned Communist rulers of one-party states have no doubt.

Law is to moralise and improve the population: freedom is being freed from servitude and superstition. So laws are then to be interpreted by underlying intentions, not by what is actually written. But a democratic socialist argument needs to be more subtle because more genuinely libertarian. To the democratic socialist liberty and equality are not to be confused and are both equally valued. An enforced equality would be unjust because unfree in principle, and anyway unworkable in practice and invariably an oppressive and often a bloody debacle when attempted. But liberty for the poor is, indeed, hideously restricted, not merely by their life-chances but in clearly measurable and dramatically different life-expectancies. Therefore the quality and quantity of liberty will be enhanced the more egalitarian a country can become, if it becomes so in a voluntary and widely acceptable manner. But if either "liberty" or "equality" is made the sole criterion of public policy, the result is injustice.

So when should we legislate against discrimination and intolerance? It depends, of course, what one means by these two terms, and what one thinks can be and ought to be the role of the state.

Dr Peter Morris in a thoughtful article, "Being Discriminatory About Discrimination" (in *Politics*, No 1, 1986), has recently drawn attention to the existence of a pressure group called VOAD. Their name denotes the widest possible generality of protest – Voluntary Organisation Against Discrimination. And in September 1987 Mr Ken Livingstone MP was reported as having a one-line Private Member's Bill up his sleeve: to declare all discrimination illegal. Such aspirations come close to what Albert Camus once called "metaphysical revolt". But VOAD, in fact, is a worthy voluntary organisation founded to obtain for the physically disabled legislation against discrimination analogous to that of the Race Relations Act 1965. The name sounds, however, both to Dr Morris's discriminatory ear and mine, meaninglessly general. Surely discrimination needs both a subject and an object, something specified done against a group described? But we readily understand what is meant by discrimination against the disabled and against the physically and mentally handicapped. We think, if we have ordinary human decency, that firms *should* employ people who *can do* a specified job irrespective of other physical handicaps or perhaps just appearance. We notice that some firms do it as a matter of deliberate policy – like the BBC – and others, like the High Street banks, not at all or not up front. Certainly we think it unjust if the disabled or the disfigured are passed over for someone less, or even equally, qualified. But I suspect that VOAD would go further, quite understandably, and argue for either or both of these propositions: (a) that if there are extra costs involved in enabling a handicapped person access, say, to the desk or bench, these should be met either by the employer or the state; or (b) that even if some physically or mentally handicapped persons are not quite as efficient as some others, yet firms of over a certain size should be required by law to employ such and such a percentage. Unlike with race and sex discrimination, there is a problem when it is admitted and obvious that the job cannot be done quite as well, or without additional costs. Very deep water occurs almost as soon as one leaves the obvious shallows. For one could put the question: is the discrimination relevant to the task? And if so, should the state make some other compensation to the disadvantaged person rather than force, for however plausible a public good, an economic liability upon an employer whose efficiency is also commonly supposed to be a public good?

For "discrimination" has come to have two quite opposed meanings. Obviously its basic meaning is simply to distinguish between things, but to many the term has now become entirely pejorative. One does not blink much, if at all, when someone boasts that they are "against all forms of discrimination". One thinks one knows what they mean, probably something like this: "I am against all forms of discrimination which are not relevant to the task at hand or are motivated by irrelevant prejudices against certain categories of people." If one says, "I don't like the look of that chap", this cannot be thought relevant to judgment of the worth of his or her concert performance. (This is to leave aside whether it is prudent for a pianist at the Wigmore Hall to upset the conventions of the occasion and the expectations of that kind of audience by adopting the dress and manners of a Punk Rock personality.) And surely one does and must discriminate between one performance and another – however this is done, however difficult it is to talk sensibly about reasoning in aesthetic judgments, just as difficult but as necessary as in ethics or in political judgments?

For an older meaning of "discrimination" is precisely the making of such judgments. Discrimination was seen as a virtue. To call someone a person of "great discrimination" meant that they were sensitive to difficult distinctions. "Discrimination" was a mixture of empathy and good judgment – an actual judgment has to be made, it is not simply understanding or contemplation; so one discriminates in favour of Bach and against Bartok. To discriminate even about moral matters is not always to moralise. The legendary actress said: "I am no prude but I am not promiscuous. I discriminate." And George Santayana said that he did not favour more chastity but simply more delicacy. To discriminate is not necessarily to condemn: "For myself, I simply prefer post-modernism", or watching West Ham. Not everyone would agree, however. Some would say that all such discriminations are arbitrary even if they are not hurtful ("I know, you just think I've got no taste"). So it comes to be believed that people should not be hurt or disadvantaged by arbitrary judgments of any kind. "Prizes for everyone", or no prizes at all and no competitive sport. ("Honorary degree, indeed; now can you see what they've done to you!") Such opinions are by no means a preserve of the ultra-Left. The folk philosopher Schultz sees it as endemic in bourgeois American society. "Charlie Brown, Charlie Brown! Gee, you were dim in school today." "Whad ya mean, 'dim'?" "I mean you got the answers wrong." "I thought you only had to be sincere." Lionel Trilling in a famous review of the Kinsey Report on human sexuality (reprinted in his *The Liberal Imagination*) saw it as exemplifying a democratic belief that all facts are equal, that all patterns of statistically significant behaviour are therefore valid. Such a belief was perhaps liberating in some respects, he said, but destructive of sensibility and discrimination in others. Aristotle had said that the fallacy of pure democracy was the belief that because men are equal in some things therefore they are equal in all.

Discrimination is not merely a virtue in aesthetic judgments, it is very close to the idea of "discretionary judgment" which Richard Titmus once argued in a famous article in *The Political Quarterly* (Vol. 42, No. 2) was essential for the just application of the complicated rules of the Supplementary Benefit Commission by counter staff (and that therefore these staff were scandalously under-trained and under-educated compared to the framers of the discretionary rules themselves). If "profiles" of pupils, for instance, are to supplement written and external examinations, discrimination will grow more important not less. Without discrimination there is only

7

inflexible bureaucracy, no individual case can truly be "considered on its merits". Discretion is also close to the idea of "good political judgment", which plainly people possess to rather different degrees – even politicians. Ronald Beiner has cogently argued in a recent book, *Political Judgment*, that it is a virtue more often found among observers than among fervid activists. It is a rare player who can assess the strategies and tactics of a game as well as a knowledgeable, experienced and reasonably dispassionate spectator – even if the spectator is powerless to intervene. Lionel Trilling saw discrimination as the supreme liberal virtue both in aesthetic and in moral judgments.

So it is foolish to think that all discrimination is unjust. It depends what one is talking about. All types of discrimination are prescriptive, positively or negatively; something is judged good or bad and an action is taken as a consequence (even if the action is only to express the judgment publicly, the attempt to influence). To say that all discrimination is bad, undemocratic, hurtful and/or elitist, is the same kind of fallacy as to say that any exercise of authority is authoritarian. Just as we should discriminate, relevantly, tolerantly, cautiously, wisely and well, so we should respect authority – when the person claiming or recognised as having authority is fulfilling a function that is widely accepted as needed and exercises it openly with some special skill or knowledge widely agreed to be in the public interest. But someone is authoritarian, indeed, when he or she tries to generalise the authority they have for specific and acceptable purposes into other and irrelevant spheres. Our noble ancestors were more sensible than modern trendies to protest against the abuse and *extension* of authority, to demand *limitation*, specification and accountability, not to denounce any exercise of authority as authoritarian, or any act of discrimination as bad.

When is discrimination unjust? Eileen Fry has recently defined (in *Politics*, No. 1, 1985) two common but unsatisfactory accounts of unjust discrimination, which she calls "the intentional view" and the "proportional view", and usefully suggests a better one, which she calls the "counterfactual criterion".

The intentional view "holds that a necessary condition of an action being described as discriminatory is that the agent's intention in acting is to discriminate". If someone is not hired or is sacked because they are black, the employer's action is plainly discriminatory. But if a university department offers places strictly according

8

Can we Legislate against Discrimination?

to merit as determined by GCE results which results in no black applicants being successful, this could not be called discriminatory by the intentionality criterion. So to make the absence of an intent to discriminate a condition of a policy being condemned as discriminatory is, she rightly argues, too restrictive as a guide to social policy. And, I would add, intentions can be frustrated and the unintended consequences of policies can be more significant than the premeditated intentions. Also someone may be radically prejudiced, but partly because he or she knows that we suspect and are watching, nothing much happens. And if we are wise we may think that it is easier to make prejudiced people behave politely than it is to "eradicate prejudice" (as is sometimes proclaimed to be the object of teaching on race relations in secondary schools – for one, two or at the most three hours a week).

The proportional view holds that the intention of the agent is irrelevant and that only the result should be considered. "An action is discriminatory if it results in a larger proportion of people of one type than another being treated in a certain way." The university department, however fair, objective and dreadfully time-consuming are its selection procedures, is discriminatory if the result is "a larger proportion of whites than blacks" relative to qualified applicants, or the society is discriminatory if the proportion of whites to blacks admitted is simply very different from that of the age group in society as a whole. This is, indeed, what people often mean by discrimination. I think Eileen Fry's example would have been even stronger if put in terms of the employment of unskilled school-leavers in a supermarket or a High Street chain-store. Some would think that it is not the relative proportions that can constitute discrimination but the proportions of those with equal qualifications. Admittedly others say that one had to look at "the system" as a whole, the huge discrimination against blacks as a whole, so it is no accident that they are poor and as under-qualified as most of the poor; and it is no better to discriminate against people because they are poor than just because they are black. Indeed, as a matter of fact, it is at the bottom of the labour market that racial discrimination in employment is most flagrant and obvious. Yet the difficulty with the "proportional view" is, indeed, that it makes the class of discriminatory actions potentially an impossible large one. You are being discriminated against both because you are black and because you are poor (and poverty is even more difficult to forbid by legislation).

9

Yes, society as a whole is discriminatory. We could just as well throw in the sponge and sit down and wait for the revolution. And, even on an individual level of false consciousness, what if most of the friends I ask to my home are black, Jewish, homosexual or otherwise foreign – am I discriminating against the plods and the normals? Or what if I only ask a black to my house because he or she is black? This action is surely discriminatory, even if unimportant and silly.

So Fry invokes *"a counterfactual criterion"*: "an action is discriminatory if it results in people being treated differently than they would have been had they been different in some respect" – as in the common cry, "if I was a man you bloody well wouldn't treat me like that!" or "If I was white you'd be all over me". I am discriminating against someone if I treat them differently than I would have done if they had been of a different ethnic group. If I refuse a job to a black fellow it is discriminatory if I could have offered it to him and would have offered it to him had he been a proper white man. My motive may not, of course, arise from overt racial prejudice, but from the tradition of employment or the known views of other workers (which is why intentionality is often difficult to pin down); or the unfortunate man may have been "one black too many" in a strictly controlled, well-meant and enforced quota system (which then might not be discrimination on the proportionality view).

Yet if discrimination can be good or bad, is it ever right to discriminate racially? Some say it is, when we discriminate against a majority in favour of a disadvantaged minority: that reverse discrimination or *positive discrimination* should be enshrined in public law, whether for compensation, to overcome prejudice or to set a trend going. Under such a policy, to follow the useful counterfactual criterion, in certain situations blacks would be better off than they would have been if they were white and whites worse off than they would have been if they were black. Turning everything on its head may be what we often want to do, as in the anarchist imagination of Dario Fo, but it may not be either justice or what is popularly acceptable as justice; no guide indeed, as Bentham would have put it, to rational grounds for legislation.

Suppose we wished to legislate to end discrimination against blacks and women in employment. The grounds for doing this are obvious. Prejudice must play some part in explaining the dramatic

10

disproportion of young blacks unemployed and women under-employed. Two strategies could be pursued. All firms over a certain size would have, subject to legal sanctions, to bring their whole work force over a period of time up to the proportionality of women and blacks actively seeking work. And where special qualifications or skills are needed, entrance standards could be lowered somewhat in the hope that over the years the same proportionality could be obtained.

With unskilled jobs there are not insurmountable problems, except political will. And I assume that a serious policy of positive discrimination would not leave it to individuals to have to prove discrimination, or – as at present – to an understaffed statutory body to take cases through the courts after exhausting conciliatory procedures. Employment statistics would speak for themselves. It is hard to see why there need be any real impairment of efficiency: certainly it would be an interference with the freedom of employers, but not in any manner necessarily harmful to their material interests in employing people at all. With semi-skilled occupations the effect could be appreciable: to shift some training from the schools and FE colleges to in-service or day-release training. But training for industry and training by industry is a shifty borderland at best, full of mutual delusion, deceit and humbug among employers, educationalists and politicians alike. And where objective entrance standards have to be lowered, they might only be lowered marginally; and most of us are well aware that such differences can soon be made up. GCE results, for example, are not a good predictor of final degree results. And a National Curriculum will almost certainly do no better: many people do grow and mature over two, three or four years. Motivation and good teaching can make up for a lot of differences at the point of entry – as shown by the experience of mature students without normal qualifications at the Open University, Birkbeck College, Goldsmiths' College and elsewhere. Detail is infinitely arguable but if there was a will there would be a way and the practical consequences, whether for industrial and commercial efficiency or for educational standards, are unlikely to be great. It probably wouldn't make any appreciable difference at all. (At least no one is silly enough to claim that efficiency and standards would necessarily *improve* if such discriminations were ended – as the original suffragettes argued would happen to the whole tone of society, just as their opponents believed that Naval

11

Estimates would never again pass the House of Commons. It is the *injustice* that is the primary issue even where systematic discrimination, as in South Africa, is also inefficient.)

Objections of principle would arise, however, when better qualified whites or males were excluded from jobs or places by either a quota system or discriminatory lowering of standards in favour of the groups discriminated against. The United States Federal Courts, for instance, seem to be drawing a line (in an admittedly somewhat confused situation) between, on the one hand, legislation for equal opportunity and fair employment practices and, on the other, positive discrimination rules for college entry when unsuccessful but better qualified white candidates brought suit. It seems to offend against natural justice to make some individuals, as it were, innocent and accidental victims of measures designed to correct an historical collective wrong, a collective wrong involving deep-rooted social and economic inequalities. Certainly it offends against what ordinary people think is justice. It is quite another matter to use public law far more strongly than we have yet done in mainland Britain against employment practices and admissions procedures that deliberately or needlessly exclude some groups of people, even if they are not designed to be deliberately racially or sexually discriminatory.

The case of religious discrimination in employment in Northern Ireland is interesting. Since 1976 there has been the Fair Employment (Northern Ireland) Act which makes discriminatory hiring illegal and which encourages employers to subscribe to a declaration of intent to implement "the principle of equality of opportunity". More recently failure to subscribe to such a declaration entails a firm losing public grants and contracts. It has some effect, even if currently unemployment among Catholics runs at about 25 per cent and among Protestants at 13 per cent (and that in a situation where one can assume a rough equality of schooling). Of course it will take another two decades before the results of the old blatant discrimination decline so far as to give, positively, anything like proportionality of employment in large firms and, negatively, an equitable proportionality of unemployment. Some would argue of such laws that the dogged officials of the Fair Employment Agency and of the Equal Opportunities Commission should have been given more teeth and have used them to bite hard more often. But all sides recognise that with majority opinion and behaviour still hostile even to the principle of equal opportunities, the limits of manoeuvre are narrow and to apply positive discrimination on any large scale would result in bitter strikes at the best and violent riots at the worst.

Recently a series of American states have enacted the "MacBride Principles". These require American companies trading in these states not to do business with or invest in any firm in Northern Ireland which cannot prove that it has abolished religious discrimination in hiring but, beyond that, prove also that it practises positive discrimination in favour of, some drafts say, "the minority", others say "minorities". And the MacBride principles demand special training programmes "to assist minority employees to advance to higher paying jobs requiring greater skills". (This fits Eileen Fry's "counterfactual" definition of discrimination perfectly. "Sorry George, you're not eligible for the scheme. For one thing, you're over-qualified, and for another you'd have to be a Papist.") Now it is far from clear whether the United States Supreme Court will sustain these ventures of New York, Massachusetts and Connecticut etc. into foreign policy, nor whether the Bills are meant to destabilise Northern Ireland by wrecking investment rather than to steer it to the havens of the righteous. One standard clause demands that employees must "guarantee the safety of minority employees travelling to and from work"! Americans opposed to such legislation, just as British Government spokesmen and even John Hume, all point out that the principle of positive discrimination would contradict the established principal of "equal opportunity" in the 1976 Act. There seems no way around this dilemma. The basic problem is, of course, that the social conditions for genuine "equality of opportunity" need to predate by far the morning of that individual job interview.

In general, quite apart from Northern Ireland, the argument is strong that positive discrimination is inequitable to other individuals accidentally disadvantaged. And the social costs of trying to enforce such a policy throughout British industry might well be too high: disruptive, stirring prejudice swiftly rather than allaying it gradually and lastingly. When the United States Supreme Court finally moved against statutory segregation in schools, in *Brown et al versus the United States* (1954), it enjoined School Boards to desegregate with "deliberate speed". It did not allow deliberate prevarication and infinite delay, as a small multitude of subsequent actions and cases showed, but it recognised that, in matters of such deep prejudice

13

and tradition, time is needed. Legislation can be effective, but only if conceived as one part of broad strategy through time – not as the single easy answer.

Short of legislation, there is obvious sense in the state itself setting an example (if the Government chooses). With regard to the employment of women in the civil service, to a large degree over the years it has; but as regards their prospects of promotion and share of higher level jobs, the occupational profile still demonstrates shameful injustice to women. The same is true of the judiciary and, most unhappily, the police service. But at least some black faces are through the station door and behind the counter. The police claim that recruitment endeavours are now strenuous but that sufficient recruits at the standard are not forthcoming – perhaps, indeed quite likely, as with recruitment of Catholics for the Royal Ulster Constabulary. So here, indeed, would be a case for some positive discrimination. Of course black applicants would have to be shown to have scored far higher on personality factors in the entrance tests to compensate for a greater flexibility about the CSEs and "O" levels, but as an experienced examiner, both in higher and secondary education, I'm reasonably sure the entry boards could fit that one up, quietly and without fuss, if the will was stronger and the views of the Police Federation were slightly more public-spirited in all respects.

Do we count the BBC and the Independent Broadcasting Authority as part of the state? In some senses, yes. They are statutory bodies, public quasi-monopolies. And with the exception of no other institution except Parliament they are treated as an embodiment of the national image and consciousness. They are often in a better position than the government machine itself to set a public example of positive discrimination; certainly they can act with greater speed and visible presence. Think of the emergence of black presenters and personalities, particularly on television. And remarkably more women in publicly prominent positions than a decade ago. Is this really a case of positive discrimination? Or is it actually tougher for them to get there, needing, like black footballers, more consistent merit? One simply will never know. But some of them must be the result of a quiet policy of positive discrimination rather than a timely consequence of demographic and educational change. There is no apparent diminution of standards. Perhaps the mark sheets of interviewing panels might show a difference, and positive policy directives could have favoured some blacks and some women over some white males. But such positions are not strictly competitive on purely objective scales of assessment, as are most public examinations and university and polytechnic entrance. It partly depends on what qualities you are looking for. Black skins and female characteristics should be highly relevant. In such employment procedures there must be safeguards against nepotism, favouritism, partisanship and corruption; but considerations stemming from broadly agreed public policy can be relevant, need not be excluded. One presumes it was not always a matter of marks that rather suddenly produced so many soft Irish accents on the airwaves and Ulster brogues giving us the bad weather. For a long time the BBC has tried, with obvious success, to deemphasise "RP" (received pronunciation), which must have involved some discrimination against well-qualified candidates with marbles in their mouths from the English public schools. Imagine, however, the difficulties of trying to achieve this through legislation. Government, through example and public policy, could do much more to combat unjustifiable discrimination even without bringing in new legislation and raising basic issues of liberty. It could put its own house in order first (as some local authorities have begun to do), in the civil service and perhaps one day even in the party itself, or at least the party machine over which it has more control. Example is extremely important as a trigger for social change. The role of television is essentially exemplary (and very important for that) rather than a serious contribution to reducing black unemployment.

Of course there is some mockery and cynicism about the search for a token woman and a token black for every damned committee. Professional black women are headhunted with indecent fervour. But if "tokenism" is partly a fraud and often a deliberate delaying tactic or buying off, it is also a foot-in-the-door. It may not be enough. The motives of the white male majority may be suspect and self-protective, but their reaction shows that some general pressures of opinion can reach them. Politics works like that. The pressure just has to kept up and increased. Once there is a foot in the door, it is far more difficult to close. A great deal more positive discrimination can be done by institutions informally that might offend principles of natural justice if attempted by legislation. In a modest way, for instance, I've quite often practised a form of positive discrimination in appointing or commissioning women. I mean that if two candidates are roughly or arguably equal in their

15

claims, then gender becomes a relevant factor, especially if one glances at the male majority around one and thinks what a disappointment most of them have been compared to that early promise shown at interview. If the will is there. Or not. Once upon a time I was an external assessor for the appointment of a Statutory Lecturer at the University College of Galway. The language of the University of Ireland Act was clear. If two candidates were of equal merit in the subject, preference must be given to the one who spoke Irish, or spoke it better in a specially convened second interview. We were advised from on high that there could never be such a thing in nature as two candidates of exactly equal merit. But if the field had been tight at the final fence, I'd have discriminated in favour of a woman or a black – had there been one.

Legislation is more likely to be successful in removing or prohibiting obvious discriminatory practices than in attempting to obtain proportionality, still less a positive discrimination. On matters that depend on people's behaviour changing, it is difficult for legislation to work if it runs too far in front of public opinion. Consider the utter failure of statutory attempts to control prices and incomes. But also consider that when the proposals for the breath-analyser or nosebag and tougher speed limits came forward, the RAC and the AA's representatives advised Barbara Castle, then Minister of Transport, that the measures would be unworkable, would lead to a lack of respect for the law akin to the attitude of the respectable drinking public under American prohibition, would bring the police and the middle classes into similar and continual conflict. Her judgment that this was rubbish, that they either did not know or were misrepresenting the views of their members, was quickly confirmed by an opinion survey commissioned by her department; and eventually by the result of the legislation. The survey showed that few motorists liked the idea but they nearly all accepted the need for the new law dourly. It was still only the workers who felt that the police were getting at them the whole time.

This may be a good parable for racial and sexual discrimination. The rational target is not agreement to positive discrimination nor a fermented outbreak of spontaneous love between ethnic groups, but is simply acceptance of each other and of procedures for equality of opportunity. Any legislation intending a mass effect on behaviour can only work when public opinion will at least accept it. There is a lack of serious studies of kinds of legislation that actually

16

need public support to work, or at least which are unworkable with widespread non-compliance. (We are much better at studying campaigns than at monitoring results.) In political life not everything is agreement or rejection: for many purposes it is enough that people will accept something. No Government, for instance, can hope for agreement to any constitutional settlement in Northern Ireland – a high level of acceptance would be grand.

Sometimes we set our sights, meaning well, too high. Let me illustrate by raising the related question of tolerance and intolerance. How far should we tolerate intolerance? Can we legislate against intolerance?

The trouble with Americans was, Martin Chuzzlewit's manservant remarked, that "they have so much liberty they can't help taking a few liberties with it". We only obey the maxim that what is good for the goose is good for the gander (or vice versa) grudgingly. We do not always approve of the use to which others put their liberty. Liberty, said Orwell, "is telling people what they do not want to hear" – absurd as a general definition of liberty but a vivid characteristic of it.

People can use their liberties in ways of which we deeply disapprove, often with good reason. But when are the reasons strong enough truly to say, "There ought to be a law"? The debate is endless but generally a minimal view (and views should be minimal) picks out actions which threaten the ability of others to exercise their proper liberties, clear and present danger to the safety of the state, assault and theft and – in the great language of the Common Law – "incitement to a breach of the peace". But short of actual violence it can sometimes be thought that to defame or abuse someone grossly and solely on the grounds of their race, religion or sexual identification, should be illegal. That people who do this should be reviled, morally condemned, even ostracised, I have no doubt; but should they be punished by law? The debate is familiar and it partly turns on our fears that to proscribe any opinion, even dishonestly held, can be the thin end of the wedge given the propensity to oppression inherent in all government; but to allow some things to be said publicly at all – for example racial abuse – puts an intolerable constraint on the objects of the abuse, always fellow human beings, often fellow citizens, to restrain themselves from striking back. And others single out obscenity and pornography as intolerably offensive to women.

It is worth reminding ourselves, therefore, that all tolerance, however benign, contains an element of disapproval. Tolerance historically is not the same as indifference (see *Political Theory and Practice*, Crick, 1973). People did care passionately about religious commitments, but sometimes were willing, partly for philosophical and partly for prudential reasons, to limit their reactions. And it was for God to punish heretics, not men. Think of the first statute of the reign of William and Mary, "The Act of Toleration to Dissenting Protestants ..." The power is there and the object of toleration is named. The country still felt threatened by religious diversity, official policy still frowned on dissent, but it was not to be persecuted or proscribed generally (except for membership of universities, commissions in the army, membership of Parliament and of most of the professions). It was not tolerant enough, by our standards, indeed to some of the best minds of the time, but it was tolerant in the sense that it gave an area of freedom to a group of which the state generally disapproved, and the state had the undoubted power to give or withhold. I cannot attach any meaning to my being tolerant about things over which I have no power or influence.

A tolerant society and a permissive society are very different ideas: the one limits disapproval and the other manifests total indifference or a belief that "anything goes". Actually a society using "anything goes" as a rule simply couldn't work. There must be some conventional moral rules. We may not take all of them that seriously but we must observe most of them or else it would be collisions all the time – as if there was no arbitrary rule of the road. Now it is a fallacy to think that the opposite of tolerance, or the negation of tolerance, is intolerance: it is indifference. For I negate indifference not by intolerance but by caring for the issues, and consciously tolerating, to some degree, different behaviour. The opposite of intolerance is not indifference, but some firm rival view: the negation of intolerance is love or conversion, being taken over by the other side.

This logical point fits in with the observed psychological phenomenon that extremists often don't lapse into or achieve sweet tolerance and moderation, but can abruptly change sides, adopt some rival harsh fanaticism. The intolerant mind with the fanatic heart lives in an either/or world. (Alas, it is so hard to find truculent

18

moderates; the old republican spirit needs reviving.) The tolerant person is a pluralist, he or she observes different moral codes or ways of life within a nation or wider community and has some familiarity, sympathy even, with several. She or he can manage this pluralistic moral economy by experience and by continual, usually conscious, compromises. If we did not have a consciousness of living among different and authentic moral codes, calling for disapprovals as well as limited acceptances, we would be accepting everything, therefore indifferent, permissive, dwelling in a kind of could-not-care-lessitude – wholly cynical and undiscriminating. The conservative accepts everything as he finds it, the anarchist accepts everything as it can be imagined as an arena for personality. For any such society of total scepticism to work, it has to have, of course, clear and rigid conventions (as Hume was well aware), like a Tory club or an anarchist commune.

I stress this element of *disapproval* in tolerance, rather than the equally real dimension of *acceptance*, because I hold to the view (to begin to summarise all this very simply) that if we modern liberals and democratic socialists were not so inhibited in expressing *moral* disapprovals publicly, there would not be felt so much need for public law in these difficult areas. I want to see far greater ethnic and sexual equality – they are parts of and test cases for the idea of an egalitarian society: but I am convinced that we have to do it for the most part by ourselves collectively, by persuasion, writing, education, above all by example. The courts can only deal with extreme cases and the public law can only provide a broad framework for social action, not itself a constant series of socially transforming legal interventions. For such interventions to work they would need, in any case, considerable and constant public support. State intervention is not always appropriate to social change. Some broad framework of legislation is needed to set standards, and some positive discrimination is desirable in symbolically important areas that can have an exemplary effect elsewhere. Why is it left to campaigning organisations to point to the fact that so few young blacks are to be seen in banks? Surely all shareholders and customers are not racist – more likely they are indifferent, when they should not be. They should be intolerant of the banks' indifference. I like Gellner's maxim: social tolerance and intellectual intolerance.

We need to condemn what we think is wrong and label what we think is nonsense, nonsense. Demands to censor obscenity and

19

pornography (dangerous areas for law, indeed) would be less strong if those who oppose *all* censorship (or so they say) so strongly gave a little time to denouncing rubbish and condemning, indeed, much that is called pornography (see *Crime, Rape and Gin*, Crick, 1974). I sympathise with those feminists who sometimes use aggressive and direct tactics against people who make their living by pornographic images of the female body, indeed see most of this as not just offensive to women but as anti-sexual, the negation of eroticism. But if I call a play both pornographic and bad, this no more constitutes a cry to have it banned than if I call another trivial and silly (only a cry for sensible people not to waste their time and money). The trouble is that as soon as some idiot demands that a play or a film is banned (not being able conceptually to distinguish between law and morality), another load of idiots (with a similar conceptual hang-up) spring up (usually in the ICA, *City Limits* or *Time Out*) to say that it is a work of art or "authentic anti-art", therefore untouchable, or that something else like it one day could be a work of art, or have faint elements of authenticity about it. When élites turn permissive rather than tolerant, ordinary people give ready support to politicians and popular journalists who bellow, "There ought to be a law." They may just want it condemned, or to hear the healthy cry of the home supporters, "What a load of rubbish!" I believe in public opinion. I far prefer it to constricting laws. But the literary and artistic élite have to try to reach it and influence it, not to demand both to be left alone and to be given a privileged position.

To think that tolerance is the antithesis of intolerance can actually lead to false optimism. Consider the most elaborate and large-scale study of race relations in modern Britain, E.J.B. Rose and associates, *Colour and Citizenship: A Report on Modern British Race Relations* (OUP, 1969). A survey was commissioned that ranked respondents on a conventional scale. At one end were the "Prejudiced" (a mere 10 per cent), at the other 35 per cent "Tolerant" (hurrah!) and in between came a shifty 17 per cent "Prejudice-inclined" and a wobbly 38 per cent "Tolerant-inclined".

Jacob Adorno in his *Authoritarian Personality* first used such a scale, with authoritarian traits at one end and democratic at the other. But such conceptualisings can be very misleading. Adorno argued that a state was likely to be authoritarian when its leadership élite had those kinds of character traits, and democratic if democratic. But Edward Shils argued, in a famous review in *Social Research*, that no democratic polity was likely to hold together for five minutes that could not make use of both these allegedly antithetical personality types, socialise a fair number of the authoritarian types and make the democrats reasonably tough-minded in their own defence. In *Colour and Citizenship*'s survey is someone in the ranks of the "Prejudiced" 10 per cent necessarily intolerant? He may be well aware of his prejudices, and lean over backwards to be nice to blacks, Jews or women or whatever. His expressed beliefs or even intentions could be awful but his actual behaviour could be impeccable, perhaps just the way he was brought up. I've known such people. Or is a man certified "Tolerant" necessarily devoid of prejudice? Consider the editor of a liberal-minded quality newspaper who works among beautiful (white) people who detest what is happening in South Africa and North Balham, but he lives nowhere near Balham and happens not to employ any blacks on the editorial and senior management floor (quite a lot down below, however) and never entertains British blacks, only visiting heads of state or American actors. Can his behaviour be called "tolerant" or "unprejudiced" when the issue simply doesn't arise, or he doesn't let it? He is neither overtly prejudiced nor capable of running up any kind of score for intoler-ance on even the most subtle attitude survey; but does he deserve the accolade of "tolerant" (if that is something positive, capable of disapprovals, and restraints) rather than "indifferent"? I think employers have to be put to the behavioural, not just the attitudinal test. My imaginary editor would be in an excellent position to practise prominent positive discrimination.

Perhaps the darker point is that racial and sexual prejudices are very hard to eradicate, but easier to contain. I've used this example before, and it caused terrible misunderstanding; but let me try again. I could admit to some prejudice against homosexuals, and, indeed, rationalise it. Unfair to women. "How will the world be populated!?" Sometimes a nepotic free-masonry. Absurd claims to preeminence in the arts. A code of behaviour impossible to generalise as a moral rule to satisfy Kant. Some worries about seduction of the young. And not merely no homoerotic feelings myself, but a tingle of revulsion. Finally, a great rage at their rape of a good and common English word to now render many great lines ludicrous. Never can the great joke come cleanly again, that the

Beggar's Opera made Gay rich and Rich (the theatre owner) gay. But I was strongly for the abolition of section 40 of the Criminal Code, and am strongly against discrimination (except in a few cases where I think it relevant – teaching in single sex boys' schools, for obvious example). I cannot see any conceivable case for positive discrimination, however. Yet I know several gays as friends. Out of civility I reluctantly use the term they now choose. I had a very dear friend once who was a homosexual. My tolerance had a strong cognitive element, as they say, not simply moral: I needed to know his tastes and habits in order to know on what occasions to meet, when to stay and when to leave. I say "my" tolerance, for the point is unavoidable that it is the majority who have to and should tolerate minorities, or in that case and in those days the one whose promiscuity was legal had to tolerate the one whose faithfulness was illegal. Of course some, for this reason, say that all tolerance is condescension: they don't want tolerance but full acceptance, even love. Sorry, that is too much. We live by our exclusions as well as our inclusions. Groups like individuals often get along best by knowing each other well enough to know when to keep a distance as well as when to mingle. In a pluralist society public law may need to be invoked both to help preserve communities, and also to ensure that the young of either sex can leave them.

Bagehot was right. One cannot make men good by Act of Parliament. We can and must use the state to create a *more* economically equal society so that people can exercise their liberties more fully, but it is better that it is done by enabling people to help themselves. Mrs Thatcher is half right, in rhetoric at least; but to help everyone to help themselves as others can means massive income support and redistribution of incomes through the tax system. Positive discrimination in taxation according to income is a sound principle of social justice. We need to combat mass unemployment and wages so low that many people in employment are also in poverty; but by devices like negative income tax, redistribution through the tax system for a guaranteed minimum wage, not by the state assuming or resuming direct control of industry or attempting to control prices and incomes.

There is a general revulsion from too much state control, state enterprise, standardised welfare and centralisation. Mrs Thatcher has part caught the mood of revulsion from "the gentlemen in

Whitehall know best" and part fermented it, but like the "there ought to be a law" individualist she has also added to centralisation by irrational dislike of liberties actually being exercised in local government and in public sector education. Her rate-capping, then her destruction of the rating system and her educational policies are creating a centralisation of power possibly greater than the decentralisation effected by her war on Quangos and campaign for privatisation.

Yet things will never go back to what they were before. The post-war welfare state was too rule-bound and too apt to do good for people through professional social workers, etc., rather than finding ways of enabling people, in groups and individually, in a variety of forms, cooperative, municipal and commercial, to do good for themselves. The welfare state, the new Leviathan, was benign and well-meaning but it was inhabited only by civil servants, social workers and clients. There were also politicians, but they were only supposed to mediate, not to change anything; and there were taxpayers who were to pay for it all. Actually, despite Tory legend, the revolt did not come from the taxpayers. Several surveys have recently shown that while everyone says they would like lower taxes, most people also say they would rather pay more if it could restore the over-stretched Health Service and the run-down schools. I think the revolt came because people began to see the professionals not merely as too interventionist, but as a self-preservation society. Even occasional readers of the popular press will be aware that the NUPE (National Union of Public Employees) campaign against Health Service cuts, like the NUT's (National Union of Teachers) to save the schools, was pictured as flagrant self-interest: jobs for the boys. Unfair, grossly exaggerated; but they could not see that they were not the people to make the case. The professionals by becoming too organised have then treated the public either as clients or as ungrateful and stupid dupes of a new rabble-rousing Conservatism and a popular Press, rather than as active agents. "We are all here on earth to help each other", Auden parodied, "but what the others are here for, God only knows."

There is a lot of talk now in the Labour Party about "an enabling state", neither a command state nor a welfare providing state. There is a reappraisal of the whole idea that the central state is necessarily able to achieve, or should even attempt to achieve, uniform social justice, including racial and sexual equality, etc. The dispersal of power, not its concentration, may actually get more done, though not always in the same way or even the same direction, let alone at the same speed. There will be much greater variation in outcomes than reformers previously envisaged, whatever the actual reality – which they always attributed to the failure of particular plans, not to central planning in general. Individualism and liberty are now taken back into the democratic socialist Pantheon. Labour's version of an individual at his or her best is still a more sociable and a less competitive animal than Thatcher's Man (also more North British than pseudo-American), but the difference is no longer absolute. Egalitarianism in many parts of the country and in some sections of society is now the style, in dress, manners and friendships; but it is less tied to ideas of formal economic equality. And respect for traditional communities is now a hidden common bond between much Labour sentiment and the values of the Old Tories among the "Wets" – as can come into the open in bizarre alliances for protests of local conservationists or environmentalists.

Amid all these changes it seems to me reasonably clear that reformers will never go back to a simple faith that with the right legislation from Whitehall and Westminster racial equality can be achieved, sexual equality, positive discrimination for the handicapped, the Health Service restored and rendered uniformly swift and good, all schools brought to much the same level. We have now learned, the hard way, that in a civilised society we do not just want unjustified discriminations in public provision abolished, we also want to discriminate more carefully about different kinds of provisions, and therefore sources of provision, for ethnic groups, women with different views and with different circumstances, local preferences for health and educational priorities, etc. Moreover, we do not all want the same things.

More taxable income should stay in the regions to be taxed or be put at the disposal of regional and local authorities. We shouldn't insist that everyone bakes the same cake and cuts it into the same portions. The state can enable more choices to be made and define an acceptable minimum (acceptable, by the way, to people in that position as well as to those who imagine they are paying for it personally); but if the state attempts a direct and universal equitable provision, it will fail. We do live in a pluralistic society, not an homogenous one. We do have different cultures, values and interests quite apart from social class. Therefore there are limits to

24

what the general rules of law can achieve by way of justice in such a situation. In such a situation one just has to trust to political mechanisms of bargaining, conciliation and compromise, and to a culture that still has some general common sense of equity or fairness and of altruism as well as individual self-assertion. We don't want less local politics, we want more; only less national politics. Politics doesn't always work well. But one can try again without having to bring in a major piece of legislation in every instance, and hope that the courts will do what parliament intended. Legislate for reform, by all means, but to create devolved, enabling structures, functional as well as territorial, that ordinary people can influence if not always operate directly. What's so bad in parent power in school government? Because it is her idea? But will it yield the result she expects? We must see.

Reformers must not automatically defend the professionals against the people. We must challenge the Prime Minister's assumptions about what people really believe, and can be persuaded to believe. Laws codify and express the necessary relationships of a society. Laws do not create these relationships.

HARDY PERENNIALS

The Right to Protest

JOHN ALDERSON

The rise and maintenance of liberal democracy in Britain owes much to protest, both lawful and unlawful. From Magna Carta, conceded in 1215 to protesting barons by a reluctant monarch, down to the present, the contribution of protest to the commonwealth provides a lengthy roll. As Sir John Harrington said in the sixteenth century:

> Treason doth never prosper;
> What's the reason?
> For if it prosper
> none dare call it treason.

Equally it has to be acknowledged that misguided and failed protest has added to the sum of human misery.

The unredressed grievances and protests of the Commons against the King, the Civil War, the end of the divine right of kings, the Great Reform movement in the nineteenth century, the founding of the trades union movement, and the suffragette movement of later years, are amongst the salient protest movements of our democratic pedigree. The unwritten constitution and the established Church are amongst the progeny of protest. And the very word has named a whole religious movement. Not content with protest in the home-lands, the spirit spreads and joins similar movements worldwide, so that dissidents protesting against tyranny become our modern heroes and heroines.

This is the bright side of protest. The positive. And this is the side with which this essay is concerned.

The relationship between rights and power is worthy of note. Politics being concerned with the power to govern there is a constant tendency, a need perhaps, for governments to seek an accretion of

29

power. This may in turn induce protest from subjects whose activation of any right or freedom to protest may make the task of governing more difficult. On the other hand rights or freedoms to assemble, to process, and to exercise freedom of speech offer a safety valve. This acts as an insurance against driving protest below the surface where it may take on more sinister forms. In seeking to acquire protection against arbitrary power and undue repression, subjects, particularly vulnerable minority groups, need to be constantly sensitive to the use of this and other rights.

In fact the great universal struggle for human rights is to be seen against the background of human suffering brought about by excessive state power, its abuses and corruption. The taming and harnessing of power is one of the tasks of protest. But reason requires that protest itself needs to spring from and to recognise a liberal sentiment, since romantic revivalist passion and the protest which its enthusiasm engenders can be inimical to both the interests of the individual and free social cooperation. In his book *Power*, written before the Second World War (1938), the late Bertrand Russell warned that "To admire collective enthusiasm is reckless and irresponsible, for its fruits are fierceness, war, death, and slavery."

There are two ways in which consideration may be given to the question of the right to protest. When it be proved that there is no legal right to protest in Britain, for example, there still remains the need to consider the existence of a moral right to do so. To some there may be occasion to place a moral principle above a legal one. This of course is the stuff of which martyrs are made, leading to sacrifice for a cause or causes in both religious and secular society. Vladimir Bukovsky informs us in his book *To Build a Castle* (the story of his life as a dissenter) that for reading poems in Mayakovsky Square in Moscow, he and his friends were arrested by the KGB. "We perceived the Manifesto of Man as a summons to resistance," he says. "I'll go out on the square and into the city's ear. I'll hammer a cry of despair."

His arrest was the beginning of his twelve years in prison, labour camp, and psychiatric hospital. The price of one man's protest. Others of course fared worse.

In Western democracies such as Britain the protester may also be in conflict with the rule of law. This conflict is illustrated by the question of conscientious objection in war time. Pacifists of both religious and secular persuasions place their moral right to protest against the taking of life above their legal duty to wage war and to kill. The same moral principle and reasoning lie behind much of contemporary protest against the manufacture, possession and threatened use of nuclear weapons. Since some people regard them as the ultimate madness and evil they deem it to be their moral right to break laws, mostly in a non-violent manner, as a form of protest. It is even persuasively argued by people such as George Delft, in *Humanising Hell*, that the manufacture and possession of nuclear weapons is itself contrary to international law. If this be true, it is argued, then governments have compromised their own moral position and therefore are morally at least in no better position than protesters who contravene laws.

It is always a matter of surprise for people who belong to nations with written constitutions to discover than whilst the British enjoy many freedoms their constitution is not a written one. Where written constitutions speak of positive rights the British tradition is to speak in negative terms. For example, whilst there is an obligation in law on A not to interfere with B's freedom to pass along the highway, this of itself does not confer a positive right on B, though the effect may be the same. Thus, a public assembly to protest, which on the face of it is lawful, becomes unlawful if it obstructs B's so-called "right of way".

That there are different ways of looking at such constitutional niceties is amusingly illustrated by a story S.E. Finer reports as once going the rounds of Soviet-controlled Eastern Europe:

> In England everything that is not prohibited is permitted. In France everything that is prohibited is permitted. In Germany everything that is not permitted is prohibited. In the USSR everything that is permitted is prohibited.

Not only is there no guaranteed right in English law to protest but neither is there any guaranteed right to hold a public meeting. If we do not have such rights then, it may be asked, what do we have? It would be more accurate to say that although we do not have a right to such things we do have freedom to do them. We have that freedom because the law has not taken it away, though it does limit its exercise. As we shall see, meetings and processions are subject to restrictive laws and police powers.

From time to time our freedoms can be diminished, extinguished, or subjected to a variety of controls. This is particularly the case where freedom to protest in public places is concerned. Freedoms are not likely to be enlarged under the British tradition since from the outset it is the notion of complete freedom which the law seeks to modify. Even the famous Speaker's Corner in Hyde Park in London is subject to ministerial regulation, and the same applies to Trafalgar Square, another well-known venue for popular protest. It is of interest to note that both venues were designated as public meeting places following outbreaks of public disorder and public clashes with the police when people were seeking to demonstrate and protest publicly in central London during the nineteenth century. Freedoms may also be suspended by Emergency Regulations promulgated by the Privy Council during a national emergency. Freedom of movement which may impede emergency operations may be suspended, property may be commandeered, and rationing of food, fuel and power may be imposed.

The law therefore does not confer an explicit right of protest but it circumscribes our freedom to do so, and what is left can be enjoyed. The notion of freedom may permit of degrees therefore; whereas right is a right or it is nothing.

It is in the exercise of freedoms that we become aware of attracting obligations.

When the law imposes obligations it does so by seeking to balance conflicting claims. Thus the freedom to act in a given way, e.g. to protest, attracts an obligation in doing so not to disproportionately interfere with other persons' freedoms or with society's interests. When, for example, in a trade dispute pickets seek to persuade fellow workers who are not on strike to join them they exercise a freedom; but should they obstruct the workers' freedom to pass, the balance of the mutual exercise of freedoms is disturbed. That of course is to express what can be a complicated legal matter in a simple way, but in highly charged and volatile situations the maintenance of such a balance by the police and trades union officials is not always easy.

So far we have been concerned to consider the question of the right or the freedom to protest, but the question may be raised as to whether there is a duty to protest. Her Majesty's Parliamentary Opposition have of course a duty to oppose the Government of the day as part of their constitutional function. But can it be said that such a duty lies on individuals and groups? There may not be a legal duty but what about a moral one? It is in this context that minorities who may feel that their causes are not adequately represented in Parliament wish to use their freedom of protest to draw attention to their plight. Civil rights protests of various kinds provide examples of this need. But is there a duty?

Consider what might happen if one lived in a society where through apathy nobody ever protested about anything no matter how obnoxious the laws became. Such a society might soon become an appalling one when judged against civilised standards. Equally if one lived in a society where everybody was constantly protesting against the smallest govermental peccadillo life would become intolerable. In other words if there be a moral burden to protest it should be well aimed, and be for proper reasons, difficult though this may be to define. But it can hardly be denied that there is a moral duty to protest when a society is governed unfairly, unjustly, or in a corrupt or slipshod manner. It may be argued that in parliamentary democracies the people can protest every five years or so by casting their votes in the election of a new government. In practice however it is possible to have a permanent majority which can deny the protest votes of minorities who are unable to bring about their desired changes. When this situation exists the freedom to protest outside the parliamentary system is of great importance to such minorities.

Many people consider that the failure adequately to protest at the rise of European Fascism in the 1920s and 1930s was a failure of moral duty, whilst others point out that protesting was a highly dangerous business which led to imprisonment, to torture, and to death. In the Epilogue to his great biography of Adolf Hitler, Alan Bullock comments: "The Germans, however, were not the only people who preferred in the 1930s not to know what was happening and refused to call evil things by their true names." In various ways the British, French, Italians, the Poles and the Russians all failed when seeking "to buy Hitler off or use him to their own advantage".

33

Liberty and Legislation

This example of failure to protest may seem too vast in the context of life in Britain in the 1980s and the many smaller, separate issues which now generate domestic protest. Perhaps however it is only a matter of degree.

The Public Order Act of 1936 was passed by Parliament to control political rallies and marches by the British Union of Fascists and the counter-demonstrations which such rallies provoked. It was an historic statute since for the first time it provided a statutory power for the banning of marches and processions of protest and demonstration. The common law had largely been concerned with action to restore order after disorder had taken place. The new and controversial power was a preventive one. The police were empowered to direct and to route processions, but a ban could only come from the Home Secretary. Where a chief police officer believed that a march would cause serious disorder which would not be amenable to control he could seek a ban through the local authority to the Home Secretary. In London the Commissioner of Police applied directly to the Home Secretary. There was no power to require meetings and marches of protest to be notified to the police, though most organisers did so. During the 1970s and 1980s there were numerous protest marches which ended in widespread public disorder, and in two cases in fatal injuries. The police more often came under physical attack and began to respond with a steadily escalating counter-violence. It became necessary to review not only police training and equipment but also the law. Following disturbances in Southall, London, in April 1979, when Asian youths assembled to protest against a National Front political rally during the general election, and when a New Zealand demonstrator was killed, some alleged by a blow from a police officer, the Home Secretary set in motion a review of the law. Stimulated by a Green Paper (Cmd 7891) in 1980 and a White Paper (Cmd 9510) in 1985 the debate attracted considerable interest. Proposals were made to give new powers to the police to control protest, as well as other processions and assemblies, and for the first time to require organisers to inform the police of their intentions in advance.

In 1986 the new Public Order Act came into force. Protest movements had to face some reduction of their freedoms. As Professor D.G.T. Williams has pointed out, differing philosophies on this question of demonstration were expressed in debate. What

34

he calls the "disruption" and the "safety valve" philosophies. Assemblies of protest, it was said in the House of Lords debate (Lord Beloff), should receive less support than in the past. Freedom for people to move around without interruption, it was said, was "of infinitely greater importance than guaranteeing the right to hold public meetings and to march in procession". On the other hand the advocates of the "safety valve" view (Lord Scarman, and others) believed that

> our society has become so complicated and our representative system of government so remote to many fellow citizens, that there has to be an alternative way of expressing dissent other than the constitutional way of doing it through representative government.

It may make for easier government and public convenience to restrict the tradition of marching and assembling for protest, but it would be a dangerous and a foolish idea to believe that public protest can somehow be laid aside as belonging to a bygone age. The scale of injustice, cruelty, and tyranny in the world in 1988 cries out for continuing protest of various forms including the democratic and peaceful marches and assemblies which in the 1960s helped to achieve greater civil rights in the USA and in many other nations, whilst the same phenomenon, sometimes more disorderly, hastened the end of U.S. participation in the Vietnam War. The duty to protest is as undeniable as the need.

Although there is no statutory right to protest by procession and assembly in their domestic law, the British have such a right under the European Convention on Human Rights.

Drawn up within the Council of Europe, the European Convention on Human Rights was signed on 4th November 1950 by the British and other member states and came into force on 3rd September 1953.

The Articles which are germane to the subject being discussed here are Articles 10 and 11. Article 10 holds that

> Everyone has the right to freedom of expression. This right shall include freedom to hold opinions and to receive and impart information and ideas without interference by public authority and regardless of frontiers.

(Had this kind of European provision existed in the 1920s and 1930s it might and probably would have made it much more difficult for the Fascist and other extreme forms of government to take hold.) The second positive right in this context is that provided for by Article 11. It holds that

> Everyone has the right to freedom of peaceful assembly and to freedom of association with others, including the right to join trade unions for the protection of his interests.

Of course the right is restricted to "freedom of peaceful assembly", and further the rule of law must have its place as is enacted by paragraphs 2 of Articles 10 and 11.

Article 10(2) requires that "since it [freedom of expression] carries with it duties and responsibilities" it

> may be subject to such formalities, conditions, restrictions or penalties as are prescribed by law in a democratic society in the interests of national security, territorial integrity or public safety, for the prevention of disorder or crime, for the protection of health or morals, for the protection of the reputation or rights of others, for preventing the disclosure of information received in confidence, or for maintaining the impartiality of the judiciary.

Article 11(2) carries a similar proviso.

It will be seen that under the European Convention an adequate balance is sought between the right to protest and the right to govern. Protesters who break the law for their cause have to accept their torment as good martyrs have always done! Another point of interest in both Articles is the reference in the sub-sections (2) to the question of the interests of national security and public safety, for this brings us to consider the question of "subversion" in due course.

It has been held by the European Court of Human Rights that freedom of expression (Article 10) constitutes one of the essential foundations of democratic society, one of the basic conditions for its progress and for the development of every man (judgment of the Court of 7 December 1976, Handyside Case, Series A, No.24). It is also held that freedom of expression is applicable not only to information or ideas favourably received but also to those that "offend, shock or disturb either the State or any sector of the population". The European Commission on Human

Rights was of the view that seeking to persuade members of the armed forces to disobey military orders which rendered a particular person liable to prosecution for "incitement to disaffection" properly justified a prosecution under Article 10, paragraph 2 of the Convention. In this case the person concerned was a pacifist, and pacifism as a philosophy fell within the ambit of freedom of thought and conscience protected by Article 9, but it was held that the protester was not manifesting her belief in the sense of Article 9 (Report of the Commission of 12 October 1978, Application No. 7050/75).

In another case under Article 11 the Commission recorded: "The freedom of assembly is a major part of the political and social life of any country. It is an essential part of the activities of political parties." It found that the prohibition of public meetings for political purposes, the requirement of permission from the police authority to hold such meetings in private and the authorisation of the military authority for the holding of indoor lectures were not consistent with Article 11. Under this particular case the Commission held that the unfettered right of allocation of these authorities went towards creating a police state (Report of the Commission, 5 November 1969, Yearbook 12, p.170). There are also a number of cases where the Commission has held that the banning of meetings and procession for a restricted period because of fears for public safety, such bans being under the democratic laws of a State, were not in contravention of the Convention. Powers given to the authorities under the Public Order Act of 1986 are clearly within the provisions of the European Convention on Human Rights Article 11.

The extremes in controlling freedom of protest are to be found in those states which are very authoritarian, dictatorial, or totalitarian. Elsewhere there are varying degrees of control.

In 1985 the Home Affairs Committee of the House of Commons published the findings of their inquiries into the Police Special Branch. Protesters and their organisations may fall to the covert scrutiny or surveillance of the police through Special Branch (and MI5). The Home Office guidelines on the work of a Special Branch are published in the Select Committee Report of 1985, from which it will be seen how protest by individuals and groups might bring them to Special Branch attention:

A Special Branch gathers information about threats to public order. Such information will enable the Branch to provide assessments of whatever marches, meetings, demonstrations and pickets pose any threat to public order and help the officer to determine an appropriate level of policing.

It also

assists the Security Service [MI5, MI6] in defending the realm against attempts at espionage and sabotage or from the actions of persons and organisations whether directed from within or without the country which may be judged to be subversive to the State.

It is this concept of "subversion" which poses problems. The Home Office Guidelines on Work of a Special Branch define "subversion":

Subversive activities are those which threaten the safety or well being of the State, and which are intended to undermine or overthrow Parliamentary democracy by political, industrial or violent means.

There is no reference in this definition to the law. To be a "subversive" therefore one does not have to be in breach of the law.

There are two parts to "subversion" as will be seen. It must threaten the safety or well-being of the state (but what does that mean?) and actions must be intended (constructively as well as directly?) to undermine (change?) parliamentary democracy by political (lawful?), industrial (lawful?) or violent means. Various combinations of the elements of the definition of subversion can result in lawful protesters being subject to Special Branch surveillance and records which in turn may result in injustice, for example public service careers may be damaged, government contracts denied and so on. Some of us believe that efforts should be made to define subversion in terms which would involve illegal activity as opposed to nuisance, inconvenience, and the like. Undercover police encroachments on lawful protest and protesters are undesirable and unnecessary, it is felt. The following suggested definition was put before the Home Affairs Committee by myself:

For the purposes of civil policing, subversive activities are those activities directly or indirectly involving criminal

38

conduct, which threaten national security, or which are calculated to overthrow or undermine parliamentary democracy and the institutions of the state.

In his report into what is known as "the Profumo Affair" in 1963, Lord Denning was of the view that the term "subversive" should relate to "people who would contemplate the overthrow of government by unlawful means". In other words the protest would need to involve activity which, it could be fairly held, the protesters should have known was against the law. If not, then it is no business of the police to maintain files, to intercept telephone calls and to examine mail, all of which are part of the government's business when laws are broken or threatened, and only then, under the very restrictive provisions of the law. This then is a convenient place to turn to consider the wider role of the police in relation to protest.

Protest which involves marches, processions and static demonstrations and meetings are almost always likely to involve the police. London being the capital city is always likely to be the stage on which protest both national and international is carried out. But in the most unlikely of places the announcement that a nuclear power station, a motorway, an institution for criminals, and so on is to be built, is likely to result in protest which requires police assistance, and sometimes law enforcement. It cannot be stressed too strongly that the police in a democracy have a positive duty to facilitate the enjoyment of freedoms. That is why the police have to secure the free passage of the highway, to assist industrial pickets to enjoy the right to communicate to workers, to protect public speakers who may arouse indignation or worse, and so on. Freedom to protest in public would be less meaningful if the police were not committed to ensuring that it was unimpeded within the Queen's Peace. It is salutary to be reminded that during its early years the processions of the newly created Salvation Army were often the subject of violent attack from other protesters, sometimes hooligan groups, who formed a counter-force called the Skeleton Army. Troops were called out and the Riot Act was proclaimed in Worthing in 1884. Earlier in Weston-Super-Mare Salvation Army leaders had been arrested for proceeding with a march contrary to a ban placed upon it by the local magistrates. The inability of the police in small provincial towns to protect Salvation Army processions from violent attack seemed a characteristic of the times.

A more contemporary example of this problem facing the police when they have to decide upon the choice between seeking to ban a procession or to protect and facilitate its progress is well illustrated by the events of Saturday 13 August 1977 in Lewisham, when the National Front marched through the busy streets in a provocative manner, much to the distress and anger of local residents, particularly those belonging to ethnic minorities. The police faced a dilemma. Were they in the interests of freedom to follow tradition and protect and facilitate a march, albeit odious in its characteristics, or were they to seek a ban under the Public Order Act 1936? In the end the police decided not to seek to ban the march but to police the route and to provide protection for the marchers against the violence which had been threatened by opposing factions. The Lewisham Council went so far as to apply to the High Court for an Order of Mandamus requring the Commissioner of Police to seek to have the march banned. The application was refused. Here was a march for political purposes with racial characteristics and though legal and provided with police protection, it was to become the subject of great protest before it began. Once it began the protest turned from non-violent to violent attack. Over 3,000 police officers were deployed. The violent attacks on the police by the counter-demonstrators who used bottles, bricks, and other assorted missiles resulted in a large number of casualties. Two hundred and seventy police and sixty members of the public were injured.

Writing in his memoirs, *McNee's Law*, Sir David McNee, Commissioner of Police at the time of the Lewisham affair sets out clearly the dilemma which faces the police in these matters. He was sufficiently influenced by the Lewisham events to seek a ban on similar marches in the months that followed.

Under the provisions of Part II of the Public Order Act of 1986 the police have been given greater powers in the regulation of processions and assemblies. These new statutory powers, which are not without their doubters and critics, are in addition to those which already exist under the common law. In future those wishing to organise a procession in protest are obliged to supply the police with written notice of their intentions at least six days before the event. The Act describes public processions intended "to demonstrate support for or opposition to the views or actions of any person or body of persons" or "to publicise a cause or campaign" or "to mark or commemorate an event" as requring notice to the police. There are some exceptions to the general rule. Spontaneous procession leaving no time for notice may be exempted but there are some imponderables yet to be clarified in practice. The idea behind the notice is to give the police and others such as highway authorities time to plan routes and supervision to avoid undue disruption of day-to-day use of public highways.

It is of interest in this connection to note that Lord Scarman, who was not in favour of similar provisions in his report on the Red Lion Square disturbances in 1978, expressed a different view following the Brixton disorders in 1981, when he included recommendations in his report that the Public Order Act of 1936 should be amended to include "a requirement of advance notice of a procession to the police". Sir Robert Mark, Commissioner of Police of the Metropolis (1972–1977), had always advocated the need for the police to have adequate notice of processions in public places and included such a suggestion in evidence to Lord Scarman at the time of the Red Lion Inquiry. But the Public Order Act of 1986 goes further than either Lord Scarman or Sir Robert Mark had envisaged by giving new powers to the police to impose conditions on public assemblies as well as on processions.

It has always been regarded as desirable that the police should be seen as taking no particular stance regarding political activity and that they should not be placed in a position where decisions of a party political nature are concerned. The decision to impose conditions on public assemblies therefore will have to be handled by the police with particular sensitivity when political passions are involved. It is compatible with the order-maintenance function of the police that they should have power to regulate both public proccssions and assemblies, and the 1986 Act refines their powers to do this. It speaks of "serious public disorder", "serious damage to property", "serious disruption to the life of the community, and intimidation" (the latter with strike picketing in mind) as justifying the imposition of conditions. As with so many of these police powers which impinge on the rights of protesters to freedom of speech and assembly the high quality of police understanding and reasonableness is crucial to success. There will always be occasions when conflict of view between protesters and the police will arise. When this does happen so much depends on the attitudes of the court for the safeguarding of freedoms which are nowhere written down as such. Failing these safeguards then public opinion is the final court of appeal.

It is a measure of the tension and complexities of our contemporary society that the police have gradually been transformed from a universal corpus of ordinary police officers performing all manner of general duties, including public order maintenance, to one which now in part approaches the quasi-military-order police model of continental Europe and elsewhere. As the plural society of the 1960s developed its many-faceted nature and the ethnic diversity of the inner city neighbourhoods became marked, the perceived need to protest increased. The Civil Rights Movement fuelled by the Martin Luther King protests on behalf of black U.S. citizens touched a chord in the feelings of oppressed people in many countries.

In the United Kingdom the Roman Catholic and Republican minority of Northern Ireland took to the streets in protest against the injustices meted out to their kind by the Provincial Government and condoned in Whitehall (see Cameron Report 1969 Cmd 532). Protest attracted violence to which it reacted with sometimes devastating consequences. The police and the Army were caught up in a public order crisis which continues to plague us and which has given rise to the most damaging terrorist campaign. The training and equipping of the police in Northern Ireland to respond in quasi-military fashion was later to serve as a model for police on mainland Britain.

The international furore over the excesses of the war in Vietnam found expression on the streets of London and elsewhere in 1968. The police resisted the temptation to abandon by now traditional methods of using ordinary foot police without special equipment to maintain order in such places as Grosvenor Square where in 1968 tens of thousands of protesters sought to lay siege to the U.S. Embassy. Violence was kept to a low level indeed, by international standards of the day and by present-day British experience. Writing in the *Sunday Times* on 27th October 1968 about the Grosvenor Square demonstrations, Miss Mary Macarthy suggested it was "a unique improbable event, something to cherish in our memory book, for, short of Utopia, we shall not see it again".

Plastic shields were first issued to the British police folllowing injuries from the throwing of missiles at the 1976 Notting Hill Carnival. Later, following riots in St Paul's (Bristol), Brixton, and other cities in 1980 and 1981, military-style helmets and flame-proof uniforms were issued to police formations, and following the riot on the Broadwater Farm Estate in Tottenham, London, in 1985 the police were equipped with plastic bullets, C.S. gas and armoured vehicles, which had proved the mainstay of Britain's colonial police and Royal Ulster Constabulary riot formations. Britain now has a quasi-military police potential for dealing with violent protest. These changes in our institution of police can bring little satisfaction to those who had come to believe that the British had found some special formula for dealing with control of public protest. Perhaps it all goes to confirm that a democratic society will inevitably get the police it deserves as it responds to new pressures.

No consideration of the right to protest would be complete without special reference to the traditional form of industrial protest through picketing and demonstrating.

After more than a hundred years of the recognition of industrial picketing as a democratic mechanism the official Code of Practice issued by the Department of Employment says: "There is no legal 'right to picket' as such but peaceful picketing has long been recognised as lawful." The Code itself imposes no legal obligations and failure to observe it does not by itself render anyone liable to proceedings. In the light of the misunderstandings and bitterness which can affect all the parties involved in an industrial dispute, it is perhaps regrettable that no attempt has been made adequately to define the legal rights of workers involved in such disputes. Too often it is left to the police and union officials to work these things out in a hostile environment where clear thinking is at a premium.

The Code of Practice on Picketing seeks to outline the law. Sections "B" and "C" outline the provisions of the civil and criminal law respectively and Section "D" describes the role of the police in enforcing the law. The Code also gives guidance on good practice on the conducting of picketing. In most cases the officials of the unions involved and the police arrange matters amicably, but there are notorious cases where feelings of injustice and unfairness run so high that violence is in attendance.

The miners' strike of 1984/5 was without doubt one of the most important and serious disputes of its kind for at least sixty years, that is since the General Strike of 1926. In the context of the right or the freedom to protest it merits special attention. It began as a protest

43

against the alleged peremptory nature of the decision by the NCB to close some working coal mines which were said to be uneconomic. It was the first major industrial dispute to test the Conservative Government's industrial legislation, or at least potentially to do so. In the event the National Coal Board decided not to invoke the powers provided by the Employment Acts of 1980 and 1982. These two Acts provided, amongst other things, powers to fine trades unions and to sequestrate their funds should they fail to control picketing and protest within the limits set down. The legislation sought to restrict picketing of a place of work to those who were employed there. Secondary picketing, that is people picketing premises at which they were not employed, could be in breach of the civil, not the criminal, law. The police were not competent to enforce the civil provisions, which required that employers should do so. The National Coal Board having decided not to do this, control of the protest fell more and more to the police and to the criminal courts. This in turn drew many striking and picketing miners into conflict with the police over the rights and wrongs of conducting protest during industrial disputes. It no doubt increased the degree of violence between the pickets and the police.

A typical argument would be along the following lines. Some hundreds of striking miners would turn up to picket and to persuade working miners to join them. The Code of Practice on picketing provides that organisers should ensure that "the number of pickets does not exceed six at any entrance to a workplace; frequently a smaller number will be appropriate". Miners complained that the police were unfairly restricting their traditional rights and in any case that the police had no responsibility for enforcing the civil law. The police on the other hand argued that their task was to uphold the law, to keep the peace, and to facilitate the entry of non-striking miners into workplaces; mass picketing was obstructive and intimidating, both of which could give rise to arrest and charge for criminal offences. Sometimes violence took place, which only added to an already bitter situation. At the peak of the strike in June 1984 some 10,000 pickets massed against a very large force of police at Orgreave in South Yorkshire. Protest had taken on dimensions never seen before as mounted and riot police in their new formations and with their new equipment clashed with pickets, resulting in many injuries and arrests.

From the early days of the strike there were allegations and counter-allegations concerning freedom of assembly, procession, and protest, which caused the National Council of Civil Liberties to constitute an independent inquiry. Their terms of reference were –

> To inquire into and thereby establish the fullest possible account and the civil liberties implications of the role of the police, the police authorities and the criminal courts in the events arising from and relating to the NUM dispute which began in March 1984 (see NCCL Report 1984).

The evidence which the Inquiry was able to gather and to consider indicated that the events had dislocated the constitutional arrangements for police accountability and that there now existed a need for a fundamental review of our police system. It appeared to some that somehow the police had been left to solve or to break the strike by impeding the exercise of the rights of persuasion and protest aimed at bringing out the miners who were still at work. Others were of the view that the police were properly protecting working miners and ensuring their freedom of passage. As in all such complicated and protracted events, both had right on their side at times which only served to perpetuate feelings of grievance. This was a protest in which many tens of thousands of miners and their families suffered greatly for their belief in the rightness of their protest. It may be rightly concluded that it was a sad affair.

The story of this episode in the industrial life of the country, of its police and courts, and of the many side issues involved, is far too complicated and lengthy for fuller treatment in an essay of this kind, but it is a story nevertheless of immense importance to the tradition of the freedom to protest and of other freedoms. The growing body of literature on the subject should be referred to for more detailed treatment.

The Public Order Act of 1986 does not specifically refer to picketing or industrial disputes at all but merely makes general provisions which might apply to such issues. The police discretion and powers under the legislation already referred to will, as usual, bring industrial protesters and pickets into a relationship with the police and it is on that relationship that the quality of freedom to protest and its scope will be worked out. That it should be worked out fairly is as important for the police as for the protesters since the police in their non-public order role, for example in the normal course of investigating and detecting crime, require the cooperation and help of people similar to those whose freedoms to protest they are not only to control but to control fairly. The wise use of police discretion and the genuine effort not to go too far in their protest on the part of the pickets and demonstrators is the formula for resolution of this aspect of conflict.

That protest is of the essence of true democratic activity is axiomatic. There is little problem in getting agreement to such an assertion. It is on the capacity of an institution or of a society in its political traditions and mechanisms to successfully manage protest that so much depends.

A protest can extend from a lone voice on a box at a street corner to a riot or even to a civil war. Whether the former degenerates into the latter sometimes depends on the skill and with which early protest is handled. Certainly there is an abundance of examples in history to illustrate that failure to redress genuine grievance in its early stages has called for a very heavy price indeed later on. Even in contemporary Western democracies, a government so powerfully entrenched that it may not feel troubled by the agitation of its enemies, detractors or of its powerless minorities, may court the danger of violent reaction. Terrorism has been described as the protest of the powerless and we have witnessed a handful of idealistic youth hold the world's mightiest nation at bay through selective hostage-taking. Nor will the banning of protest avail without ruthless determination to silence the brave. We have witnessed dissenters bring international opprobrium upon powerful nations too, and gradually force them to relax their denial of freedom to protest. How a nation safeguards the freedom of the meanest and least powerful of its people to protest, and how it goes about redressing the just grievances of those and of others, will determine in part its degree of civilisation and its right to a place in the pantheon of nations. As for the people, they are constantly challenged by the need for eternal vigilance and by such sentiments as those of Edmund Burke in his speech on arrival at Bristol on 13 October 1774:

> The only liberty I mean, is a liberty connected with order; that not only exists along with order and virtue but, which cannot exist at all without them.

Obscenity:
Manners and Morals in
the Media

JAMES FERMAN

"We had fed the heart on fantasies
The heart's grown brutal from the fare."
W.B. Yeats
'Meditations in Time of Civil War'

In most fields, the criminal law deals only with the outer limits of the permissible. Editorial standards in the media operate for the most part well inside those limits, with the criminal law invoked chiefly against publications which have as their primary function the exploitation of those limits through material traded as "forbidden fruit". In a free society, the regulation of such material is always problematic, with social mores shifting from generation to generation – and not always in the same direction.

In Britain in the early days of cinema, prosecutions were brought not for obscenity, but for breaches of licensing conditions, and when certification became the rule in 1923, legal actions ceased for half a century until sex suddenly became a burning media issue in most Western countries. The Obscene Publications Act 1959 had exempted theatre, cinema, and broadcasting from the provisions of the Act, since all were subject to formal regulation by public authorities. The extent to which British society has, until recently, found such institutions congenial derives largely from an unbroken and perhaps originally feudal tradition of social networks and obligations which were imposed on and accepted by all members of society, whatever their status. Voluntary codes of practice are still widely accepted in Britain, and public authorities like the BBC, the

47

Independent Broadcasting Authority, the Cable Television Authority, the Advertising Standards Authority, and the British Board of Film Classification (the BBFC) have for many years been entrusted with responsibility for media standards.

American institutions are more legalistic, adhering to principles enshrined in a written Constitution where all rights derive from the fundamental principles of liberty and equality. In Britain, it has seemed natural to refer to a third guiding principle, fraternity, which derives from the communal or associative traditions of British society. Far from being mere pious aspiration, the principle of fraternity carries great practical implications, finding direct expression even in the law of the land. Lord Denning has written that the whole of the English law of criminal negligence, and indeed the biggest change in civil law this century, derives from the commandment to love thy neighbour enunciated by Lord Atkins in 1932, when he ruled that, even if a man cannot love his neighbour, he must still refrain from harming him, and that in law his neighbour was anyone who was so closely and directly affected by his actions that he ought to have had that in mind when he acted. The English law of negligence is based on the principle of fraternity, which in turn has its roots in the English common law. It is unsurprising, therefore, that the statutory approach to obscenity should also be grounded in our civilised concern for the obligations we owe our fellow men.

The test of obscenity laid down in the Obscene Publications Act 1959 derives from the common-law offence of obscene libel, which rests on

> whether the tendency of the matter charged as obscenity is to deprave and corrupt those whose minds are open to such immoral influence and into whose hands such a publication might fall. [*Hicklin* (1868)]

Parliament discarded the phrase "those whose minds are open to such immoral influence", with its overtones of whether or not a gentleman would let his servants read such and such a book, since the words "deprave and corrupt" already carried the sense of "immoral influence", together with a tacit assumption that writings or other works of the imagination could have the effect of tending to make men wicked. This is still the essence of the test, according to which an article shall be deemed to be obscene if its effect or (where the article comprises two or more distinct items) the effect of any one of its items is, if taken as a whole, such as to tend to deprave and corrupt persons who are likely, having regard to all the relevant circumstances, to read, see or hear the matter contained or embodied in it. [section 1(1)]

A defence is provided in section 4(1) of the Act for cases in which "it is proved that publication ... is justified as being for the public good on the ground that it is in the interests of science, literature, art or learning, or other objects of general concern". When, in 1968, a new Theatres Act swept away the censorshop of plays by the Lord Chamberlain, it was replaced with the 1959 test of obscenity, but added a qualifying provision that no case could be brought without the consent of the Attorney General. The public good defence for performances which were proved to be "in the interests of drama, opera, ballet or any other art, or of literature or learning" omitted the words "or other objects of general concern", thereby rejecting the so-called "therapeutic defence" according to which pornography was claimed to be "psychologically beneficial" to some persons "in that it relieves their sexual tensions and may divert them from anti-social activities". The Court of Appeal had ruled that whether or not such material might be "beneficial to those who were sexually repressed or perverted or deviant" did not make its publication "an object of *general* concern", since otherwise any form of pornography could be defended on the ground that it was beneficial to some people, if not to the public at large. This distinction soon proved acceptable to juries, who were increasingly inclined to acquit matter which depicted or described apparently normal, healthy or pleasurable sex between consenting adults. It was films depicting behaviour which seemed perverse or deviant which were seen as more suitable for private therapy than for public consumption, since the possibility of harm to at least a proportion of the wider public could not be ruled out.

The European Convention for the Protection of Human Rights and Fundamental Freedoms, to which the United Kingdom is signatory, enshrines the right to freedom of expression, but acknowledges the extent to which its exercise carries with it duties and responsibilities, including the "prevention of disorder and crime" and the "protection of health or morals". It is fair to say that the British obscenity test is one of the few in the world which attempts to focus specifically on the "protection of health or morals".

Since harm was the guiding principle, section 2(4) provided that "a person publishing an article shall not be proceeded against for an offence at common law ... where it is of the essence of the offence that the matter is obscene". But this protection would not be available to theatre, cinema and broadcasting, since all had been specifically excluded from the provisions of the Act. The theatre was given its own legal status in the Theatres Act 1968, but the anomalous position of the cinema was not revealed until 1975, when the President and Secretary of the BBFC were charged with aiding and abetting an indecent exhibition, namely the showing by Classic Cinemas Ltd of the Swedish sex-education film *Language of Love*. The magistrate dismissed the case against Lord Harlech and Stephen Murphy on the grounds that they had acted in good faith and with due care and attention to the issues involved. The error, if such it was, was an honest error of judgment, but Classic Cinemas Ltd were committed for trial at the Old Bailey to determine whether the film itself was indeed grossly indecent. This same charge had first been brought against the sequel, *More about the Language of Love*, which was refused a certificate by the BBFC but granted a local "X" by the GLC. A charge of public exhibition of indecent acts or things had not been brought for 100 years, since a showman was convicted of keeping a booth on Epsom Downs for the purpose of an indecent exhibition. The Law Commission, in reviewing such cases, said that to the extent that they "disclose a consistent principle, they seem to indicate a species of public nuisance, where to do the act is enough to constitute the offence, and innocent motive is irrelevant".

The *More About the Language of Love* case, *R v. Jacey (London) Ltd and Others* (1975), demonstrated clearly that showing a film on licensed premises could be indicted as an indecent public exhibition. Indeed, the judge had directed the jury's attention to the final minutes of the film, which depicted a couple making love in explicit anatomical detail, some of which was photographed in close shot. If this is not grossly indecent, he asked, you may be led to wonder what is. The jury took twenty minutes to return a verdict of guilty.

A year later, in *R v. Classic Cinemas Ltd ex parte Blackburn*, the jury considered the film's predecessor, *Language of Love*, and returned an acquittal after only seventeen minutes. The case had taken two weeks at the Old Bailey, the first devoted to legal argument before the jury was sworn. In this case, the question of *mens rea* was crucial, the defence arguing the relevance of the BBFC's decision to refuse a national certificate in 1970 so that the film could first be assessed by a representative sample of local licensing authorities who were more closely in touch with community standards. When elected councillors were given the chance to judge the film, 127 councils voted to approve its exhibition to adult audiences, whilst seven went so far as to permit entry to 14-year-olds. Thus, when the film was resubmitted to the Board in 1973, it was classified "X" (18) for nationwide release, with only a few scattered councils maintaining their ban on local screenings. At the Old Bailey, the defence argued that after such painstaking tests of public taste, their clients must have had an honest mind in relation to its subsequent exhibition. The test of outrage was also considered, and was countered by evidence that in the two years from July 1973 to June 1975, the film had been shown in 475 cinemas before an audience of approximately one and a half million people without a single complaint to the police or any local authorities until the present case. This, it was argued, failed to meet Lord Simon's definition of outrage in *Knuller v. DPP* (1972), that "outrage in public decency goes considerably beyond offending the susceptibilities of, or even shocking, reasonable people". The lack of protest was accepted by the jury as proof of the lack of outrage.

The verdict ultimately turned on the test of indecency formulated by Lord Reid in the same case: "indecency includes anything which an ordinary decent man or woman would find to be shocking, disgusting and revolting." Comparable judgments used terms like "lewd", "offensive", "recognised standards of propriety" and "the ordinary modesty of the average man", all of them largely subjective responses to behaviour which is legal in itself, but which becomes unacceptable when viewed by others. These are all, in effect, tests of manners, not morals, since propriety is a measure of the appropriateness of public behaviour to a particular time or place.

The relevance of such a test to works of art, particularly literature, which deals with private, not public behaviour, is hard to see. "If art teaches anything," said Joseph Brodsky, the expatriate Russian poet in his Nobel Acceptance Speech of 1987, "... it is the privateness of the human condition," and this privateness is maintained even when the experience is reenacted in public, or semi-public, surroundings. The Indecency is a singularly inappropriate test for regulating dramatic depictions of intimacy, particularly where the audience has expressed a conscious choice to view the performance through the purchase of tickets. It is reasonable, of course, for communities to impose limits on the circumstances of public or semi-public performance, provided there is also a degree of privilege attaching to performances for which the public has made an informed choice. Classification by audience age has proved an acceptable limitation to impose on a cinema audience, and may also warn of the type of experience on offer. But such protection derives from licensing conditions which are stricter than those in the theatre, where shows like *Oh, Calcutta!* had to rely on advisory "adults only" notices at the box-office.

It is unsurprising that the cinema should have sought legal parity with the theatre on questions of obscenity, which it did in a petition forwarded to the Home Secretary by the BBFC in 1977 on behalf of the Cinema Consultative Committee, which comprised delegates from the film industry and from all the associations of local licensing authorities in Great Britain and Northern Ireland. The local councils had seen the legal implications of common-law indecency in the writ of mandamus awarded against the Greater London Council for granting a local "X" certificate to the film *More About the Language of Love.*

The Law Commission had strongly recommended in its 1976 Report on Conspiracy and Criminal Law Reform that cinema films should be brought within the scope of the Obscene Publications Act, since Parliament's supposition that "such exhibitions ... are most unlikely ... to be prosecuted" had already proved unfounded. The Commission had taken much of its case from the evidence of the BBFC, differing only in proposing that the private exhibition of films on domestic occasions should not be subject to criminal sanction provided that no person under 16 was present and no charge was made for the exhibition or for anything provided in connection with it. If the 1959 Act had proved itself suitable only for the control of sexual depictions or descriptions where the question was one of manners rather than morals, then the recommendation of the Commission might have been acceptable, since sex between consenting adults in private was no longer a matter for the British criminal law. But the Board was concerned far less about the private use of "blue movies" as an aphrodisiac than about the increasing taste for sadism and other "bizarre practices" in films and about the worrying influx into Britain of child pornography. Were such matter to find its way into the domestic blue-film market, the Board argued, it could have a very real tendency to deprave and corrupt, not just those of 16, but of any age, who had been encouraged to view such material in private. At the very least, we urged, the age of exemption should be raised from 16 to 18.

When the Commission's proposals were incorporated into the Criminal Law Act 1977, the Board took pains to convince the Home Office that the viewing of films in private could as easily become a social activity, with some persons at greater risk in a private flat than in a public cinema. As a result, no exemption was provided in the 1977 Act for private showings of films in domestic dwellings. Instead, the amendment simply deleted the proviso excluding cinema films from the range of publications caught by the 1959 Act, which already extended to anything "containing or embodying material to be read or looked at or both, any sound record, and any film or other record of a picture or pictures". The words "or other record" became crucial with the growth of the video industry, when the "deprave and corrupt" test was used with great effect to stem the tide of what became known as "video nasties", where viewing in private was no defence.

The Board also succeeded in 1977 in persuading Ministers that, since the deprave and corrupt test would be applied by the BBFC in assessing the suitability of films for exhibition to the public, those same films should not suffer "double jeopardy" in the sense of being subject both to censorship through prior restraint and also to the risk of private prosecutions for obscenity. The result was a consent provision like that of the Theatres Act 1968, whereby no proceedings could be instituted except by or with the consent of the Director of Public Prosecutions (the DPP). Interestingly, no similar safeguard has yet been considered appropriate for the video industry under the terms of the Video Recordings Act 1984.

Although law reform was at hand, the government found it politic in 1977 to set up a Home Office Committee on Obscenity, Indecency, Violence and Film Censorship under the Chairmanship of the Cambridge Professor of Philosophy, Bernard Williams. This distinguished Committee conducted the widest-ranging review of the subject ever undertaken in Britain, and among its conclusions published in November 1979 were two far-reaching proposals:

(1) that save where persons under 16 have been exploited for sexual purposes or persons of any age have been made to suffer actual physical harm, sexual depictions should no longer be subject to the criminal law; and

(2) that violent and sadistic sexual depictions on film constituted such a major social problem that film censorship even for adults should continue.

This latter recommendation surprised many who had expected a liberal/academic working party of "the great and the good" to turn their backs on the idea of retaining a paternalistic and arguably outmoded system of adult censorship. But if some members of the Williams Committee had started out with such an attitude, a look at the evidence seemed to have converted them. Indeed, so firmly did they reject the view that adults should be given the right to choose their own cinema entertainment − "whatever turns you on", as the saying went − that their Report marked the beginning of a historic swing of the pendulum away from what can now be seen as the libertarian heyday of British media law. After the Williams Report, it was very hard to argue convincingly for a *laissez-faire* approach to screen entertainment. The advent of video confirmed the need for vigilance, but it was Williams who marshalled the evidence, and did so in cogent terms:

> We should make the point that the violence we have seen on film (from films refused a certificate, or cut before the film could be certified) far exceeds in nastiness anything likely to be seen on television. It is not simply the extremity of the violence which concerns us: we found it extremely disturbing that highly explicit depictions of mutilation, savagery, menace and humiliation should be presented for the entertainment of an audience in a way that appeared to emphasise the pleasures of sadism. Indeed, some of the film sequences we saw seemed to have no purpose or justification other than to reinforce or sell the idea that it can be highly pleasurable to inflict injury, pain or humiliation (often in a sexual context) on others. [Williams, para 12.10]

In such circumstances, it seemed surprising that the Report

should recommend the repeal of the Obscene Publications Act and consequent decriminalisation of all forms of publication other than those narrowly defined as causing actual harm to performers, whilst urging for films, and films alone, the continuation of an administrative system of prior restraint. Even more surprising was the Committee's rejection of the "deprave and corrupt" test, since the selling of the idea that sadism can be highly pleasurable, as described above, or the reinforcing of that idea in those already attracted to it, must surely epitomise what was intended by the phrase "deprave and corrupt", at least as that test is interpreted by the BBFC.

In its evidence to Williams, the Board had strongly supported the statutory test of obscenity because of its unique relevance to the sort of films which were repeatedly found most pernicious. Sadly, the Board was virtually alone in this support, and to understand why, we must return for a moment to the sixties, when the test was used almost exclusively to curb the spread of erotica.

The Williams Report offers a compendium of disenchantment with the 1959 test based on a decade or more of misinterpretation. Thus in *R v Stanley* (1965), Lord Chief Justice Parker explained the meaning of the terms "indecent" and "obscene" by suggesting that they both convey the same idea, "namely, offending against recognised standards of propriety, indecent being at the lower end of the scale and obscene at the upper end". This sliding-scale approach might still have relevance to the Post Office Act, on which that case turned, but it has little to do with obscenity as defined in the 1959 Act. Nor, in our view, has Lord Parker's observation, that "an indecent article is not necessarily obscene, whereas an obscene article almost certainly must be indecent". Certainly, when videos celebrating rape and sexual torture were brought before juries under the deprave-and-corrupt test, questions of indecency as measured by degrees of visual explicitness proved immaterial. Whether or not genitalia were seen, either in long shot or close-up, was far less to the point than whether the sexual behaviour displayed was criminal in itself and yet presented solely for the purposes of sexual arousal.

Even in the sixties, the words "a tendency to deprave and corrupt" had led the courts from manners to morals. Lord Justice Salmon tried to elucidate the sort of tendencies that might be caught, such as "(1) to induce erotic desires of a heterosexual kind, or (2) to promote homosexuality or other sexual perversions, or (3) drug-taking, or (4) brutal violence". The range was wide, but only the first two attracted much notice, the Arts Council Working Party pointing out in 1969 that since these were not crimes at all, how could it be "a heavily punishable crime to 'induce' these particular non-crimes?" If obscenity laws were really about sexual conformity, their Report continued, then "no Royal Commission could ... draw an intelligible line between what is acceptable and what is not acceptable ... [nor could] such a Commission find any evidence that anyone has been corrupted or ... depraved by pornography". The 1959 Act was a law "to regulate the evolution of private *mores*", said the Report, begging the question of what particular weight was to be given to this word "mores". Were "mores" matters of serious concern to the community, for example, and what significance ought they to have in a court of law? Mr Justice Stable told a jury that the words "to deprave and corrupt" must not be construed as "to shock and disgust", which is not a criminal offence, the argument Lord Gardiner had deployed in gaining an acquittal in the *Lady Chatterley* case. Yet if this were indeed the law, then surely the Act must have had as its object something of greater moment than the nudie magazines and rude pamphlets which British juries were asked so regularly to assess for depravity. If the tests were truly designed for the control of "anti-social influences in the arts", as the Report said, then how could the law seem other than misconceived when a decade or more of legal scrutiny and barristers' banter had been publicly squandered on the anti-social potential of pubic hair, the peculiar dangers of which seemed clearer to the police than to juries.

A decade later, society had begun to sense the triviality of this approach – "splitting pubic hairs", as the BBFC described it. Few British juries had ever been happy "to equate ordinary sexual desire with depravity", as the Working Party would have had it, but Williams a decade later was equally wrong in assuming that the 1959 test was therefore null and void. Juries, faced with depictions of bestiality, sexual sadism or child pornography, had proved perfectly capable of deciding the issue "on an assessment of evil consequences which", the Arts Council had mistakenly predicted, they can "have no means of judging". Indeed, it was the "anti-social" focus of the obscenity test which had proved to be its singular virtue, since when juries drew the line, they did so on grounds of morals, not manners.

If the focus was clear, however, the psychological process of depraving and corrupting could still be open to misconception. Thus the Greater London Council proposed in their evidence to Williams that the law should prohibit any depictions "which purport to portray an unlawful sexual act", a course which might have ruled out sin as a serious subject for filmed drama. Not only tragedy would feel the ban, but comedy, too, since all drama begins with human frailty, and none so universal and absurd as the propensity of mankind to behave badly. From *Macbeth* to *Peter Rabbit*, the world's most popular stories have explored unlawful impulses. But it is treatment, not subject matter, which determines the stance of the artist – not the "what", but the "how" and the "why" – and studies of wickedness, even those which depict the crime in all its brutality, may nevertheless illuminate, appal or even deter. Art, particularly great art, is, like religion, concerned with moral imperfections, but it can be perfectly moral in confronting them.

A more penetrating comment on the statutory test advanced in that 1959 Report was that it sought to control a mere "tendency". Incitement to criminality was already covered by the law of incitement, they argued, and to the extent that the Obscenity Acts add "a mere unintentional tendency toward crime as a punishable offence, they are to be deplored". This is the line taken by the United States Supreme Court, which rejected the "bad tendency" grounds for abridging freedom of expression because it lacked the all-important factor of "clear and present danger". The answer put by proponents of the British approach is that the effect of publications or performances is rarely to incite directly whether to crime or anything else. What these works do, or tend to do, not so much singly, perhaps, as in series, is to set in train through the sheer repetition of their demeaning view of women, for example, or their glamorisation of crime, what is known in behaviouristic terms as a process of conditioning, the "drip-drip" effect of popular parlance. It is the subtlety of this insidious process which blinds us to its true power – which is the power of advertising, of education, of good or bad parenting. The power of cinema was recognised by Hitler and Stalin alike. It was Goebbels who said: "The best propaganda is not that which is always revealing itself: the best propaganda is that which works invisibly, penetrates the whole of life without the public having any knowledge at all of the propagandist's initiative." When the propagandist is also a pornographer whose motives are those of the marketplace, the law must match subtlety with subtlety.

57

We live in an age of media saturation where the attention span bestowed on images and voices on the screen may be far greater during the years of maturation than the time and attention given to more traditional bulwarks of a civilised society. And when we examine those repetitive media messages, we find amongst them those which dull, which desensitise, and which may ultimately disinhibit by eroding the internalised constraints which are part and parcel of the civilising process, constraints we used to learn at our mother's knee, and which we discard at our peril.

Amongst the films criminalised by the British obscenity test are a number of American porno films which celebrate incest as a stimulating variant on the standard range of sexual pleasure. For Freud, incest was not just some strange psychological quirk: the capacity, he argued, was as universal as the opportunity. Father-daughter incest, and particularly stepfather-daughter incest, is an increasingly reported and prosecuted form of child sexual abuse, and the urgent need for prevention outweighs the value of any *post hoc* cures, penal or therapeutic. If men who take advantage of their own daughters are simply choosing the object of least resistance, then we dare not tamper with the ancient, world-wide, multi-cultural taboo against such conduct. Yet since the early 1970s, sex films have treated father-daughter incest as just another staple of erotic entertainment. BBFC policy follows British law in ruling out all such depictions lest they come to exercise a normalising, disinhibiting influence on men who have the power *and* the opportunity to do untold harm to their offspring. The attraction of such films lies apparently in the offer of illicit sexual pleasure to men whose sexual confidence is at such a low ebb as to make them unlikely or unable to resist. Such inducements can be caught by British law as having a clearly defined "tendency to deprave and corrupt".

The same potential exists in rape films which confirm "macho" myths about the sexiness of male power and aggression by suggesting the invariable gratitude of rape victims for the satisfying, liberating attentions of the rapist. If inadequate men need the fantasy stimulus of a simulated female orgasm in order to perform at all, then perhaps such scenes have a therapeutic role to play in psycho-sexual conditioning. But when the narrative is rape, and the sounds of pleasure are preceded by cries for help from an unwilling victim, then the messages are mixed indeed. If failure to attract a willing partner leads some men to choose an unwilling one, or if, having failed repeatedly in the sexual stakes, such men find redress in humiliating and punishing one emblematic woman for the inaccessibility of all women, then society has failed in its role of socialising the male sex drive at its point of maximum danger and loss of control. In most cultures, men are conditioned by upbringing to develop inhibitions against inflicting harm, particularly on women. It is a matter of concern when such healthy and necessary taboos are eroded by the tawdry pleasures and pressures of pornography. When market forces cultivate such tastes, then forces of another kind must supervene.

Films endorsing or encouraging depravity are not granted a BBFC certificate in Britain, and few such films were available as evidence to Royal Commissions until the advent of video. The relative ignorance of judges and barristers about such films led the Criminal Bar Association to testify to Williams in 1978 that the deprave-and-corrupt test had outlived its usefulness, which led that Committee to recommend replacement of the criminal test by a scheme of prohibition based on physical rather than psychological harm to (1) children involved in child pornography, and (2) humans or animals involved in so-called "snuff movies". Everything else except for films was to be tackled through a scheme of restriction based on the offensiveness to reasonable people of unrestricted access to the material in question.

Some earlier critics of the deprave-and-corrupt test had suggested a return to a test based on "outrage", with the Longford Report proposing in 1972 that an article might be deemed to be obscene "if its effect, taken as a whole, is to outrage contemporary standards of decency or humanity accepted by the public at large". The word "humanity" borrowed some of its force from the 1959 approach, but the rest of the definition would have taken us back to a test of manners based on an assumption of consensus which is at worst suspect and at best unproven, but which is to be measured only by outrage, surely an irrational and wholly subjective response.

From the opposite camp, the Defence of Literature and the Arts Society supported a similar test of outrage by proposing to Williams that:

> a person commits an offence if, for payment or not, he knowingly exposes or delivers to another person who has not consented to receive it any item which, on the ground that matter contained or embodied in it –

59

(a) is concerned with human or animal sexuality, or
(b) depicts violence or cruelty, or
(c) is gruesome or disgusting,

may, if taken as a whole, be expected to outrage the majority of persons who are likely, having regard to all relevant circumstances, to read, see or hear it.

Recognising that consent must be based on a true appreciation of contents, this proposal reveals a strange inability to grasp the extent to which a work of art can rarely if ever be described or paraphrased with perfect accuracy. A great critic may evoke what it was like to attend a historic performance, but only a genius can provide an equivalent emotional experience. Nor can a notice in the foyer adequately forewarn an audience of a work's potential for outrage. But even if it could, are we to outlaw the artist's capacity to shock, to appal, to disturb profoundly in the interests of truth? If outrage were the sole test of legality in the arts, then the Impressionists would never have been allowed to organise the Salon des Refusés, Edvard Munch would have been driven into permanent exile, and the score of Stravinsky's *Rite of Spring* would be gathering dust in some criminal museum like the Italian negative of Bertolucci's *Last Tango in Paris*. Outrage condemned Shostakovitch, and it is an odd test indeed to be proposed in the defence of literature and the arts.

A major difficulty with such a test is that familiarity may breed tolerance rather than contempt. Expectations reshaped by mores are no longer so easily affronted. Victorians disregarded, or perhaps frequented, child prostitutes in the Strand until re-sensitised to the evil by a reformist campaign. This is a point not taken by Lord Denning when he declares in *R v. Greater London Council* ex parte *Blackburn* (1976) that the

> common-law offence has proved to be a far better stop upon pornography than the 1959 Act. For this simple reason: pornography shocks and disgusts decent people, but it does not tend to deprave and corrupt them. They revolt from it and turn away from it. If asked, they will be quite ready to say that it is grossly indecent, but far less ready to say that it tends to deprave or corrupt.

In practice, few juries have ever supposed that ordinary people turn away so consistently from the sort of pornography brought before

British courts in the 1960s and 1970s. Where they do tend to turn away is in cases where the effect of the work is aversive because its purpose is aversive and the intention to shock or appal is successfully realised. Intention alone is not sufficient, however; if it were, the accused need only argue that he never meant the effect he produced. The 1959 obscenity test is one of effect, which directs the jury's attention to the extent to which a work tends to encourage such feelings of aversion or revulsion rather than of corruption or depravity. It was the failure to put this "aversive" defence to the jury with any clarity which resulted in the notorious quashing of two obscenity convictions during the 1960s. It was also the issue weighed by the DPP before declining to prosecute Pasolini's film *Salo* in 1977.

In the GLC case, which was the last in which a cinema film had been subject to charges of indecency, Lord Justice Bridge agreed with Lord Denning that the common-law test still applied to films, but went on:

> I cannot say I feel any enthusiasm for the result. The statutory test of obscenity has been much criticised, and with good reason. But I don't know how many people today would accept as an appropriate test of criminality what is "shocking, disgusting and revolting".

Definitions were always crucial in this debate, and the Church of England Board for Social Responsibility in its submission to Williams made a useful contribution to clarifying the distinctions between terms like *eroticism, pornography*, and *obscenity*:

> *Erotic* publications and artefacts "reflect and celebrate the sexual nature and life of men and women" in the context of the total human personality (a definition usefully extended by Williams in observing that the purpose of the erotic is primarily to *express* sexual excitement rather than to cause it).
> *Pornography* is "the representation of sexual relations" divorced from "a context of personal caring or affection". It trivialises sexual relationships by treating them in mechanistic fashion, its purpose being "the stimulation of sexual desires in the reader or viewer". The word "pornography" meant originally "the writings of prostitutes", which "provides an apt analogy for the prostitution of human sexuality which is a feature of pornography".

61

Obscenity "represents a much more fundamental assault on men and women and what it means to be human ... [it distorts] human personality by depicting it as deprived of those characteristics which are essential to humanity [since] common to all obscene productions is the degradation of persons and of relations between persons".

The submission argued further that it would

be misleading to categorise as pornography works of art or literature merely because they were capable of being treated primarily as sources of sexual stimulation. If there is an honest portrayal of human life and relationships, however extreme, we consider that a production can be judged according to the canons of aesthetic criticism. The fact that it may be interpreted by some readers or viewers as pornographic is secondary.

The Church of England did not support the view that pornography *per se* should be criminalised; there are other means of control than the criminal law. But when it turns to obscenity, their report contrasts the cruelty or violence depicted in Goya's *Disasters of War* or *King Lear*, which appeal "to our shared humanity", with depictions of a more prurient kind which "invite us to collude in degrading it". The law's concern, it was argued, is with "the attractive presentation of a degraded humanity", the effects of which may "include, but not be confined to, consequential actions".

The honorary legal adviser to the Nationwide Festival of Light had criticised the deprave-and-corrupt test in *The Daily Telegraph* precisely because it had been so applied, arguing, in a plain man's version of Lord Denning, that

Everyone knows – except the depraved and corrupt – that obscenity depraves and corrupts all who condone or delight in it ... but when a jury hears [that] they must decide whether, taken as a whole, it has a tendency to deprave and corrupt ... they are easily bewildered and confused. ... In the "Oz" case, the Appeal Court ruled, in effect, that for the purposes of the Obscene Publications Act 1959 the word "obscene" meant, *and meant only*, "a tendency to deprave and corrupt." If Parliament had intended that, why did it not call the Act the "Depraving and Corrupting Publications Act"?

It was the value and aptness of a "Depraving and Corrupting Publications Act" which later became manifest later when the worst of the so-called "video nasties" were found by judges and juries alike to have the effect of selling and reinforcing the pleasures of sadism. The law of incitement could never have caught such publications; the obscenity test proved more than adequate. The question to be answered is not whether the deprave-and-corrupt test is necessary in a modern society – that has now been conceded – but whether it is sufficient to catch the full range of material which "the protection of health and morals" requires? It is a strong test certainly, which means it is also a narrow one, but that, too, is appropriate in a free society.

Above all, the deprave-and-corrupt test carries the sense of something "strikingly or importantly *bad* or *evil*", to quote the words of an educationalist in *The Times* (1977), who continued:

> It is hard to see how sexuality as such – I mean, when not combined with overt physical disruption such as torture or castration – can be a candidate for the genuinely obscene. ...
> It could only seem so to those who see sexuality as something essentially disruptive, invading, and dangerous.

Unpredictably, in the post-AIDS world, sex has begun to carry just such overtones. But in law, as in human relations, the case to be made must still be based on social responsibility.

And here we come back, as always, to the views of John Stuart Mill:

> the sole end for which mankind are warranted, individually or collectively, in interfering with the liberty of action of any of their number, is self-protection. That the only purpose for which power can be rightfully exercised over any member of a civilised community, against his will, is to prevent harm to others. His own good, either physical or moral, is not a sufficient warrant. (*On Liberty*)

Professor H.L.A. Hart in his book *Law, Liberty and Morality* (1963) argued that the law was not and ought not to be a tool for "the enforcement of morals", in particular in the field of sexual morals, where the activities condemned may "involve nothing that would ordinarily be thought of as harm to other persons". On the other hand, "society could not exist without a morality which mirrored and supplemented the law's proscription of conduct injurious to others". It is the moral law which governs interpersonal relationships that must be reflected in statute law, suggesting a field of public morality which is the preserve of the state and a field of private morality which is not. Even in the private sphere, however, Hart modified Mill's principle by justifying a degree of paternalism, since there are those who may be seriously harmed even with their own consent.

Ronald Dworkin, Oxford Professor of Jurisprudence, clarifies this fundamental principle that concern for the rights of others must rest on their own personal welfare and not on some sense of the "general benefit":

> A state may be justified in overriding or limiting rights [only if] *competing rights* ... would be jeopardised if the right in question were not limited. [But] we must recognise as competing rights only the rights of other members of society *as individuals. (Taking Rights Seriously,* 1977)

There is an even more fundamental principle here, the principle of fraternity, without which the "deprave-and-corrupt" test would be meaningless. In a more recent book, *Law's Empire,* Professor Dworkin returns to this concept:

> political legitimacy – the right of a political community to treat its members as having obligations in virtue of collective community decisions – is to be found not in the hard terrain of contracts or duties of justice or obligations of fair play that might hold among strangers, where philosophers have hoped to find it, but in the more fertile ground of fraternity, community, and their attendant obligations.

In the light of the revolution in gender attitudes in Western society in the past decade, it is perhaps ironical that the most significant application of British obscenity law in recent years, at least in relation to films and videos, derives almost wholly from the fraternal obligations which men owe to women.

If fraternity is the foundation stone of the British approach to obscenity, through the courts and the public authorities, then it is relevant to discover the extent to which such a principle plays any part at all in the regulation of obscene matter in the United States, given the fact that the USA produces the vast majority of publications which appear before the courts of America, Europe and the free world.

The First Amendment of the Constitution stipulates that "Congress shall make no law ... abridging the freedom of speech, or of the press", while the Fifth states that no one shall "be deprived of life, liberty, or property without due process of law". After the Civil War, a Fourteenth Amendment was added binding state legislatures and courts in similar terms, so that protection against prior censorship was guaranteed, but not protection against proceedings for obscenity.

In the 1930s, the Supreme Court began to widen its interpretation of free speech to include writings and films of little or no artistic merit, provided they did not include "licentious" speech, the forms of which were listed in 1942 as libel, slander, insulting or "fighting" words, and obscenity, all of which were excluded from First Amendment protection. In *Roth v. US* (1957), the definition of free speech was extended to "unorthodox ideas, controversial ideas ... But implicit in the history of the First Amendment is the rejection of obscenity as utterly without redeeming social importance." Yet the word "obscenity" was qualified: "Sex and obscenity are not synonymous. Obscene material is material which deals with sex in a manner appealing to prurient interest."

In 1959, the Supreme Court ruled that a state ban on "the exhibition of a motion picture [*Lady Chatterley's Lover*] because that picture advocates an idea – that adultery under certain circumstances may be proper behaviour –" was unconstitutional, since the First Amendment's basic guarantee is of freedom to advocate ideas not necessarily "conventional or shared by a majority". Obscene matter could be outlawed only to the extent that it went beyond ideas to become an "incitement to action or an excitation".

In 1966, the Court ruled that a publication which is not obscene might be regarded as such if distributed in a lascivious manner, and in 1968, that the law's jurisdiction did not "reach into the privacy of one's home ... [whereas] public distribution ... might intrude upon the sensibilities or privacy of the general public ...". The test of obscenity still required proof that the matter was "utterly without redeeming social value", but it was not long before social value was claimed for sex, a Californian judge declaring himself unable to find such lack of social value in a film which "appeals to the normal

65

interest in sex and nudity which the average person has in such matters".

In 1973 the tide turned with a 5-to-4 majority ruling by the Supreme Court in *Miller v California* that obscenity, as narrowly defined, was not protected by the First Amendment, and that each state could set its own standard: "People in different States vary in their tastes and attitudes, and this diversity is not to be strangled by the absolutism of imposed uniformity." Above all, the three-part test of obscenity adopted by the Court in 1966 was strengthened, laying down three essential conditions, all of which would have to be satisfied in every case:

(1) that "the average person, applying contemporary community standards, would find that the work, taken as a whole, appeals to the prurient interest";
(2) that "the work depicts or describes, in a patently offensive way, sexual conduct specifically defined by the applicable state law";
(3) that "the work, taken as a whole, lacks serious literary, artistic, political, or scientific value."

The effect of the second condition was to require the laws of individual states to define specifically the kinds of sexual conduct which would be subject to regulation if presented in a patently offensive way. And a reference to "ultimate sexual acts, normal or perverted", had the unintended effect of limiting obscenity to hardcore pornography only.

The importance of public decorum was reaffirmed by the Court in another 1973 ruling that

> the right of privacy did not extend so far as to confer a protected right on consenting adults to pursue their own choice in the matter of watching obscene and pornographic motion pictures within a theatre ... [even one] not open to minors and which gave patrons due notice of the kind of entertainment provided.

In 1977, the Court made it clear that the kinds of sexual conduct specified in *Miller* were not exclusive. Sado-masochism was added to the list, the first acknowledgment of the obscene potential of violence or cruelty. But violence unconnected with sex was still not caught by the *Miller* test, since obscenity was defined as necessarily including some "patently offensive" representation of "sexual conduct" which, being "lewd and obscene", could form "no

66

essential part of any exposition of ideas". Whether or not depictions of violence could form an essential part of such a discourse was not considered, since the Court's focus was on sex, the "crass commercial exploitation" of which can debase and distort a "key relationship of human existence, central to family life, community welfare, and the development of human personality".

The difference between American and British approaches to obscenity law lies in the harms they seek to curtail and in their comprehension of the processes by which those harms are inflicted. In Britain, the deprave-and-corrupt test is intended to curb the anti-social influence of obscene matter as measured by the consequence to others of changes in the attitudes or behaviour of reader or viewer. In America, obscenity law protects the reader or viewer against harms he may inflict on himself, by whatever process those harms may be inflicted. Nor need the courts assess the extent to which such harms are measurable against any standard of consequential morality. All that need be proved is that the matter is of a certain type and the manner of presentation patently offensive. This would, in Britain, be a test of indecency, not obscenity.

To understand how such an emphasis gained ascendancy in US jurisprudence, one needs to go beyond legal questions to those of history and politics. The pendulum has swung on both sides of the Atlantic, and if the sexual habits of urban America had been transformed in the 1960s by the so-called sexual revolution, then the small-town traditions of middle America found their own political voice a decade later, and with it a judicial response from the highest court in the land. It is not necessary here to weigh the relative merits of successive waves of public sentiment, and it is too early to guess the judgments of history, but differences between American and British obscenity law can be assessed on their technical merits, and the consequences are significant.

The American test relies wholly on community standards, which may cover an entire range of social conventions without necessarily embracing aspects of public morality adequate to the behaviour portrayed or the vile exploitation of that behaviour by the work itself. Community standards may embrace moral principles or they may not. The Nuremburg courts rejected the plea of the defendants that they were only obeying the community standards of their day, since the gravity of their crimes had to be weighed against the highest moral standards of humanity, not the customs of the age or the community. Where freedom of expression is at stake, the same ethical standards are relevant, particularly where the works in question offer sexual excitation through scenes of rape or torture.

Even by the modest standards of the Supreme Court, American obscenity law has had little measurable effect since 1973. Hardcore porn is openly traded in the cities and exhibited in cinemas and video shops across the country, despite experimental zoning restrictions in certain areas, yet there has been little or no attempt in the courts or the legislatures to discriminate between the greater and lesser dangers it represents. A hopeful and insufficiently applauded shift in emphasis was signalled in 1986 by the Report of the Attorney General's Commission on Pornography, which sought to identify the relative harms caused by various forms of pornography, thus making it possible to draw up a list of priorities. The first significant result has been a nationally coordinated programme of enforcement against the spread of child pornography in the United States. The next priority will be the flourishing trade in sexually violent films, videos and magazines, but here the Supreme Court rulings could prove an embarrassment.

In 1976, the film *Ilsa, She-wolf of the SS* was brought before the courts of New York State on a charge of obscenity, but the case was dismissed because the judge found nothing which could properly be covered by the Miller test, no "lewd exhibition of the genitals", no representations of "ultimate sexual acts, normal or perverted". Indeed, the film could not be described as hardcore pornography at all. In Britain, the same film was refused a cinema certficate by the BBFC in August 1976 because of its prurient sexual exploitation of torture and the brutal degradation of concentration camp prisoners, male and female. The Board's monthly report commented as follows:

> Because the film includes no genital close-ups or explicit sexual activity, it has played in many parts of the world, occasionally with a classification less restrictive than that given to so-called "hardcore" sex films. England is one of the few countries in which the legal tradition provides a test which can distinguish between the natural and the unnatural, the civilised and the barbarous. This work seems to us to be truly depraving and corrupting, unlike some sex films which offend solely on grounds of impropriety. The distinction between manners and

morals is exemplified by this film, and we can see no possibility
of our offering it a certificate for public exhibition.

With the *Miller* test, the US Supreme Court had established a
judicial equation between the terms "pornography" and "obscenity"
with the result that the kinds of harm they do can be neither
distinguished nor assessed. Williams characterised "pornography"
as combining the explicit description or representation of sexual
matter with a function or intention to arouse the viewer sexually.
The offence this may cause is attributed to the fact that it "crosses the
line between private and public since it makes available ... some
sexual act of a private kind ... for a voyeuristic interest". This is
compounded when it "not only exists for private consumption, but is
publicly displayed ... [or] forced on the attentions of those who have
not even volunteered to be voyeurs" (para 7.7).

But that offence is one against propriety, against what a community may find appropriate to a particular time or place. The issue
is one of manners, not morals, and the degree of impropriety may be
proportionate to the degree of explicitness as measured along a
continuum running from softcore to hardcore. That this is not the
only dimension along which one can or must discriminate became
fully apparent to juries when confronted with the "video nasties" of
the 1980s, where the verdicts surprised some observers by turning
more often on the morality or immorality of the conduct portrayed
and the moral stance taken towards it by the film-maker than on the
affront caused to the viewer.

British cinema licences have for most of this century prohibited
the exhibition of films which are "likely to encourage or incite to
crime", which anticipated the deprave-and-corrupt test of 1959.
American cinemas show films celebrating rape, which can be
judged obscene only if the act is depicted or described in a "patently
offensive way". Whether or not the act is criminal is immaterial,
since it is the explicitness of depiction which renders it obscene.

There is nothing in the British test to exclude such a focus,
provided there is also a clear sense of harms which flow from it. But
the case must rest on whether the depiction of sex on the level of
gross anatomical detail, divorced from feeling and personal
relationships, carries a probable consequence for the viewer of
changes in attitudes or behaviour of a significantly harmful or anti-
social kind. In the age of AIDS and other incurable forms of

venereal disease, new moral attitudes are gaining ground, and juries might well be led towards the view that explicit sexual depictions are degrading to such an extent as to exercise a depraving and corrupt influence on future conduct. But one hopes they would have reached this view on grounds not of personal taste or fashion, but on a calculus of harm which J.S. Mill would have recognised and respected.

In 1986–87, Parliament considered two new definitions of obscenity in Private Member's Bills tabled by Winston Churchill MP and Gerald Howarth MP. Both Bills would have preserved the deprave-and-corrupt test, significant in itself, but would have added a new test, sufficient in its own right for the work to be deemed obscene. The Churchill Bill in 1986 included a list of proscribed depictions any one of which would attract a conviction for obscenity irrespective of context or effect on the viewer. The inadequacy of such an approach was exposed in Standing Committee. In 1987, the Howarth Bill took a different route, proposing to add an alternative test based on whether or not the work in question was "grossly offensive to a reasonable person". No defence was provided for circumstances in which a reasonable person had made a conscious and informed choice to read, see or hear the work in question, provided only that some other reasonable person found it "grossly offensive" for him to have done so. This was a return to the test of outrage, with all its faults, but it met little outrage in Standing Committee and fell only because of the dissolution of Parliament for the 1987 General Election. Were such a test to be adopted in future, it would reintroduce into British obscenity law a wholly subjective assessment of taste and decency with respect to works of art and public communications, and it would do so by amending an Act which was designed to focus solely on the question of harm.

In practice, the criminal law is a particularly blunt instrument for policing works of the imagination, yet the alternatives are equally unattractive. The Williams Committee suggested for films a system of state regulation by a public authority, with powers to ban but no criminal law to provide the grounds for such a ban. The BBFC opposed this, preferring to apply the law, not make it. But any law which is capable of setting limits across the whole range of publications must acknowledge the risks inherent in the very concept of limits. In an open society, the law must do neither too much nor too little, which is why the shifting sands of community standards have their place in the field of indecency, but not obscenity, the latter being a far more serious offence and one properly grounded in the fundamental values without which no civilised society can survive.

If a new test of obscenity is to be considered, then it must catch works which endanger not governments, but society itself. It is their anti-social influence in that deep sense which is at issue, and which can be measured only by the extent to which such works encourage conduct which threatens the rights and freedoms of others to enjoy a peaceful and secure life under the law. Such a test much be wide enough to safeguard public morality, yet narrow enough not to encroach on private taste or conscience. It must balance the claims of freedom and responsibility. The current British test meets all those requirements, but if clarification is needed, then the following is an attempt to interpret the test in the light of practical experience in applying it to films and video recordings. It draws on the form of words suggested by the Williams Committee for their scheme of prohibition, and the purpose is simply to redefine the essence of the deprave-and-corrupt approach for those for whom the old form of words seems too far removed from the values and habits of today:

> The exhibition or supply of any film, video or sound recording or any other publication shall be prohibited by law if the manner in which it depicts or describes violence or sexual activity or crime is such as, when taken as a whole, to encourage the imitation or toleration of behaviour which is seriously harmful to society by a significant proportion of those who are likely, having regard to all the relevant circumstances, to read, see, or hear the matter contained or embodied in it.

In applying such a test, no jury should require expert evidence, since it is not the psychological or sociological effect, but the moral effect that must be considered, in accordance with their own experience as responsible adults. Questions of right and wrong are properly decided in criminal cases by juries chosen at random to represent the popular will. Adults are familiar with day-to-day questions of morality or immorality and the extent to which good citizens may be turned into bad citizens or bad citizens into worse. What is different about obscenity is that the test requires a jury to pronounce a work wholly unfit for publication in a civilised society, which implies an immoral influence of a strikingly serious kind. It is

71

a judgment about moral *limits* and one which reasonable adults can properly be expected to make in a democratic community.

Indecency in public displays is and should remain a separate if lesser offence. The Indecent Displays (Control) Act 1981 was sound in principle, but so narrow in application that it has rarely if ever been tested in the courts. If the scope of that measure were widened to take in the contents of magazines which are easily accessible to persons under 18, it would form a useful adjunct to the powers of the police. A Home Office Amendment to the Churchill Bill provided a model of how this might be done and was the only section of that ill-judged proposal which received unanimous support in Standing Committee. It would almost certainly have been given the same support by the full House had it not been attached to a Bill to reform obscenity law, with which it had no clear or logical connection. In America, the dissemination to children of material which is indecent but not obscene is a separate issue, and the Supreme Court has upheld state legislation to protect children from exposure to such material where accessibility to children is a particular feature of the medium in question. On that principle, it seems correct that an amendment to extend controls to the contents of magazines should be added to the Indecent Displays (Control) Act, section 1(5) of which was drafted so as to *exclude* from "displayed matter" caught by the test "any part of that matter which is *not exposed to view*". Using the Churchill amendment as a model, the words "exposed to view" could be deleted and replaced so as to limit such exclusion to "any part of that matter which is neither visible nor accessible to persons under the age of 18, or which, if so accessible, is not kept in a wrapping which, while intact, prevents that matter from being seen". The test of indecency would be the traditional common-law test, directing the jury's attention not to their own subjective responses, but to their sense of the propriety of the average man. It is here alone that community standards are both necessary and sufficient as a test of criminality. Manners change, and the verdict must ultimately rest on the jury's sense of what their own community would or should tolerate on environmental grounds at a particular moment in social history.

If the public are to be protected from gratuitous affront, then this will involve applying the manners test not only to public displays but to any matter which invades the privacy of individuals without their consent, which of course extends to unsolicited matter sent through the post. It has been said in defence of such publications that those who allow themselves to be depicted indecently are thereby "waiving their own privacy rather than impeding or intruding upon that of others". But that is to ignore the possible effect of indecent displays on the unwary viewer, which may be to invade the realm of the most private emotions and to play on these in an unsettling and intrusive fashion, utterly without permission. The best protection against such unwanted intrusion is a code of manners as between strangers, and one that can be breached only by mutual consent. Where such consent is knowingly given by adult citizens, the only restrictions which a free society ought to impose are those designed for the prevention of harm.

The involvement of children as viewers or participants in material classed as indecent or obscene presents a species of harm almost universally acknowledged. In Britain in 1978, the Protection of Children Act extended the scope of the earlier Indecency with Children Act 1960 to cover indecent photographs, still or moving, of children under the age of 16. All forms of publishing are subject to the Act, including distributing or exhibiting films or videos, so that works imported from abroad may be caught irrespective of context, circumstances or intention. The 1960 Act had protected only those children under 14, so the decision to raise the age limit to coincide with the statutory age of consent seemed sensible and uncontentious. But the test itself was also changed, from gross indecency, which like the deprave-and-corrupt test had been adequate to catch most child pornography, to the lesser test of indecency, the precise meaning of which is left to the jury to assess according to their own standards of propriety for children or young people. The effect of this Act has been to inspire a greater sense of caution in British film-makers regarding the involvement of children in immodest or suggestive photography, and restrictions on importing such material might well spread these considerations abroad.

British law has also sought to control real cruelty to animals in film-making, forbidding not only the staging of such scenes, but their public exhibition as well. The Cinematograph Films (Animals) Act 1937, like the Protection of Children Act, limits the range of material which may be imported into Britain for public exhibition or distribution, and it was once hoped, vainly, that such a law might provide the model for similar limitations in other countries. Were

73

such laws to be extended to the treatment of humans as well as animals, as suggested by the Williams Committee, the international community might find such an example more appealing. Films or videos of sadism, actual or simulated, have been traded widely on the international scene since the 1970s, the most notorious being the film *Snuff*, which purports to show the actual gang rape and murder of a prostitute in Argentina who is then physically dismembered before the camera. Rumours of such "snuff" movies had been carefully fostered in the New York Press with accounts of private screenings at Mafia parties, and when it was claimed that one had been acquired for public exhibition, it was advertised with the slogan: "Blood Money, the film that could only be made in South America ... where Life is CHEAP!" The police were said to have had no grounds for intervention unless the scene were shown to be the record of a real murder, so the posters dared the police to prove it real and the public to prove it not. In Britain, most juries would find it depraving and corrupting to solicit members of the public to become voyeurs of an actual rape, murder, and dismemberment, but a new criminal test based not on the effect of the work, but on the circumstances of its production could provide one more useful link in the chain of criminal provisions which modern media law requires.

To go further in curtailing the freedom of expression would be, almost certainly, to go too far. "Freedom", said Oliver Wendell Holmes, "is freedom for the thought we hate", since if we deny the rights of the odious, we may also threaten the rights of the unpopular, which in time may become the wisdom of posterity. Constitutional guarantees of freedom of speech and of the press arose in America in response to the efforts of George III to suppress dissent through seditious libel laws and the licensing of the press. Jefferson's purpose in the First Amendment was to stop all future American lawmakers from making it a crime for people to criticise their own government. The extent to which such rights might justifiably embrace ideas unrelated to government or public affairs, ideas of no value at all, or cloaked in images of a sexual or violent nature, has long exercised the finest minds not only in American jurisprudence, but in Europe and the Commonwealth as well.

That debate is a continuing one, and amongst the principles most importantly at stake is that of artistic freedom, the right of the individual artist to explore the dark side of human experience and to draw unpopular conclusions from his own, perhaps partial, vision. The true nature and worth of such pursuits may elude their contemporaries, since history tends to impose a time-lag on the degree to which the public can keep in touch with the sensibilities of the artist. Difficult modes of speech may be coined to convey difficult themes, but the private nature of the artist's invention is what gives it its power. "A work of art", said Joseph Brodsky, "of literature especially ... addresses a man *tête à tête*, entering with him into direct relations." It is this intimacy which permits and often begets intensity, and the world of the spirit is much the poorer when such works are suppressed.

Amongst such considerations, however, there must still be room for the needs of society, for what the European Convention calls "the protection of health or morals". If some media products can have effects which are subtle, persuasive and demonstratively anti-social, not by the standards of the day or the ruling party, but by the ethical standards which define civilisation, then no society can ignore the matter. It will always be hard for the courts to distinguish between what is harmful and what is merely unpleasant or challenging, but it is a task which society must confront for its own good. The future of a culture may depend on where and how it draws the line. If dross is the price we pay for freedom of expression, there is nevertheless a point at which such dross may become pernicious.

In reflecting on the conflicts between freedom and responsibility, Burke said:

> Men are qualified for civil liberty in exact proportion to their disposition to put moral chains upon their own appetites ... Society cannot exist unless a controlling appetite upon will and power be placed somewhere, and the less of it there is within, the more there is without.

It is still in the working out of that complex moral equation that the challenge lies, but in the two hundred years since Burke, we are little nearer to finding a wholly adequate, much less ideal, solution.

The Mentally Ill and the Power of the State

LARRY GOSTIN

Since the time of Blackwell there has been an assumption that all
citizens have the right to choose their own destiny, with the
exception of children and the mentally ill. For these two groups
there is no absolute right of self-determination. They are thought to
be incompetent to determine where their interests lie. Children, of
course, have parents to guide their destiny until they reach the age of
majority. The mentally ill, however, are often assumed incompetent
for life, so that it is the state which should make decisions for them.

Thus, when decisions are to be made about the liberty or
autonomy of mentally ill people, they are made not by the individual, but by the state – through the use of civil commitment or on
the grounds of criminal insanity. Moreover, the *purpose* of this
compulsory intervention is thought to be benign, so that it is
unnecessary to provide rights and safeguards.

The power of the state to deprive a mentally ill person of liberty
persists today, although we are beginning to recognise that even the
state must prove its case before an independent court or tribunal.

There is certainly a worldwide human rights movement for the
mentally ill – no less important than the movement for blacks and
women. Yet the civil and social status of the mentally ill, even today,
needs great improvement.

Below I will examine the three basic assumptions which have
perennially justified state intervention over the mentally ill –
incompetence, dangerousness, and the need for treatment. I will
then propose five human rights principles which should govern the
modern relationship between the mentally ill person and the state.

To understand the relationship between the state and the mentally ill person, it is necessary to examine the traditional assumptions (which persist even today) which were said to justify removal of the rights and liberties of a whole class of people.

First, mentally ill people were presumed *incompetent* to make decisions for themselves (Brakel, Parry & Weiner, *The Mentally Disordered and the Laws*, 1985). This assumed general incompetence was thought to justify a whole array of decisions – for example, hospitalisation, consent to treatment, contracts, voting, access to the courts. We now know that mental illness is not wholly disabling. Mentally ill people are not incompetent all of the time; nor are they incompetent with respect to all decisions. Before a mentally ill person is deprived of any right or privilege, the question must be put: is the person capable of understanding and acting responsibly in that particular area? For example, a mentally ill person who does not fully appreciate the need for hospital care may, nonetheless, know that major antipsychotic medication causes him severe and distressful adverse effects; or he may understand the implications of a contract including a marriage contract; or he may understand full well the difference between the political parties and have a clear voting preference. Thus, before any right or privilege is denied a mentally ill person, the state should prove before an independent court or tribunal that the person is incapable of exercising the right or privilege.

The second traditional assumption is that mentally ill people are *dangerous*. This is a particularly pernicious assumption, and is founded upon the most basic logical error. There is little doubt that there can be causal association between mental illness and violent behaviour (Stone, A., in Roth and Bluglass, eds., *Psychiatry, Human Rights and the Law*, 1985). John Hinckley's attempt to murder President Reagan was intimately bound to a complex set of delusions about the President and an actress, Jodi Foster. Peter Sutcliffe, the Yorkshire Ripper, heard voices demanding that he harm prostitutes.

The law has had a doctrinal confusion in these and hundreds of other cases through the ages. Are these people mad or bad? Should they be treated or punished? Strangely, John Hinckley was found not guilty by reason of insanity and admitted to Saint Elizabeth's Hospital in Washington, D.C. But, when doctors tried to give him a therapeutic leave of absence, the public clamour for revenge was so great that the hospital was forced to keep him in. The Yorkshire

Ripper, on the other hand, was found guilty and sentenced to prison. It took years after the receipt of clear and convincing psychiatric evidence that he was insane, to transfer Sutcliffe to a special hospital. The line between punishment, prevention and therapy in these cases is a fine one.

The fundamental error in logic is to infer from a small number of cases such as those of Sutcliffe and Hinckley, that many or all mentally ill are potentially dangerous. The fact is that the mentally ill as a class are probably less dangerous than some in the population at large. They are more likely to be depressed, insular, and vulnerable than aggressive or dangerous.

Perhaps more importantly, psychiatrists cannot predict future dangerous behaviour. Numerous studies now show that psychiatrists differ among themselves when predicting dangerousness from similar or identical sets of clinical facts. Further, they tend to overpredict dangerousness. Thus, in any case where a mentally ill person is predicted to be dangerous, the chances are that he or she will engage in no criminal or violent behaviour (Monahan, J., *Predicting Violent Behavior*, 1981).

These facts substantially undermine the moral authority of the state to confine mentally ill people under its police power. The police power can be exercised to protect the public. But if a mentally ill person has committed no offence, what is the police power justification for civil commitment? If it is impossible to say who will, and will not, engage in dangerous behaviour, on what basis can the state confine mentally ill people?

The final traditional assumption is that depriving mentally ill persons of their liberties or right to consent to *treatment* is necessary for their own good. This is perhaps the most convenient and complacent assumption. It is easy to assume that our actions are benevolent and that we are doing good. If the state is doing a service for mentally ill persons, not punishing them, then it has no need to prove the necessity for civil confinement and mandatory treatment (Gostin, *A Human Condition*, Vol.2, 1977). Indeed, if we assume that the state is acting benevolently, there is even no need to prove that the intervention is beneficial to the person. The label – "treatment" – has a magical quality which transcends all the difficult burdens of proof which the state usually has to bear before it can use compulsion.

There are clearly instances where the use of mental hospitals is a thinly veiled disguise for preventive confinement or punishment, as in the case of Hinckley or Sutcliffe. One further example is a patient currently detained in Broadmoor Hospital. The patient committed a heinous sexual offence and murder of a young boy. He was convicted and spent six years in prison. After his discharge from prison he sought treatment in a mental hospital on an informal basis, suffering from depression. When the hospital discovered his previous criminal record he was involuntarily detained and transferred to Broadmoor, where he remains today nearly twenty years later. What this demonstrates is that, under the guise of "treatment" the mental health system can be as, or more, punitive than the criminal justice system. This is not to suggest that the patient was not dangerous or did not deserve a long period of confinement, but only that civil confinement statutes can be just as effective in confining a person for a long period of time as the criminal courts. Indeed, because mental health does not have a tradition of justice and proportionality between length of sentence and gravity of the offence, it can be a more restrictive alternative.

When a decision is taken to send someone to a mental hospital, as opposed to a prison, the person can be treated against his will. To some this is as great an intrusion on the person's rights as confinement itself (Szasz, *Insanity, the Idea and its Consequences*, 1987). To others, it is the *sine que non* of civil commitment, for without compulsory treatment the psychiatrists cannot provide effective therapy (Stone, 1985).

These two extreme positions are both based upon dogmatic views of mental illness. The anti-psychiatry movement assumes that mental illness is a social construct designed to exercise the power of the state over vulnerable individuals. The pro-psychiatric position assumes that all treatment is good treatment even if patients cannot now appreciate the benefits. Later, when they see the world as we do, they will thank us. The intermediate position is one the law should subscribe to – viz, there are some narrow instances where treatment can be imposed upon an unwilling patient; but those circumstances need to be clearly demonstrated before a dispassionate court or tribunal. What needs to be demonstrated is that the treatment is beneficial, has no disproportionate adverse effects, and that the patient clearly cannot assess the benefits and risks.

For centuries it was simply assumed that, if a person was committed to a mental hospital, the psychiatrist could then impose whatever treatment was thought necessary for the health of the patient. In *A Human Condition*, Vol.I, (Gostin, 1975) I observed:

> Legal concern for the welfare and rights of the psychiatric patient has traditionally ceased at the hospital door on the assumption that, while the law could reasonably set procedural and substantive standards in respect of compulsory admission, it could not interfere in the clinical relationship which must be established following admission. The traditional legal view resulted in the failure of mental health legislation to establish general principles protecting the position of detained psychiatric patients to decide what treatment they should receive.

Since that time there has been a revolution in mental health law throughout North America and the Commonwealth (Gordon & Verdon-Jones, in *Law and Mental Health*, Vol.2, ed. Weisstub, 1986). The impact of this new law, by and large, has been to tighten the criteria and procedures for civil commitment. But few countries have made great improvements in the area of consent to treatment.

The Mental Health Act 1983 in England and Wales is one of the more interesting pieces of modern legislation. The 1983 Act creates a series of formal obstacles in cases where treatments are to be administered to detained patients. The consent provisions apply to any patient "liable to be detained", except those admitted under short-term powers or remanded to hospital for report. Several categories of treatment are dealt with differently. First, psycho-surgery and other forms of treatment as may be specified by regulations or a code of practice cannot be given unless the patient consents *and* a second opinion is obtained. A medical practitioner and two other persons appointed by the Mental Health Act Commission must certify in writing that the patient is competent and has consented. The medical practitioner, moreover, must certify in writing that, having regard to the likelihood of the treatment alleviating or preventing a deterioration of the patient's condition, it should be given. Further, before giving a certificate, the medical practitioner must consult with two other persons who have been professionally concerned with the patient's treatment, one of whom is a nurse and the other neither a nurse nor a doctor.

These arrangements represent one of the basic departures from traditional common law assumptions contained in the Act. Specific treatments which give rise to special concern cannot be given even with the consent of the patient, unless there is independent verification that the patient is competent to give consent and that the treatment is effective. This departure from the common law principle respecting a voluntary therapeutic relationship between doctor and patient is further undermined by the fact that the provisions requiring consent and a second opinion apply to patients not liable to be detained. This is an instance where departure from traditional legal norms may be justified. This is because of the difficulties of obtaining a voluntary and informed consent from psychiatric patients; the potenially hazardous or irreversible nature of the treatment on patients; and the need to control the psychiatric profession in its use of treatments which may not be fully established (Gostin, "Psychosurgery: A Hazardous and Unestablished Treatment?" in *Journal of Social Welfare Law*, 1982).

The second category of treatment applies to the administration of medicine by any means and treatments to be specified in regulations; the regulations include electro-convulsive therapy. These treatments cannot be given unless the patient consents or a second opinion is obtained. The consent must be confirmed by a certification in writing by the responsible medical officer (RMO) *or* by a medical practitioner appointed by the Mental Health Act Commission. The second opinion must be given by a medical practitioner appointed by the Commission who must certify in writing that the patient is not capable of giving consent or has not consented but that, having regard to the likelihood of it alleviating or preventing a deterioration in his condition, the treatment should be given. Before making a certificate the doctor must consult a nurse and another professional (not being a doctor or a nurse) who is professionally concerned with the patient's treatment.

The need for a second opinion does not arise in the case of "administration of drugs by any means" until three months after the drug was first administered. However, the "three month rule" would not apply to treatments listed in regulations or the code of practice.

The Act provides that all other forms of treatment for mental disorder which are not included in the provisions outlined above may be given without the need to obtain a consent or a second opinion. This could conceivably include potentially intrusive forms

81

of treatment such as behaviour modification, physical restraint and seclusion.

The Act provides, for the first time in the history of the law of England and Wales, specific authority to impose somatic treatment upon a patient who understands the nature and purpose of the treatment, but expressly withholds consent.

In psychiatry and law the entire edifice of forcible treatment is erected upon the presumed incompetence of patients to consent to medical procedures. Any other position would be arbitrary; if patients have the capability reasonably to understand the nature and purpose of treatment there is no more justification for disregarding their own conceptions of their self-interest than there is in the case of any other patients – whether physically or psychiatrically disabled.

The Act establishes intricately detailed regulation of consent, treatment and second opinions. Consents or certificates under the Act may relate to plans of treatment which may specify a number of different forms of treatment. Where a certificate is given for a plan of treatment it provides authority for the administration of all the diverse forms of treatment within the plan. The Act upholds the common law right to withdraw consent, but only subject to broad emergency provisions. Urgent treatment can be given without the need for consent or a second opinion. The "urgent treatment" provisions are broadly based and include the right to prevent "a serious deterioration in the patient's condition" or to "alleviate serious suffering". There are exceptions for hazardous or irreversible treatments which are defined tautologically in the Act.

The consent to treatment provisions, on their face, appear to be a triumph of legalism; they are complex and require the doctor to proceed through a number of procedural obstacles prior to the administration of certain treatments. If closely examined, however, the consent provisions represent a return to legal formalism, but do not provide an effective safeguard for the unconsenting patient, except in respect of treatments requiring consent *and* a second opinion. The form of second opinion is medical with a duty only to consult other professionals. Professional self-regulation is always open to the criticism that it is not sufficiently open, rigorous, and dispassionate. The duty to consult other professionals was very much a compromise measure arrived at by the House of Commons Standing Committee. First, it represented an attempt by the

Committee to legislate for good practice by requiring doctors to operate on a multidisciplinary basis; second, it was viewed as a greater safeguard for the patient if a more widely-based second opinion was invoked. The difficulty with the compromise is not only that the role of non-medical professionals is part of a constitutional – not a decision-making – process, but also that those professionals are not independent. As part of the therapeutic team at the hospital who originally devised the treatment, they will not be in a position effectively to question their own treatment programme.

The foregoing assumptions about the mentally ill have persisted for centuries. But the civil rights revolution in the 1960s and 1970s injected notions of "rights" and "safeguards" in mental health. Much of the progress was generated by a series of court cases in the United States (Brakel, Parry & Weiner, 1985), Europe (Gostin, 1975, 1977), and the Commonwealth (Gordon & Verdon-Jones, 1986).

In this section I will develop a set of five human rights principles which should govern the relationship of the mentally ill individual and the state. In doing so I will trace the landmark human rights decisions in the field, and forecast where the human rights movement will be heading.

1. The Right to Humane, Dignified and Professional Treatment

Mentally ill people should possess one human right more important than any other – the entitlement to humane, dignified and professional treatment (Gostin, "The Ideology of Entitlement: The Application of Contemporary Legal Approaches to Psychiatry" in Bean, ed., *Mental Illness: Changes and Trends*, 1983). The principle of humane, dignified and professional treatment is derived from a number of international documents which all have regard to the essential dignity and worth of human beings. The Universal Declaration of Human Rights (U.N., 1948), the International Covenant of Civil and Political Rights (U.N., 1966), and the European Convention for the Protection of Human Rights and Fundamental Freedoms (Council of Europe, 1971) all prohibit inhuman or degrading treatment. The International Covenant of Economic, Social and Cultural Rights (U.N., 1966) implements these basic principles in the mental health context by proclaiming the right to medical services to promote the "highest attainable standard of physical and mental health". In addition, the U.N. International Declaration of Disabled Persons (U.N., 1975) states that disabled (including mentally disabled) people have the right to psychological treatment, rehabilitation and other services to help them develop their capabilities to the maximum, and to hasten their social integration.

These existing declarations have been used as a model for proposed human rights guarantees intended directly to protect mentally ill people. The Daes report to the United Nations in 1982 encourages all States to "see new ways of humanizing the care of the [mental] patient by observing the humanitarian elements and the quality of care and treatment"; and providing "care in a humane physical and psychological environment, qualified staff in sufficient numbers and an individualized treatment plan for every patient". The U.N. Declaration on the Rights of the Mentally Ill proposed in the Daes Report states (Article 4): "Every patient shall be treated with humanity and respect for the inherent dignity of the human person." "Every patient shall, in particular, have the right to protection from exploitation, abuse and degrading treatment."

The only international body which has specifically considered the application of these human rights principles in Mental Health is the European Commission of Human Rights. In *Ashingdane v. the United Kingdom*, the Commission said, in *obiter dicta*, that incarceration of mental patients in appalling conditions would be inhuman and degrading treatment prohibited under Article 3 of the European Convention.

In *A. v the United Kingdom* (1980), the Commission heard a claim from a mental patient at Broadmoor Hospital in England that he was treated in an inhuman and degrading manner. The Commission approved a detailed settlement requiring the U.K. government to adopt minimum standards for the seclusion of mental patients.

In *B. v the United Kingdom* (1981), the European Commission considered a claim of inadequate conditions and treatment at Broadmoor Hospital: overcrowding, fire hazards, lack of occupation and stimulation, and infrequently seeing the responsible medical officer. The Commission did not find a violation of Article 3 on the facts of the case because no single element of the case amounted to inhuman or degrading treatment or punishment. A bewildered dissent, however, asked why a critical combination of inadequate conditions could not add up to a violation of Article 3 in the absence of a single horrific example of maltreatment or punishment.

2. The Right to a Full and Impartial Judicial Hearing Before Involuntary Loss of Liberty

It is a basic jurisprudence principle that all people are entitled to a full and impartial judicial hearing prior to loss of liberty. The same principle should operate to protect mentally ill people from involuntary hospitalization without sufficient medical evidence and social justification. Where society is to withdraw the most basic right to liberty because it believes the person cannot rationally exercise choice and requires compulsory treatment, it must give that person the opportunity to refute those propositions before an impartial decision-maker.

There is strong justification under international law for the human rights principle that all involuntary mental patients have a right to judicial review. The International Convention of Civil and Political Rights (1966) has been signed by 84 states including Japan. Article 9(4) of the Covenant provides:

> Anyone who is deprived of his liberty by arrest or detention shall be entitled to take proceedings before a court, in order that such court may decide without delay on the lawfulness of his detention and order his release if the detention is not lawful.

Article 5(4) of the European Convention of Human Rights (1971) contains virtually the same language, which was construed by the European Court of Human Rights in two landmark mental health cases. There were three distinct questions decided by the European Court (Gostin, "Human Rights, Judicial Review and the Mentally Disordered Offender" in *Criminal Law Review*, 1982): (i) Does the concept of judicial review refer only to the initial admissions decision or does it imply a right of periodic review? (ii) What is the scope of judicial review? (iii) What are the required characteristics of a court?

The European Court in *Winterwerp v the Netherlands* (1979) found that the principal justification for involuntary detention in a mental hospital is "unsoundness of mind". Unsoundness of mind is subject to change, amelioration and cure. The reasons initially warranting confinement may cease to exist; it must, therefore, be shown that the unsoundness of mind continues throughout the period of detention. The Court in *Winterwerp*'s case concluded that "a review of lawfulness must be available at reasonable intervals".

The European Court in *Winterwerp*'s case expressly reserved its decision as to the scope of judicial review; this was despite a written brief from the government of the United Kingdom inviting the Court to limit the scope of review to the formal lawfulness of the detention, not to its material justification. The government of the United Kingdom (1979) said that in drafting the European Convention it was envisaged that the prerogative writ of *habeas corpus* was a constitutionally sufficient method of judicial review.

The European Court in *X. v the United Kingdom* (1981) rejected this view and decided that Article 5(4) requires a review wider than *habeas corpus*. Article 5(4) requires not only a judicial determination of whether the detention is in conformity with the domestic law, but also whether the detention is justified on its merits.

In Article 5(4) the word "court" does not signify a court of law of the classic kind, integrated into the judicial character and which affords minimum procedural guarantees to the parties. The most important characteristic of a court is "independence of the executive and of the parties to the case".

The procedural guarantees in mental health cases have been broadly specified in *Winterwerp*'s case (1979):

> It is essential that the person concerned should have access to a court and the opportunity to be heard in person or, where necessary, through some form of representation ... Mental illness may entail restricting or modifying the manner of exercise of such a right, but it cannot justify impairing the very essence of the right. Indeed, special procedural safeguards may prove called for in order to protect the interests of persons who, on account of their mental disabilities, are not fully capable of acting for themselves.

The European Commission has been asked on two occasions to specify what the "special procedural safeguards" are for mentally ill people (Gostin, *Mental Health Services and the Law*, 1986). In both cases the Commission did not ultimately decide the matter because the government of the United Kingdom conceded the human rights principle by enacting the required guarantees on the domestic law. *Barclay-Maguire v the United Kingdom* (1980) was concerned with the delays in which Mental Health Review tribunals hear cases. There were inordinate delays of several weeks or months between the application to the tribunal and the hearing. The Mental Health Review Tribunal Rules of Procedure (England and Wales, 1983) were amended to require a "speedy and just determination". *Collins v the United Kingdom* (1982) concerned the right to publicly funded representation and procedural fairness. The procedural questions included withholding relevant reports from the patient, excluding the patient during parts of the hearing, and failing to give detailed reasons for the decision. A decision in this case was avoided by a regulatory amendment guaranteeing legal aid for tribunal representation (Law Society, 1982) and a complete change in the Mental Health Review Tribunal Rules of Procedure (1983).

International law, then, requires a court or tribunal to hold a substantive hearing in which the patient or his representative can present medical and social evidence to determine if there is justification for detention in a mental hospital. A hearing before a court or tribunal must take place before, or soon after, the initial admission, and, thereafter, at reasonable intervals. These broad human rights principles are applied below to the law in Japan.

The concept of *judicial review* has been closely associated with a legalistic approach, inappropriately exported from the United States to another cultural context. Judicial approval of the admissions decision has been criticized as attaching a criminal veneer to the mentally ill, and imposing technical procedural barriers to access to medical care (Stone, Address to the International Forum on Mental Health Law Reform, Kyoto, 1987).

The purpose of judicial review is to give the individual, faced with the consequence of the drastic diminution in personal autonomy, the right of access to an independent court or tribunal. The independent decision-maker will consider all the evidence the individual can assemble to refute the case for deprivation of autonomy. It is not too much to require a society to provide the individual with the opportunity for a dispassionate review to establish clearly the need for compulsory hospitalization.

The charge that judicial review impedes access to treatment is ill-founded. It presumes that which still has to be impartially established

– *viz*, that the person requires treatment which can be most effectively given in a hospital. Mental health legislation gives psychiatrists authority to deprive a person of freedom. It is a fundamental human rights principle that the law should lay down criteria and procedures for the exercise of the authority and that a full and fair judicial process is established to review the decision. Psychiatrists who are empowered under the statute should not be dissuaded by the necessity of judicial approval, for a psychiatric judgment, like any other professional judgment, may be fallible.

It is not necessary or even desirable to transport a United States view of procedure to other countries. The objective of a hearing is to provide an open forum where the patient can actively participate; to bring together a full range of information, evidence and opinion; and to leave the decision to an independent and impartial body.

A full and fair hearing need not be undertaken by a formal court, adopting strict rules of evidence. The adversarial rules of a criminal trial such as hearsay, self-incrimination, transcripts and appeal are unnecessary to the fair and accurate resolution of a case.

The British Mental Health Review Tribunal, widely used in the Commonwealth (Gordon & Verdon-Jones, 1986), provides a good alternative model. The tribunal has a multidisciplinary membership comprising a legal chairman, a psychiatrist and a lay or social work member. The composition of a tribunal reflects the three essential elements of a mental health case – legal, medical and social. The legal chairman has the responsibility to ensure a fair procedure where full information from the patient, psychiatrists, social workers, nurses and family can be provided and evaluated. The tribunal must apply the statutory criteria for discharge stated in the relevant statute.

The medical aspect addresses the question of whether the patient is mentally ill and susceptible to treatment in hospital. The tribunal can evaluate a range of medical opinion provided by the treating psychiatrist, the medical member of the tribunal and any independent psychiatric reports submitted in evidence.

The social aspect involves a full review of the patient's family and community. The tribunal will want to explore the care, treatment, financial and social support for the patient in the community, and whether the patient can be expected to take medication outside of the hospital. A package of treatment, nursing and social support in the community can provide a more effective, less intrusive, therapeutic alternative.

Community care or aftercare is such an important aspect of a tribunal case that patients are advised to consider the seeking an independent social inquiry report which explores, and even arranges, a community support network. The social inquiry report can provide another view of the community and aftercare facilities, clarify details of the patient's home circumstances, investigate facilities for housing, treatment, social support, community care and employment that can be provided by local authorities or voluntary organizations, and comment on the appropriateness of the patient's detention in the context of less restrictive facilities which may exist in the community.

3. The Right to Representation

An important component of a right to a hearing is representation. Representation can make a tribunal hearing a most effective forum for examination of a patient's case. Representatives need not be lawyers, but should receive structured, in-depth training on the legal, medical and social aspects of a tribunal hearing. Patients are confined and may have limited capacity due to their illness or medication. They require assistance in focusing the tribunal's attention on the criteria for discharge and a fair procedure, effectively compiling, organizing, and presenting relevant medical and social testimony and written reports, and finding alternative forms of community support. Representation is also necessary for effective examination of records and testimony adduced by the hospital, some of which may be kept confidential from the patient.

The European Commission and Court of Human Rights have repeatedly emphasized the need for effective legal representation as part of the "special procedural guarantees" required in mental health cases. Further, in *Airey v Republic of Ireland* (1979), the European Court considered that the right of a person to appear in the High Court without representation would not be "effective in the sense of whether she was able to present her case properly and satisfactorily". The Court concluded that publicly financed representation was required so that her rights under the European Convention were not "theoretical or illusory", but "practical and effective". These cases suggest that where a patient has clearly expressed a desire to be represented, and where she is prevented from being represented either because the court or tribunal does not ensure that someone is appointed and/or she cannot afford representation, a claim under international human rights law conceivably could arise.

In summary, the proposal for an inquisitorial, non-adversary, tribunal hearing, with an effective and trained representative in each case is intended to ensure that all relevant legal, medical and social facts and evidence are brought to bear upon a fundamentally important decision affecting liberty and the quality of human life.

4. The Right to a Free and Open Environment and Free Communication

Patients who are receiving psychiatric services should do so in the least restrictive, most therapeutically effective environment. This requires that they are cared for in a free and open setting, and that they are not restricted in their ability to communicate.

There is a worldwide practice-trend toward open (unlocked) wards and freedom to use the telephone and postal services, to receive visitors and to consult with a lawyer or other representatives (Curran & Harding, 1978). Unfortunately, few countries have specifically guaranteed these rights in their mental health codes. For most countries, an open environment and free communication are considered enlightened professional practice and not legal rights (Weir, 1974). A strong model for a Bill of Rights for hospital patients can, however, be found in some jurisdictions, particularly in North America. In the United States, the courts (*Wyatt v Stickney* 1972) and some State legislatures (Mass. Department of Mental Health, 1985; Weir, 1974) have guaranteed a set of human rights for hospitalized patients including the right to communicate with persons outside the facility, keep clothing and personal effects, have religious freedom, be employed if possible, keep and spend money, obtain education, and not be subject to unnecessary restraint or medication (Brakel, Parry & Weiner, 1985). The overriding theme is to ensure that patients, to the extent possible, have the same freedoms of expression, privacy, and liberty as any other citizen.

The proposed Declaration on the rights of mental patients in the

Daes Report (1982) is the first international human rights document which comes close to adopting the enumerated rights approach. The Daes Report specifies the following rights which can be limited only as strictly necessary for the patient's health and the protection of himself or others: to practise religion, privacy, enjoyment of facilities for education, vocational training, reading and recreation, and the purchase of essential items for daily living including clothes, recreation and communication. The Daes Report also proposes an unlimited entitlement to communication with persons outside the hospital, fair compensation for work done by patients, and a ban on exploitation of patient labour.

The freedom to communicate is so fundamental a human right that it should never be restricted. The right to inform others of conditions and treatment in the hospital is essential to help prevent patient maltreatment and neglect. The freedom of expression is also a basic constitutional right of any person in a vibrant democracy (Gostin, *A Human Condition*, Vol.1, 1975).

In modern times, the purpose of mental health services should be to meet a person's needs. This requires care in an open, free environment. There can be no disagreement today that patients should have an entitlement to write what they want, and see who they want. Closed mental health services invite public and international mistrust, and serve no therapeutic purpose.

There has been little written on the right of patients to be free from *restraint and seclusion* within the confines of a hospital. If a voluntary or informal patient is locked in a room, placed in seclusion or prevented from leaving the hospital without lawful justification, that is false imprisonment. However, under what circumstances can a compulsorily detained patient be imprisoned or otherwise restrained? Deprivation of liberty should not authorize all forms of "lesser" constraints within the hospital premises or the withdrawal of ordinary rights. Restraint within the hospital, even of detained patients, cannot be intended for revenge, punishment or convenience. It must be justified under the legal doctrine of "necessity" – i.e., to prevent an immediate danger to self or others. Moreover, any force used must be proportionate to attaining a legitimate therapeutic objective – force should not over-extend in degree or duration (Gostin, *Mental Health Services and the Law* and *Institu-*

91

tions Observed: Towards a New Concept of Secure Provision in Mental Health, both 1986).

There are few human rights declarations or court decisions specifically guaranteeing against unnecessary restraint or seclusion for the mentally ill patient in hospital. In the United States several courts (*Youngberg v Romeo*, 1982)) and commentators (Chambers, 1972; Hoffman & Foust, 1977) have developed a principle of the "least restrictive alternative" for psychiatric treatment. The Daes Report incorporates this principle in its proposed guidelines.

The European Commission of Human Rights in *A v the United Kingdom* (1980) forced the government to adopt detailed minimum standards for the seclusion of mental patients. The applicant had been placed in seclusion in Broadmoor Hospital in unsanitary conditions, without adequate space, light, ventilation, and toilet facilities, and with virtually no activity, occupation or association. The minimum standards agreed included the required amount of floor space; natural lighting; an individual programme of recreation; association; nursing care and treatment; clothing; mattresses and bedding; toilet and sanitation; and writing and reading materials.

The human deprivation involved in restricting free communication, and in restraining or secluding patients for disproportionate durations and under degrading conditions, is of international concern. Human rights safeguards in this area are justified by the harm that can be done to human liberty and integrity, and the degree to which these activities have taken place in many countries worldwide.

5. The Right Not to be Discriminated Against on Grounds of Mental Illness

Many progressive nations which give a constitutional value to equality, specifically require equal treatment of persons regardless of such morally irrelevant factors as race or sex. Yet few nations proscribe discrimination against the mentally ill. Mentally ill people often do not enjoy the same personal and property rights as other citizens (Brakel, Parry & Weiner, 1985; Gostin, *Mental Health Services and the Law*). There is a generalized assumption that mentally ill people as a class are incapable of exercising civil rights and privileges. Accordingly, statutes and regulations in countries throughout the world concerned with mentally ill people have regulated or denied their right to vote, to serve as a juror, to marry, to rear their children, to conduct their property and affairs, to sue in a court of law, to practise certain professions, to drive a car, to hold political office, or to make a binding contract. The list is almost endless of the restrictions on the basic rights of mentally ill people, rights which the rest of society takes for granted.

These restrictive laws and regulations take as their assumption the fact that the person is incompetent to exercise rights and privileges. The law in various countries has applied these restrictions in various ways – to all mentally ill people, to all persons in mental hospital, to all compulsorily detained patients, or to all patients adjudged incompetent. Thus, the label of "mental illness", "mental patient" or "incompetent" has served as a method of restricting a whole collection of rights and privileges.

There is a slow, but perceptible, international trend towards ending these automatic deprivations of rights for a class of people (Curran & Harding, *The Law and Mental Health*, 1978). The guiding principle is that mentally ill people are capable of exercising the same civil rights and privileges – and obligations – as others in society. There is no scientific basis for assuming that mentally ill people cannot perform as well as others. In each case the question must be asked – is the person capable of functioning responsibly in the specific area of concern? A right or privilege should be limited only when an independent court or tribunal decides, on the basis of demonstrable evidence, that the person is incapable of exercising it. Mentally ill people, like others, have varied and unique skills and limitations. A mentally ill person is seldom incompetent all of the time and in relation to all activities.

The applicable human rights principle is stated in the Daes Report. Every patient has the right "to exercise all his civil, political, social or cultural rights", including the right to manage his own economic affairs, control the disposition of his assets and vote. The only limitation is where a court makes a specific finding that the person is incompetent to exercise the right; detention in hospital itself does not justify such a finding of incompetence.

This human rights principle is consistent with the jurisprudence of the European Court of Human Rights. Article 6(1) of the European Convention of Human Rights provides that "in the determination of his civil rights and obligations ... everyone is entitled to a fair and public hearing within a reasonable time by an independent and impartial tribunal established by law ...". The European Court in *Winterwerp v the Netherlands* (1979) held that where mentally ill people were divested of the capacity to administer their property there was a determination of civil rights within the meaning of Article 6(1). Thus, patients divested of the right to manage their affairs are entitled to a judicial procedure.

This essay seeks to demonstrate that the assumptions which have been used to deprive mentally ill people of their liberty and autonomy are not wholly valid. International legal principles for all citizens should apply equally to the mentally ill. I have proposed five international human rights principles which are intended to establish a baseline of human rights values to protect, and serve the special needs of, mentally ill people.

NEW POSSIBILITIES, NEW THREATS

Computers and Privacy

NORMAN LINDOP

The U.K. passport we all know and love is on the way out. In 1987 the Passport Office ceased to issue the familiar hard-backed dark blue, gold-embossed symbol of British superiority, and we now have to make do with a limp, plastic-covered, mulberry-coloured booklet which is no more impressive than those of other countries. The talisman will have become a docket, and a docket with a sinister purpose; for the change is not just to conform with the requirements of the EC but signals a fundamental change of function. The new passport will be "machine readable". This means that at any frontier anywhere in the world a border official who has at his disposal a piece of equipment which is already widely and internationally available will be able instantaneously to record the personal details from a passport without the holder realising it, and the record will be automatically read into and stored by a computer. Instead of the passport opening frontiers to the traveller without let or hindrance, it has become the means of international surveillance. Ernest Bevin's utopian vision of going to Victoria Station and travelling freely abroad without documents of identity has finally faded. It has been overtaken by the undreamt-of scale of mass travel, by the internationalisation of crime, in particular terrorism, and above all by the ubiquity of information technology. Perhaps it was after all impossibly naïve and idealistic to expect that frontiers would cease to be watched, but just what price are we paying for the security effected by border controls? Will the surveillance made possible by modern information technology only apply at the frontiers, or shall we have to live with it in our daily lives?

This is only the latest in a series of issues which have emerged as computer technology has developed and linked up with telecom-munications, and which appear to bear upon fundamental questions of individual freedom. We are all familiar with the use of computer-

97

ised mailing lists by advertisers; they, too, are now international and going into orbit via satellite transmission – in the remorseless pursuit of markets and lower unit costs. Networks of communicating computer systems, within and across frontiers, are growing all the time in the private and public sectors. Bureaucrats and civil servants the world over are fascinated by the possibilities. Already in Britain there are plans for putting into communication the computer-based personal information systems of DHSS, the Driving and Vehicle Licensing Centre, the Police National Computer and the Inland Revenue; and the embossed plastic cards with unique machine-readable numerical identifiers which are now issued automatically to all school-leavers to mark their entry into the National Insurance scheme will in a few years' time be, in effect, national identity cards. The Big Brother of "1984" will have set up in business, a few years late perhaps, but with effective tabs upon everyone.

As long ago as 1975 a Home Office White Paper "Computers and Privacy" said, unambiguously, that "the time has come when those who use computers to handle personal information, however responsible they are, can no longer remain the sole judges of whether their own systems adequately safeguard privacy", and it set out clearly the special features of computerised information systems which had implications for privacy. The speed of computers, their capacity to store, combine, retrieve and transfer data, their flexibility and the low unit cost of the work they do, all facilitate the establishment and maintenance of ever more extensive record systems, retaining more and more data, which is easily and quickly accessible from many distant points. This data can quickly be transferred from one information system to another and can be combined and transformed in ways which might not otherwise be practicable; furthermore, data held on computers is invisible and not directly intelligible so that people have more difficulty in knowing what is in the records or what is happening to them. All in all, the technology could be said to be qualitatively transforming the threat to privacy which information systems, even manually sorted card indexes, have always posed. It prompts the question whether there is not something inexorable about the mindless march of technology; are we doomed to be everlastingly in retreat before the insidious advances of electronic information systems? And just what is it that we are objecting to? What do we feel we are losing?

Throughout the 1960s, as technology, especially computer

technology, developed, pressure built up in Parliament for legislative controls. Eventually, in 1970, the Home Office took refuge in a Committee of Enquiry into whether legislation to protect people against intrusions into privacy was needed. This, the Younger Committee, reported in 1972 and its report is still a classic; it covered a wide range of activities and technological developments which might be intrusive, although it was precluded from considering the activities of government departments and other public sector organisations – a limitation about which it protested.

Sir Kenneth Younger and his colleagues had first to consider what was meant by privacy. There was and is no legal definition of privacy; indeed there is no general agreement about what it is – like happiness we cannot define it but recognise it when we have it, or more often we know when we feel we do not have it. The concept derives from an assertion by an individual against the rest of society; since we are social animals and essentially interdependent, we voluntarily (or is it involuntarily?) surrender some of the autonomy of solitary existence in return for the support which society can give us. The extent of the surrender varies from one person to another, and the assumptions about the claim to privacy also vary – not only from one person to another within a given group or society, but from one society to another and from one historical period to another. "The right to be let alone" is probably the simplest statement of the privacy claim – significantly by an American judge in the 1880s – but it *is* a claim, not a fundamental right, since what is involved is a negotiation of the frontier between individual autonomy and social accountability. At its literal face value "the right to be let alone" is a quite unreasonable claim, and would be useless as the basis of granting legal protection.

The Younger Committee made no attempt at a definitive statement on what constituted privacy, contenting itself with a summary of different approaches and attempts at definition. It examined and rejected the proposition that a general right of privacy should be legally recognised, pointing out that this was not the way in which English law had in recent centuries sought to protect the main democratic rights of citizens – neither the right of free speech nor the right of free assembly being embodied in statute law, for example. Scotland might order things differently, but in England the rule was that what was not prohibited was permitted and the debate on civil rights was therefore concerned with the balance between the acceptable limits imposed by law and the freedom of action of the individual. Since then the pressure for a Bill of Rights has built up, partly inspired by the work of the European Court of Human Rights at Strasbourg, in which successive British governments have too often been on the losing side.

However, the Younger Committee argued that such a topic as privacy, which can be subject to rapid changes in social convention, was probably best not regulated on the basis of the slow build-up of case law, which would always tend to reflect the values of an earlier period rather than of contemporary society. The Committee therefore concentrated on a series of *ad hoc* recommendations, relating to two main aspects of privacy – freedom from intrusion upon oneself, one's home, family and relationships on the one hand, and privacy of information, that is the extent to which one can determine how information about oneself shall be handled, on the other. Under the first category they considered the intrusive gathering and dissemination of information by the publicity media, the handling of credit information, unwarrantable intrusion into personal matters at work and in education and medicine, prying by neighbours and landlords, and intrusive sales methods. Under the second category they considered investigations by private detectives, industrial espionage, technical surveillance devices, and finally computers.

They made a number of recommendations about legislation in various areas. During the 15 years since Younger reported, legislation more or less along the suggested lines has followed in two of the areas where it was recommended – the 1975 Consumer Credit Act, with the establishment of the Office of Fair Trading, and the 1984 Data Protection Act, with the establishment of a Data Protection Registrar. In an era in which prevailing political opinion has opposed increases in legislation, most of the other areas have not been found appropriate for legislative action. It is true that the media have developed procedures for self-regulation to forestall all-embracing legislation, but many would question how effective this self-regulation has so far been. As such Reports go, therefore, Younger can be said to have been fairly effective, in spite of being limited by being unable to consider public sector threats to privacy. When the Data Protection Committee was set up in 1976, to redeem a pledge made by the Home Secretary when Younger reported, it had no such limitation put upon it – it was in fact the first body

100

empowered to investigate information systems in the public sector, and the Committee came to see this as a major aspect of its work. Here again, however, the terms of reference of the Committee were not entirely congenial – in its anxiety not to open Pandora's box too wide the Home Office expressly precluded the Committee from considering traditional manual or non-electronic information systems. This was increasingly felt as an irksome and illogical limitation as the work of the Committee progressed, and prompted a somewhat disingenuous argument in its Report that in the long run the distinction would lose significance, because computers would sweep the board, and there would be no manual records anyway – an improbable outcome.

The Committee was in no doubt that, so far as any data protection principles were concerned, they should be universal and not dependent upon the particular form of system or record. Although the Committee's terms of reference excluded manual records, its Report makes clear that it could not justify on grounds of logic or justice the exclusion of manual records from any data protection legislation based upon general data protection principles. Nevertheless the Act is based upon this distinction; some other countries have followed the logic and applied the legislation to all forms of information systems, whether manual or electronic, but it is not known how effective such legislation is. One of the Home Office's strongest objections to the inclusion of manual records under the legislation was what it saw as the insuperable practical obstacles to controlling such a ubiquitous traditional activity.

The extent to which a person feels threatened by other people having information about him or her varies from one person to another. My father, if correctly addressed by name by a complete stranger, would say, rather coldly, "You have the advantage of me, Sir" – he felt slightly threatened by the mere fact that a stranger knew his name. Presumably pop-stars and politicians feel otherwise, but many people like to feel they can control the extent to which their names are known; it is to them an aspect of personal privacy, and it extends to other identifiers like home address. When investigators questioned the public about privacy on behalf of the Younger Committee, 33 per cent of those asked objected to the publication of names and addresses as happens in the Electoral Roll. The idea of what has been called data privacy, the claim of the individual to control information about himself, is not confined to so-called sensitive data or information of a particularly recherché kind – it can apply to any piece of data about an identifiable individual, who is the only one who can say whether or not, in the particular context, he or she regards the data as sensitive. The context is all.

In the course of ordinary domestic, family and work-place life, each of us voluntarily gives our name and address to a wide range of agencies, authorities and individuals, usually in expectation of a service; in addition, of course, we are each of us under statutory obligations to give personal details to agencies of central and local government, whether as employed persons, voting citizens, rate-or-tax-payers or licensees (of TV, dog, car, etc). The list grows as you think about it; the average middle-class citizen with a family, a house, car, insurances, mortgage, probably gives his name and address involuntarily (i.e. statutorily) to well over twenty agencies, and as many again voluntarily, each year. And each time there is a specific context which itself frames and augments the information about the individual. We do it almost without thought – certainly without considering just what may become of the information. When yet another mail order catalogue or free gift offer pops through our letter-box, personally addressed, we probably hardly stop to think how they came to have our name and address.

Now the receipt of unsolicited junk mail may seem a relatively trivial matter (though for some, who seem to regard their letter-box as part of their person, it is an affront) – and it certainly seems effective as a marketing device. The Younger Committee pointed out that any attempt to control the distribution of unsolicited advertising matter by legislation would involve an element of censorship in determining which types of advertisement or litera-ture were permissible and which not; they recommended no action. The issue remains an irritant to many unwilling recipients, but could be left as a relatively harmless result of the publication of names and addresses, were it not for more disquieting developments.

Marketing is by its nature an expansionist, aggressive activity and those concerned with it are constantly seeking to improve their performance by increasing the scale and selectivity of their approaches. There is therefore constant commercial pressure on address lists, especially if they are preselected – i.e. compiled in a particular context which is relevant from an advertising point of view. It may be harmless enough if mail-order suppliers of garden-

102

ing sundries sell their mailing lists to publishers of gardening encyclopaedias – it is perhaps more questionable if access to share registers of companies is used to circulate shareholders with party-political propaganda about privatisation or nationalisation.

There is now a considerable market value attaching to an accurate up-to-date and selective address list, and some of the largest collections of data in the private sector, running to thirty million entries or more in some cases, are amassed in this way. It could be argued that when publication of address lists reaches this scale they are so unselective as to be innocuous; the Swedish Data Inspection Board took the opposite view when it objected to the *Readers Digest* organisation compiling its own register of all adult Swedes (roughly 9 million). The Board took the view that it was not in the national interest that such complete information about the whole nation should be in private hands and after a prolonged and bitterly fought legal battle it won – ensuring the perpetual hostility of *Readers Digest* the world over to any suggestion of data protection thereafter.

At the other end of the scale a short list of names and addresses is not necessarily harmless. It may be so, if it is a personal Christmas card list, for example; but if the same modest list were to be headed "suspected sympathisers with the X Party" (or the Y terrorist group), or "directors of companies believed to be trading with country Z" – there could be danger to those on the list if it fell into the hands of evil-minded zealots – and perhaps then the shorter the list the greater the danger. Less dramatically, but of no less threat to those concerned, the publication of even so innocuous a list as the Electoral Register can, by disclosing the addresses of those who live alone, present a distinct danger in areas where the crime rate is high.

These are simple cases of the general thesis that information is power – information about a named person can confer power over that person, and the more complete the information the greater the power. As Seigel puts it in *Computing Law* – "information is power over decision, power over capital, power over individuals, power over organisation, power over adversaries and power over the past, present and future, and [that] power lends itself to any use and abuse". Information exerts its power when it is handled – collected, stored, transferred, analysed, collated, indexed, and, of course, published, broadcast, or obtained illicitly.

Information, defined as knowledge conveyed to the mind by a statement of fact, i.e. knowledge transfer, can take many forms – it

103

can be words, figures or pictures, through the medium of speech, printing or screen, or of course any other stimulant to human senses. Information is the currency of human communication; access to it may be controlled but information itself cannot be owned, since it is in essence in the mind. It is not an offence under the Theft Act to take information. The usual legal connotations of ownership are therefore irrelevant, but the possession of information, or the ability to control it, may nevertheless be of great significance; in an entirely trivial sense the paper or computer tape on which information is recorded can be owned, and while this does not confer rights of ownership over the information itself, this distinction may seem empty if what really matters is control of access to and use of information.

Now it can be argued that the mere collection of information about named persons is not in itself necessarily wrong; even if it does offend against good taste – like the prying neighbour behind the lace curtains – it is hardly an area for the heavy hand of the law. If it is said that it is the use to which such information may be put that can be objectionable, the libertarian might well reply that gossip is an age-old way of passing the time and one of the cements of society. It can be argued that it is a citizen's right to be free to collect information about whatever and whoever he likes and to do it in any way which is not intrusive or injurious. Here again the attempt to define one man's right reduces the freedom of another – the right to observe discreetly impinges on the privacy of whoever is observed, and the claim to privacy restricts the right to observe, if right it be.

It is relevant to recall in this connection that Younger did envisage situations where mere observation could seriously impair privacy – where, for example, the person observed had a reasonable expectation that he would not be subject to observation, or had deliberately taken steps to prevent surveillance, but special technical devices, either optical or electronic (bugging), were used to spy upon him. To meet such situations Younger proposed a new offence of "unlawful surveillance by device" where it was done surreptitiously. Here the normal human facility of observation, and the normal limits to human perception, would be extended and augmented by purely technical means – and the effect of technology would be not merely quantitative or multiplicative but qualitative; a new order of threat would be created. Although several European countries have legal controls on such activities, in the U.K. the law has not been extended in this way, though there may be legal remedies in some cases for those who believe they have been harmed by the use to which the surreptitiously collected information has been put: if, for example, unauthorised entry on to property has occurred, or if there has been breach of confidence or copyright, or if conspiracy to commit a crime, civil wrong, public mischief or some outrageously immoral act can be proved. This leaves a wide range of activities in an area of unregulated uncertainty, including telephone tapping; this may be official, under Ministerial approval "in the national interest", which Parliament may be said to have condoned or sanctioned, or it may be unofficial in the interests of, say, commercial or industrial espionage, in which case an offence is committed, if only the misappropriation of electric current!

The protection of individual privacy, in the sense of anonymity, has an obvious political dimension. If the individual can fence himself off from the prying eyes or fingers of the state, can maintain his private domain in his own way without intervention by public authorities, an important aspect of political liberty is established. Here again there is a question of balance: if society has democratically determined that taxes shall be collected and revenues so received spent in certain ways, non-payment of taxes is punishable even if the defaulter is objecting on conscientious grounds to aspects of state spending – on arms, for example. All this is straightforward enough, and is at the heart of liberal democracy, respecting dissent and minority opinion within the limits of the law. How far should it be taken in respect of information handling? The freedom of information lobby advocates the maximum possible openness by state and public authorities in disclosing information they hold; the state is a great collector of personal information – should that be publicly disclosed too? It is significant that the first country to enact data protection legislation was Sweden, which has had a freedom of information regime for over 200 years; the Swedes have become accustomed to a much more limited version of personal privacy as a result. It is commonplace in Sweden, for example, that the annual declarations of personal income and of wealth made by all citizens become publicly available documents once they are received by the tax authorities; a man can conceal his income neither from his wife nor from his neighbour. All Swedes have an officially registered address and all Swedes have a personal identification number which clearly incorporates date of birth – there can be no secrecy about

105

age. With so limited a territory left for privacy, perhaps it is not surprising that the Swedes have led the way in data protection. Their privacy problems started long before computers.

This last point is important. The idea that information about identifiable individuals must be handled with care is not new; it does not arise from the use of computers to process such information, though the rapid development of computer technology in the 1950s and 1960s brought the issue into sharp relief. Together with the popular demonology associated in the public mind with these strange monsters called computers it produced a sudden upsurge of anxiety. It was in this atmosphere of unease that the Younger Committee reported; about computers it had to say that, restricted as it was to investigating private sector applications, it had no evidence of abuse, but that there was a possibility and apprehension of abuse in the future. It gave a clear hint that the threat could come from either the public or the private sectors, and it set out a number of principles for handling personal information which, as the Younger Principles, have become famous; they survive in recognisable form in the Schedule of the Data Protection Act of 1984, where they assume an unusual importance. For the first time, an Act of Parliament lays a duty upon a public official, the Data Protection Registrar, to judge whether activities shall be deemed lawful by reference to a set of principles. And although the Act is all about computerised data banks, the word computer is not mentioned in the principles. In the form in which the principles appear in the Act they relate clearly to a version which was included in the Council of Europe Convention of 1981.

The first principle is that "the information to be contained in personal data shall be obtained, and personal data shall be processed, fairly and lawfully". This sounds simple enough, yet it does mean that the data subject (to whom the information relates) and the data user (who puts it into a computer) should each see the handling of the data in the same way, and this has not always been the case when data have been disclosed to third parties, or have been collected for one ostensible purpose and used for another. Since the electoral registration officer is authorised by statute to sell copies of the electoral register, address lists from this source are fairly and lawfully obtained; objections to trading in other address lists can be circumvented if, at the time of the initial collection of information, it is made clear that addresses will be passed on unless the data subject expressly objects. As a general rule data users should give as much information as possible to data subjects about what they propose to do with the data and must on no account mislead them.

The second principle simply says that "personal data shall be held only for one or more specified and lawful purposes". Here the key words are "only" and "specified". This means that data users, when they register, must state all the purposes for which the data are likely to be used, and they must then ensure that they do not use the data in any other ways.

The third principle is that "personal data held for any purpose or purposes shall not be used or disclosed in any manner incompatible with that purpose or purposes". This sounds a very broad and fine principle, and so it is. But unfortunately the Act is framed in such a way as to permit it to be circumvented. The principle appears to prohibit disclosure of personal data to third parties; in fact such disclosure is permitted either if the data user registers his intention so to disclose, or if the circumstances are covered by one of the controversial "non-disclosure exemptions". These have been described as a fraud upon the public because, even if a data user has solemnly undertaken in his registration statement not to disclose the data to any third party, he will under the Act be deemed not to have contravened the terms of his registration if he accedes to requests from police or tax officers pleading prejudice to their enquiries. So much for fine principles.

The fourth principle is that "personal data held for any purpose or purposes shall be adequate, relevant and not excessive in relation to that purpose or those purposes" – and there is more to this than at first meets the eye. It clearly precludes the collection of data for its own sake, or just in case it might turn out to be useful; and it requires that information shall be kept for only as long as it remains relevant. It ties in with the fifth principle that "personal data shall be accurate and, where necessary, kept up-to-date" – a formidable require-ment, if taken literally, in view of the frequency with which personal details (address, etc.) can change, and also bearing in mind the possible diversity of sources of information; and who but the data subject can be the true judge of accuracy – unless of course he may have an interest in falsifying the record? Who is to judge if there is a dispute? The Act goes no further than requiring that, where there is disagreement over accuracy, the fact that there is such disagreement must be recorded. The sixth principle, that "personal data held for

107

any purpose or purposes shall not be kept longer than is necessary for that purpose or those purposes", follows from its predecessors and places a heavy responsibility on data users to ensure that they regularly weed out data once it has served its purpose. This is a new requirement for most information systems, which have simply expanded to contain ever more data, relevant and timely or not; but it is surely little more than good practice should require in the interests of efficient and economical operation. The last principle of all, the eighth, is also soundly practical, requiring security measures to protect data from unauthorised or accidental access, alteration, disclosure or destruction.

The seventh principle is different from the others, and introduces an important new right for data subjects. "An individual shall be entitled (a) at reasonable intervals and without undue delay or expense (i) to be informed by any data user whether he holds personal data of which that individual is subject, and (ii) to access to any such data held by a data user; and (b) where appropriate to have such data corrected or erased." The right of subject access is established, as is the right to have the record corrected or erased if the other data protection principles require it, but there may be a charge for it.

In accordance with the terms of the European Convention the Act provides additional safeguards for four categories of what are called sensitive data; these are information about the data subject relating to racial origin, political opinions or religious beliefs, physical or mental health or sexual life, and criminal convictions. The Home Secretary has power to modify or supplement the data protection principles to provide additional safeguards for these categories; it will be interesting to see what these additional regulations will contain.

The path to data protection legislation in Britain was a long and tortuous one. There were attempts at legislation on computers and privacy through Private Members Bills from 1961 onwards, which the Home Office, as the lead department on the subject, managed to stall successfully until 1970, when it was one of the issues which led to the setting up of the Younger Committee. When that Committee reported in 1972 there was further delay before a White Paper, *Computers and Privacy*, was published in 1975; the Data Protection Committee was established in 1976 and reported, recommending legislation, in 1978. Six more years elapsed before the Act of 1984. It is hardly an exaggeration to say that by delaying tactics the Home Office held up the legislation by more than twenty years. Why? It can hardly have been on account of the unanimous beliefs of the many Home Secretaries who passed through the department during the period – though it has to be said that only one, Roy Jenkins, showed any real interest in the issue and he did what he could to achieve action. Clearly the permanent officials were opposed to legislation and persuaded successive Home Secretaries of whatever party to follow their line. As a kind of amalgam of a Ministry of Justice (dealing with the rights of the individual) and a Department of the Interior (responsible for internal order and the integrity of the state), it would hardly be surprising for the Home Office to show symptoms of schizophrenia; it controls immigration, prisons, and drug abuse, for example, in addition to carrying responsibility for the Metropolitan Police and the Special Branch, and all these activities depend heavily on collecting and using personal information. Clearly it viewed suggestions for data protection legislation, especially those which made the inclusion of public sector computers a central point, with disfavour, and until pressure from Europe proved irresistible it was successful. Even then it ensured that there would be emasculating exemptions. Britain was almost the last country in Western Europe to legislate, though it had been in Britain that the debate had originated decades earlier.

When the Data Protection Committee came to consider the case for legislation it had no doubt that the public sector presented the greater set of problems: the complex modern government bureaucracies at national and local level are great consumers of personal information about citizens – mostly to the citizens' benefit, of course, but some of the possibilities of linkage, network-formation and hence secret profile-building about identifiable individuals seemed frightening. The Committee would have liked to secure legislation which ensured that at least the existence of every computerised system handling personal information was known: such provisions apply in other Western democracies, but the British tradition of shielding National Security matters even from Parliamentary scrutiny militated against such disclosures here. As a positive step towards ensuring some uniformity of treatment of all other non-secret operations, in both public and private sectors, the Committee strongly advocated a set of publicly known Codes of Practice, to one or other of which every user would be required to

109

subscribe. Without ever explaining quite why, the Home Office fiercely resisted this approach until late in the Bill's passage through Parliament; as a result Codes of Practice are just mentioned in the Act, and the Registrar is now busy encouraging their formulation and observance. Because they are optional, however, they cannot provide the safeguards once hoped for, and individual data users are able to register their activities in their own way.

So insistent were the Data Protection Committee that the public sector constituted the greater threat that they recommended wholesale registration of all public sector users but only piecemeal or phased registration of private sector users. In the event the Act required simultaneous, across-the-board registration of both sectors, placing an unnecessary strain on the private sector, and ensuring the greatest possible public hostility to the legislation, and the greatest possible strain on the Registrar's Office.

The Report of the Data Protection Committee was published late in 1978, a bad time for political initiatives: within a few months the new Conservative Government was in office and contenting itself with a fresh and laborious round of further consultations – there seemed little likelihood of anything being done until, in 1981, the Council of Europe, as part of its concern with human rights, opened its "Convention for the Protection of Individuals with regard to Automatic Data Processing" for signature by States which had appropriate legislation enacted. Before long there were sufficient signatories for the eventual ratification and implementation of the Convention to become certain, and the prospect loomed of Britain becoming isolated as a somewhat dubious off-shore "data haven". This was because of the vast trade which had built up in trans-border data flow – the international exchange across frontiers of electronically processed information. Britain, and especially London, had become "a cross-roads on the international data highway"; yet if Britain could not subscribe to the European Convention those who were subscribers could discriminate against Britain and refuse to handle data flows in either direction because there was no protective data legislation. This had immediate commercial implications and the Government suffered an overnight conversion, bringing forward the first Data Protection Bill in February 1983 and reviving it after the election later in the year. "Commerce, not liberty, is the motive", said *The Times*, going on to call the Bill, which became the 1984 Act, meagre and minimalist.

It was symptomatic of the British approach to the whole question that at the time the Act took effect no one knew, even to an approximation, how many data users were going to be required to register. Ten years earlier at the time of the Younger Report, it had been possible to compile a rough estimate of the number of computer installations; all thoughts were then on the powerful centralised main-frame equipment which had dominated the technology till then. By the 1980s, however, the whole aspect of the technology had changed, with profound effects on the privacy issue. The emphasis was now on the proliferation of high-capacity small-scale computers capable of greater versatility than the older machines, lending themselves to the formation of networks, and many of them deliberately designed for easy access, so that much of the mystique was being dispelled. No estimates could be made of the number of systems or the number of applications involving personal data – guesses ranged from 50,000 to 350,000. The Data Protection Registrar, in publicising a closing date of May 1986 for the receipt of registrations, had no idea how many data users ought to be registering; in the event the flow of registrations was far slower than had been hoped, but by the end of 1986 it was clear that the higher guesses were more likely to be right.

Assuming that eventually all data users handling personal data on computers are registered, what has been achieved? It would be pleasant to be able to say that, as a result, the existence of all automated personal data handling systems is known, even if not much has been vouchsafed of what they do. Unfortunately, however, because of exemption clauses which the Government insisted upon throughout the debates on the Bill, even this minimum reassurance is not possible.

Not only are personal data not protected if a Cabinet Minister certifies that exemption is required "for the purpose of safeguarding national security" (a rather vague and wide catch-all phrase) but there are other exemptions where the protection afforded by the Act is held to be "likely to prejudice" the prevention or detection of crime, the apprehension or prosecution of offenders, or the assessment or collection of any tax or duty. The decision on prejudice is presumably at the discretion of police and tax officers; if widely exercised it could set at naught some of the principal objects of the Act.

The Data Protection Act was not designed to curb the develop-

111

ment of automated data systems, but to ensure good practice on the part of users, and to give data subjects the right to interrogate users. It was designed merely to fit within the minimal requirements of the European Convention and it hardly revolutionises the data privacy scene. Nevertheless, assuming that all users are eventually registered, the data subject should be able to feel that he knows or can find out more than he knew hitherto about the extent to which he figures in the data banks. The great motive power behind information technology is ever-diminishing unit costs, so that the application of computers can be expected to continue to proliferate. Will the Act remain effective in the face of technical development?

One of the innovatory features of the Act is that the holder of the office it sets up – the Data Protection Registrar – has the task of applying a set of principles – the Data Protection Principles, set out as a Schedule to the Act. He has to judge each application for registration in the light of the Principles; to the extent that the Principles are agreed to be universal and timeless, the march of technology should present few problems, since particular technical processes are not dealt with in the Act. (Here it is superior to the American version, which attempted to describe the technology and was rapidly outdated.) What is not so clear is whether the Principles have anticipated all types of problem which the technology may throw up. It could even be that we are moving into a hitherto unknown dimension with the next steps in IT. Already we have micros everywhere, capable of linkage and "conversation" with each other, up to now by telephone link, but any day now through satellites. The electronic information explosion knows no frontiers; we may soon be enveloped in a world-encompassing atmosphere of information messages and "noise" of a variety and density not known before, able to plug in to one or a multiplicity of channels and capture information of a wide diversity of nature and origin, much of it junk. Once personal information gets into such a network it will be difficult if not impossible to restrict access to it; it could be that such an open system could be justified to the data subject as the latest desirable addition to the role of consumer in the acquisitive society – why not order one's claret from one's fireside by the keyboard direct from the château, with instant payment by electronic fund transfer at point of sale, debiting one's bank account instantaneously? With the expansion and internationalisation of markets this may become commonplace. A decade ago the Chairman of *Readers Digest* in the

112

U.K. could dismiss the pressure for legislation on data privacy as "like consumerism, a middle-class fad". Perhaps the wheel has gone full circle and the middle class is now prepared to sell its birthright of privacy for the glittering prizes of acquisition.

But that is not the end of the story; networks will not only serve the interests of the market; they bring within reach the possibility of the surveillance of whole populations, with serious implications for personal privacy. In Britain it is easy to forget that, while we may have the publicly available electoral register, we are almost alone in Europe in not requiring each citizen to have a formally registered address, and to notify changes of address to the police. It is an aspect of privacy we should take more seriously; it may seem a frail distinction to draw when armed police can batter down your front door on suspicion that a wanted person may be inside, but at least it gives the possibility of some redress, and may make it more difficult to achieve the total surveillance of society. The arrival of the jackbooted armed emissaries of the state, battering the door in the small hours of the morning, has become the epitome of political repression of right and of left, particularly in respect of dissenting minorities. It is made possible because information about citizens is held by organs of the state. So it was when the Germans over-ran Holland in 1940 and within three days had rounded up large numbers of Jews – the Dutch population records which included religious affiliation were put to sinister use, promptly and efficiently even without the aid of modern technology. We cannot afford to assume that all governments, all public servants, will always be benign and free from corruption. No legislative curb can guarantee fair and benevolent treatment for individuals irrespective of the fortunes of the political future; laws will not stop tyrants. At best the existence of some checks and balances, or statutory tripwires, may serve to alert the wary as to how things are moving. It is easy to be paranoic about IT and the future, and that is hardly justified; but constant vigilance is required.

For Information Technology is going to transform all our lives – we have hardly seen anything yet. When every new house or flat is automatically provided with plug-in points for water, electricity, *and information*, each of them offering the instant service of a widespread network, everyday life will change. Our shopping and banking habits, our home record-keeping and correspondence, local and worldwide, our legal, medical and insurance affairs, our

113

most intimate communications, could all be encompassed by our home data bank with its living connections to systems in the outside world; and by the two-way nature of those links and the ingenuity of the "hacker" or by pure mischance all our secrets could be opened to the world. The effect of IT on personal life could be as profound as that of an earlier technological innovation, the motor car. The earliest horseless carriages were regarded as socially dangerous and the first legislation to control them required that each should be accompanied by three persons – a driver, a passenger in case the driver was taken ill, and a third person walking in front carrying a red flag. If at the time of the first Red Flag Act anyone had prophesied that within 100 years horseless carriages would be careering around by the million, they would have been thought dangerously deluded; no one would have believed that society would survive such an onslaught. Yet we have adapted our lives, more or less, to the motor car; the early legislation was progressively modified as technology advanced and attitudes changed until, by a process of social adaptation and general education, the current road traffic regulations and the Highway Code together just about control the monster. We are at the Red Flag stage with IT, and it is hardly possible to anticipate how the future will work out. In addition to vigilance we need education in the responsible uses of this new extension of man's powers, otherwise we might be driven to a fruitless Luddite destruction of computers because they seem able to take on a life of their own. IT presents a challenge to the responsible society which cannot be ignored.

Interventive Reproduction

URSULA MITTWOCH

"We have a tradition that sex and reproduction must be attended by privacy, dignity and romance. It is a good tradition, provided we add a fourth attribute, namely understanding; for otherwise the fundamental life activities concerned with sex may become involved in fears, inhibitions and blind taboos." (Corner, *The Hormones in Human Reproduction*, 1964)

Ethical problems arising from discoveries, real or imagined, in the field of reproduction are not new. In 1786, J.C. Hencke, an organist in the German town of Hildesheim, published a book which set out to describe a secret of nature which the author had recently discovered. As a result of his discovery, parents would henceforth be able to select the sex of their children at will. The author regarded as unfounded the fears of those moralists who thought God's order would be destroyed if the birth of sons and daughters were determined by the parents. He argued that, on the one hand, reproduction is mainly practised by peasants and others of low rank, who could hardly be expected to show much interest in whether they produced male or female children. Whereas for those classes for whom his discovery was primarily intended, it might indeed reveal the wise intention of the Creator to prevent the sad fate of so many daughters who, because of exaggerated economic expectations, were hitherto condemned to spend their entire lives in the unmarried state.

Ethical problems do not change. What changes are the details on which different generations base their convictions. Another change within the last 200 years is in the field of reproductive biology. The fourth attribute demanded by George Corner, that of understanding, is possible for the first time in the history of civilization; but it is a

115

possibility which so far is available to only a small minority of specialists. Therefore I shall preface a discussion of the pros and cons of reproductive techniques by a brief résumé of the underlying biology.

Modern biology is based on cells. The cell is the unit of which all living organisms are composed, and most organisms contain vast numbers of them. A rough estimate tells us that an adult human individual is made up of ten million million (10^{13}) cells, a number which exceeds that of the total population of the world approximately 2000 times.

Different cells, such as blood cells, nerve cells, and muscle cells, make up the various tissues and organs of the body, but the diversity of cell types is superimposed on a common plan: each cell consists of a nucleus, which is the seat of the chromosomes, the genes, and the genetic material in general; and which is surrounded by cytoplasm, whose constituents provide the environment in which the genetic potential is actualized.

The basic similarity between cells refers not only to their general plan but also to their genetic endowment. Indeed, all the millions of cells that make up each one of us have been formed by a process of successive cell divisions, during each of which the 46 chromosomes were first faithfully duplicated, and then separated to form two new daughter cells. This process can be traced back until we arrive at a single cell which was formed at the moment of conception by the fusion of two parental germ cells, i.e. one egg and one sperm cell. This fusion cell, which is technically known as a zygote, could be regarded as the foundation stone of the new individual.

In view of the central position of the egg and sperm cell in reproductive biology, we need to look at them in a little more detail. The diverseness of their appearance gives no clue to the similarity in the origin and function of the male and female germ cells (which are also known as gametes, or marrying cells). The egg is the largest cell of the body, and in addition to its nucleus contains a relatively massive cytoplasm, whose contents provide nutrients to the zygote in the early stages of its development. By contrast, the sperm is the smallest cell of the body, whose nuclear material is packed into the smallest possible space inside the sperm head, and whose cytoplasm

116

is reduced to a thin filament, the tail, which allows the sperm to swim before fertilizing the egg.

In spite of their different appearances and functions during the actual process of fertilization, the egg and sperm cells bring equivalent portions of genetic material to the zygote and hence the future individual. They are able to do this because they are formed by a special type of cell division, during which the 46 chromosomes in the body cells of the father and the mother assort into 23 pairs, following which the two members of each pair segregate, so that the resulting germ cells receive only 23 chromosomes. Fertilization consists of the coming together of the two sets of chromosomes, 23 paternal and 23 maternal ones, so providing a new set of 46 chromosomes "yoked together" in the zygote, which is the first cell of the new individual.

The difference in size between egg and sperm is counterbalanced by the numbers in which they are produced. During the reproductive life of a woman, one egg – rarely two or more – matures at monthly intervals and is discharged at ovulation, which brings the total number of eggs that are ovulated to barely 500. In order to achieve this, almost seven million egg cell precursors are laid down in the female fetus. But this number pales into insignificance when we compare it with the prodigious number of sperm, whose output runs to a hundred million daily! Only one sperm fertilizes an egg, but it evidently requires the backup of many millions of others.

The word "sperm" is derived from the Greek meaning a "seed", and reflects the Aristotelian idea that the male semen (the latter word being derived from the Latin word for "seed") contains the formative element which grows and develops inside the mother's womb. Only within the last hundred years has it become evident that a sperm is in no way comparable to the seed of a plant, which is a multicellular reproductive structure containing the embryo of the plant. By contrast, a sperm is a single cell, a gamete, which needs to fuse with another gamete of opposite sex before the development of the embryo can be initiated.

The immense difficulties lying in the way of an understanding of the mysteries of generation, and the late stage in history when the riddle was solved, is also evident when we consider another commonly used term for the sperm cell, namely "spermatozoon". F.J. Cole (*Early Theories of Sexual Generation*, 1930) has described how in 1827, Karl von Baer achieved lasting fame by his discovery of the mammalian egg in the ovary of the dog. However, von Baer regarded the multitude of sperm cells swimming around in the semen as single-celled parasites, and he perpetuated this view by calling them "spermatozoa", i.e. sperm animals. During the 1840s, Albert von Koelliker showed that spermatozoa are not parasites, but products of cells in the testis. The coming together of egg and sperm in fertilization was observed in simple marine animals, such as sea urchins, during the course of the following four decades.

The problem of how it comes about that individuals develop as either males or females was solved, at least in principle, during the first quarter of this century. One of the 23 pairs of body cells differs in males and females, and these chromosomes are known as "sex chromosomes". Females have two equal sex chromosomes, called "X", but males have only one X chromosome, which is partnered by a smaller one, the Y chromosome. It follows that all eggs contain an X chromosome, but when spermatozoa are formed, the X separates from the Y, with the result that half the sperm contain an X, and the other half a Y chromosome. The latter will cause the development of a male, the former of a female embryo. The sex of the embryo is, therefore, predetermined at fertilization.

The human egg meets the sperm in the Fallopian tube (see Figure). During ovulation, the ripe egg is released from the ovarian follicle which contained it. It is channelled into a Fallopian tube, with the aid of the finger-like projections which surround its aperture, and which are themselves covered by numerous cilia, resembling tiny eye-lashes.

The journey of the sperm to the Fallopian tube is of necessity longer. On leaving the testis, the sperm traverses a tightly coiled convoluted tube, known as the epididymis, which eventually widens into the vas deferens. During ejaculation, the sperm is deposited into the vagina, after which it has to negotiate the cervix and the uterus, from where it enters the Fallopian tube. Of about two hundred and fifty million spermatozoa that are deposited in the vagina, two hundred may reach the Fallopian tubes.

If egg and sperm meet at the right time, one of the spermatozoa is likely to penetrate the egg. The fertilized egg, now known as a zygote, continues to move along the Fallopian tube towards the uterus, and while it does so, divides once or twice a day. This results in a ball of cells, which then proceeds to burrow into the wall of the

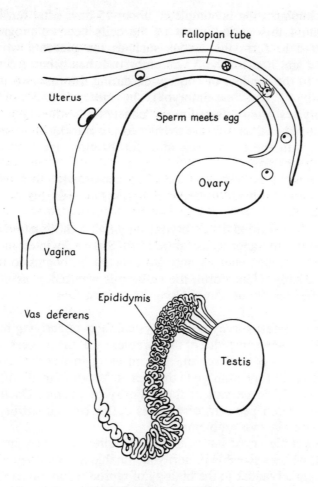

LEGEND TO FIGURE

In order to achieve fertilization, spermatozoa need to travel from the testis via the highly convoluted epididymis to the vas deferens, and, during intercourse, are deposited in the vagina, from where they continue their journey up the uterus and into the Fallopian tubes. Once a month an egg is discharged from the ovary, and is picked up into the opening of the Fallopian tube. The egg proceeds down the Fallopian tube, and if it meets spermatozoa, is likely to fuse with one of them. The proembryo continues to move down the Fallopian tube and after two weeks is ready to imbed in the wall of the uterus. (Diagram by A.J. Lee)

119

uterus. Implantation is completed about 15 days after fertilization. Throughout this period, most of the cells become progressively committed to form the tissues such as the placenta which will surround and nourish the future embryo. It has become customary to refer to the product of conception during the first two weeks as "proembryo" (or "pre-embryo"). In medical terminology the proembryo is often referred to as "conceptus", which, by referring to a past rather than a future event, has the additional advantage of neutrality. In the third week after fertilization, the embryo itself begins to develop.

It is thought that about a third of conceptuses fail to develop into an embryo. In most cases, their presence will not have been detected.

When first formed the embryo is only half a millimetre long, and bears no resemblance to its future form. Six weeks later, most of its organs are present and its outward appearance begins to resemble that of a baby. Henceforth, the embryo is referred to as a fetus. It now measures about 25mm along its longest axis.

Even the briefest survey of the physical facts underlying reproduction will convey some idea of the complexity of the process, from the formation of egg and sperm, their meeting in fertilization, to the development of the embryo in the uterus. Yet despite all difficulties, conception is successful in the majority of people. On the other hand, about ten per cent of couples suffer from infertility. These facts results in two problems.

Most people could have far more children than they are able to support, while a sizeable minority are unable to have any children at all. Recent advances in the biology of reproduction have resulted in methods and techniques which can overcome both problems. The pros and cons of the various procedures involved have been debated on many occasions with much ardour and conviction, and not a little prejudice.

To what extent should people be allowed to choose their own reproductive strategies?

Abortion

It should be evident from the preceding section that the product of conception obtained half its genetic endowment from the father's sperm, and the other half from the mother's egg. Therefore it cannot at any stage, whether as embryo or fetus, be regarded as part of its mother's body. This is not an argument against abortion, but the legitimacy of this procedure needs to be based on a concept other than that a woman may choose how she wishes to use her body.

The alleged choice is in any case short-lived. If there is a conflict between the baby's and mother's welfare after it is born, all public sympathy will have shifted away from the mother. Even if the child is a drain on her health, and she cannot cope with it, public opinion will totally condemn her if she neglects or injures her child. When contrasted with the legitimacy of abortion, this difference in attitude must be attributed to the changed status of the child as before and after birth. The argument about women's choices over their bodies is largely a red herring.

To bring up a child is not only a more protracted process than pregnancy, but is also in many ways more onerous, and certainly more expensive. Abortion usually provides the last chance for a woman to opt not to have a child (unless she is prepared to offer it for adoption) either for social reasons or because the fetus is in some way malformed. This possibility is available because the fetus is regarded as less important than the mother.

Contraception

Contraception as a problem of principle is largely, though not entirely, a thing of the past. Family planning is regarded as the norm by the majority of people in developed countries, and the threat of overpopulation in developing countries is perceived by a thinking minority in many countries as casting a shadow over the future of mankind. This of course does not mean that the opposition to birth control expressed in the early years of the century, particularly by religious authorities, has completely ended. In particular, a Papal encyclical of 1968 explicitly proscribes any action which either before, at the moment of, or after sexual intercourse, is specifically intended to prevent procreation. Nevertheless, the climate of public opinion has moved in the direction of making contraception available, in spite of legislation, which varies from country to country, aiming to restrict various aspects of the practice.

In Britain, condoms are available over the counter and from slot machines, so that anyone wishing to purchase them can do so.

However, oral contraceptives for women require a doctor's prescription, while other contraceptive devices need to be fitted in a clinic (Caroline Berry, *The Rites of Life*, 1987). Even though there are valid medical and technical reasons for this state of affairs, it can lead to difficulties for women and girls. A legal quandary can arise if the contraceptive is requested by a girl under 16 years of age. Above that age children can give consent to medical treatment, whereas children below 16 require their parents' consent.

Suppose a girl under 16 does not wish her parents to know that she is seeking contraceptive advice: the medical profession is divided between those who give priority to parental consent, and others who, in line with the General Medical Council, hold that the principle of professional confidentiality overrides that of parental consent. In 1983, Mrs Victoria Gillick sought a court order to rule the latter order of priorities illegal. She won her case on appeal, but this was subsequently overruled by the House of Lords. The outcome was clearly welcomed by those with liberal sentiments: for however much one may deplore the sexual activities of young teenagers, there can surely be little doubt that the protection of such a girl from an unwanted pregnancy must be a matter of primary importance, and, therefore, if need be, have precedence not only over the right of parents to give or withhold consent, but even over the right to information regarding their child, for whom they are legally responsible.

Artificial Insemination

Until recently, infertility was regarded as a problem for women, and hardly anything was known about reproductive problems in men. Today infertility is seen as a problem for the couple and andrology has joined gynaecology as a discipline in scientific medicine.

In order for conception to take place, a man must produce a very large number of motile spermatozoa. If the number of spermatozoa is relatively small, conception may fail to occur after natural intercourse. However, if the sperm from a number of ejaculates are stored, added together and introduced into the wife's vagina or uterus, fertilization may be successful. The techniques may also circumvent impotence and some other problems that prevent normal intercourse followed by conception.

Artificial insemination by the husband's sperm is approved by

122

many religious authorities as a means of achieving fertility in a couple who would otherwise be childless. However, the practice is condemned in a recent announcement made by the Vatican on Respect for Human Life in its Origins and on the Dignity of Procreation, which permits a child to be conceived only as a result of intercourse within marriage.

Artificial insemination by donor (AID), i.e. by a man other than the husband, can be used to achieve fertility where the husband lacks spermatozoa, or is otherwise infertile, or if the husband is a carrier of a genetic disease with a high chance of its being transmitted to a child; alternatively the husband and wife may both be carriers of the same recessive gene, so that each act of fertilization would have a 25 per cent chance of giving rise to a diseased child. The use of AID would make this an unlikely event. This procedure has attracted more opposition, both from religious authorities, who regard it as in some ways similar to adultery, and from sociologists, whose misgivings are based on two main reasons. One is that it may weaken the marriage by suggesting a "failure" on the part of the husband. The other worry is whether the child will or will not be told about his or her origin. There are differences of opinion whether the whole truth is necessarily helpful in all cases. The Warnock Committee on Human Fertilization and Embryology (1984) recommended that AID should be available on a properly organized basis and subject to licensing arrangements. The Committee also recommended that the law should be changed so that the husband could be registered as the father.

In Vitro Fertilization

Whereas artificial insemination is a simple technique, which can be carried out in an outpatients department, or even at home, *in vitro* fertilization needs to be performed by highly skilled practitioners and requires sophisticated laboratory facilities. The technique consists of four basic stages:

1. Eggs need to be collected from the woman's ovary.
2. Since spermatozoa in ejaculated semen are not yet able to penetrate the egg, the spermatozoa have to undergo careful treatment in the laboratory to achieve the maturation which normally occurs in the female reproductive tract.
3. Spermatozoa are combined with the egg.

4. After fertilization has taken place, the zygote is cultured in the laboratory for a few days and the proembryo is then placed in the woman's uterus.

In vitro fertilization was pioneered by Patrick Steptoe and Robert Edwards, and resulted in the first "test-tube baby", Louise Brown, being born in 1978. Since that time, more than 20,000 babies are thought to have been born as a result of this technique.

In vitro fertilization can restore fertility to women who ovulate but cannot conceive because their Fallopian tubes are blocked. A major cause of tubal occlusion is pelvic inflammatory disease. Once the oviduct is blocked, it is difficult to treat by surgery or other means. Since the egg cannot enter the oviduct, the treatment consists of removing it from the ovary prior to ovulation, fertilizing it in the laboratory, and placing the proembryo into the uterus where it has a chance to implant. A baby conceived by *in vitro* fertilization in this way is as genetically related to its father and mother as a normally conceived baby, and the technique is widely accepted as ethically acceptable, although not, of course, by the Catholic Church, for the reasons that have been mentioned above.

One ethical problem which does arise stems from the fact that the success rate of implantation increases with the number of embryos being implanted. In practice, women undergoing *in vitro* fertilization are treated with hormones, which causes several eggs to ripen, and they are then fertilized. The proembryoes can be frozen and stored, and their availability improves the chance of success of *in vitro* fertilizations as well as allowing a woman to have another child a year or two after the first. The status of the proembryo, and the laboratory procedures to which it may or may not be subjected, have been the subject of extensive debates and discussions.

The availability of *in vitro* fertilization opens up the further possibility that the proembryo which is eventually implanted need not originate from an egg produced by the woman herself. The procedure of egg donation, or of proembryo donation, could help some women to bear a child even though they are unable to produce their own eggs, or are bearers of a genetically transmissible disease. The Warnock Committee recommended that donation of an egg or proembryo should be permitted as a means of treating infertility, but that the techniques should be carefully controlled by licensing. The Committee further recommended openness with the children about their genetic origin.

Surrogacy

Surrogacy is an arrangement whereby a woman carries a child with the intention of handing it over to another woman after its birth. This could be a way out for a couple unable to have children because of the wife's inability to bear a child. If the wife is unable to produce eggs, or if she is the carrier of a serious genetic abnormality, the surrogate mother may also be the genetic mother of the child, and the spermatozoa may be donated by the commissioning woman's husband, either by *in vitro* fertilization or through intercourse. Alternatively, the wife may be able to produce healthy eggs but for various medical reasons not be in a position to maintain a pregnancy. In such a situation, her egg could be fertilized by her husband's sperm in vitro, and the fertilized egg be implanted in the uterus of another woman, who will bear the child, to whom she is not genetically related. This condition is referred to as full surrogacy, or uterine fostering. Of course, either type of surrogacy could be commissioned in the absence of medical reasons, with a view to providing a baby without the burden of pregnancy. For instance, if a couple opted for a full surrogacy arrangement, they could have a baby that bears the same genetic relationship to them as do children conceived in the normal way, while someone else copes with the inconvenience of pregnancy and birth.

Of all the possibilities of interventive reproduction, none has been the subject of more public opposition than surrogacy. The Warnock Committee, after expressing liberal views regarding such practices as egg donation and *in vitro* fertilization, turned to truly Draconian measures in their effort to stamp out surrogacy. The Committee not only recommended statutory provision making all surrogacy agreements illegal and therefore unenforceable in the courts, but also called for the introduction of legislation rendering it a criminal act for any person to assist in the establishment of a surrogate pregnancy. Agencies arranging contacts between potential commissioning and surrogate mothers would also be committing criminal offences. Commercial agencies for the establishment of surrogacy have since been outlawed by the 1985 Surrogacy Arrangements Act (M.D.A. Freeman in *Current Legal Problems*, 1986).

In an age when homosexuality and abortion have been legalized, what could be the reason for an otherwise progressive body like the

125

Warnock Committee to invoke the criminal law with a view to preventing a newly available reproductive technique from being practised between consenting adults? One important difference between surrogacy and homosexuality is of course that surrogacy results in the birth of a child; and it could be argued that such a child might be socially disadvantaged if the facts became known. But if all children who might be socially disadvantaged were prevented from being born, the earth would be a thinly populated planet. In the absence of more tangible evidence, the argument regarding possible harmful effects on children can be ignored.

A major argument put forward against surrogacy is "that to introduce a third party into the process of procreation which should be confined to the loving partnership between two people, is an attack on the value of the marital relationship". Since the same argument applies to *in vitro* fertilization by donor, which the Committee recommended should be available on a properly organized basis, the case against surrogacy continues as follows: "Further the intrusion is worse than in the case of AID, since the contribution of the carrying mother is greater, more intimate and personal, than the contribution of a semen donor. It is also argued that it is inconsistent with human dignity that a woman should use her uterus for financial profit and treat it as an incubator for someone else's child." The last sentence begs at least four questions, and will be analysed in some detail.

What is, or is not, consistent with human dignity is obviously a value judgment, which can neither be confirmed nor refuted; and, of course, one can think of other activities that could be construed as being inconsistent with human dignity, which are not criminalized.

The point about a woman using her uterus for financial gain poses two problems. If the loss of human dignity were dependent on the financial gain, there would be no moral and social objection to surrogacy in the absence of such gain; whereas if the condemnation refers to surrogacy under any circumstances, the question of financial gain is irrelevant. The additional use of the metaphor of the uterus as incubator is comparable to the "Rent-a-Womb" heading of the tabloids. Both are designed to convince the readership of the horror of the subject-matter.

Why should the uterus be singled out for such treatment? Supposing the sentence read: "It is also argued that it is inconsistent with human dignity that a man should use his muscles as a crane for

126

transporting someone else's goods"; or "that a woman should use her vocal cords for the delectation of others"; or "that a person should use his or her brain to work out someone else's income tax" – would these substitutes carry convictions? The fact is that we all earn our living by using parts of our bodies, and there can be no biological, or logical, reason for outlawing organs of the reproductive system. Nevertheless, according to long-standing tradition, the esteem with which different organs are regarded diminishes with their position in the body from the top downwards. George Corner recalls an article in the *Baltimore Sun* of many years ago, according to which the heart and lungs are perfectly respectable, the liver not quite, the spleen dubious and the kidneys definitely vulgar. In those days the prostate was so far below the standard of respectability that it could not even have been mentioned in the newspaper. When we turn to the uterus, not only is it situated in the abdomen, but it is also confined to women; and even in our enlightened days, it is hedged around with taboos. This is exemplified by another argument against surrogacy, namely that since there are some risks attached to pregnancy, no woman ought to be asked to undertake pregnancy for another, in order to earn money. We are not told how these risks compare with, say, working as an air hostess, or as a policewoman. Prostitution also is not without danger, but this is not usually cited as an argument for making it illegal.

Two members of the Warnock Committee dissented from the majority to the extent of permitting surrogacy as a treatment for childlessness under the general supervision of a licensing authority; and they also suggested that payment to a surrogate mother should not be a barrier to the child being adopted by the commissioning couple. The same minority report emphasized, however, that the authors concurred with the majority in their disapproval of surrogacy for convenience, and that the criminal law should be invoked to prevent agencies concerned with surrogacy arrangements being run for profit.

Of course, it is possible that the Warnock Committee saw the surrogacy issue as a kind of scapegoat, whose condemnation would allow for a certain measure of acceptance of other technological advances in reproduction, such as *in vitro* fertilization. Perhaps by joining in the public disapproval of surrogacy, and seemingly sharing the moral universe of "Disgusted of Tunbridge Wells", the Committee may have increased their sphere of influence. But in order to arrive at a balanced judgment, a more rational analysis of the factors involved is required.

There appears to be a widely, though not universally, held opinion that the degradation of the surrogate mother is increased if she receives payment for undertaking the pregnancy. Such payment, furthermore, is thought not only to detract from any generosity that might otherwise characterize her action, but altogether to cast doubt on her motives and her reliability. The activities of commercial surrogacy agencies were unanimously condemned by the Warnock Committee, although the reasons for this are not obvious. The only member of the surrogacy team who appears to be unscathed by financial considerations is the obstetrician. As long as he operates within the law, nobody seems to suggest that an obstetrician or other medical practitioner should provide his services free, or that receiving a fee makes either his motives or his reliability suspect; and clinics can legally be run for profit. Payment, it seems, is acceptable for professionals, but its legitimacy is more controversial for other ranks. It is ironical that one of the definitions of "professional" given in *The Shorter Oxford Dictionary* (1975) is "applied to one who follows, by way of profession, what is generally followed as a pastime, as a p. cricketer".

The fee paid to the surrogate mother is thought to degrade not only her, but also the child, "since for all practical purposes the child will have been bought for money". It is worth reminding oneself, therefore, that the institution of marriage, which is so often held up as the ideal against which other relationships are to be measured, is certainly not unaffected by financial considerations. Today undoubtedly a marriage involves fewer regulations regarding property between spouses than it did in the eighteenth century. But even if the dowry has all but vanished, to marry a rich husband or wife is still a means of improving one's financial situation. Who is to say what part of the loving relationship was generated by the bank account? And what is the effect on the children of a marriage entered into for economic or social reasons? Whatever the answers, neither marriage nor commercially run marriage agencies are illegal.

Those whose task it is to lay down the law on matters of ethics and morality need to ensure that their views are based on a wide knowledge of human institutions and their history. They must also lay aside their personal feelings. Most people would probably not be delighted to be told that their daughter has chosen to become a surrogate mother; but it cannot be the function of the law either to prevent unpleasant situations, or to tell one's daughter how to conduct her affairs.

Surrogacy is frequently denounced as an exploitation of the surrogate mother, but the idea that the exploitation is increased if she receives payment is surely paradoxical. One possible reason could be that in addition to a general sense of guilt associated with the organs of sex and reproduction, there is the added fact that most surrogate mothers belong to the economically disadvantaged classes; and it is arguably a case of exploitation if a woman is driven to use her reproductive organs to escape from a state of poverty.

Surrogacy however cannot bear any responsibility for our social system. If a section of the population is held to live below a minimum economic standard because of the selfish aspirations of the rest of the community, this is an act of exploitation and a reason for communal guilt. Any woman living above the poverty line may choose or refuse to become a surrogate mother, and value judgments of either exploitation by the commissioning parents or of greed on the part of the surrogate mother are misplaced.

But suppose a woman has agreed to become a surrogate mother and accepted a fee from the commissioning parents. If she subsequently changes her mind and refuses to hand the child over, the courts may allow her to keep the child, and in practice she will be unlikely to return any money, even if she were legally required to do so. This could provide an open opportunity for women to exploit couples who are desperate for a child by persuading them to hand over a substantial sum of money in lieu of a service that cannot be legally enforced.

The solution to this problem lies not in legislation but in effective screening of potential surrogate mothers. This task could probably be best handled by the surrogacy agencies, who would need to be regulated, as adoption agencies already are. By taking up references, and through medical and psychological testing, the failure rate could be minimized. It does not matter whether the agencies are voluntary or run for profit, provided they are efficient.

The spectacle of adults fighting legal battles over children is by no means confined to cases of surrogacy, although at present these will run an increased risk of litigation. The obvious solution is to reduce

129

the risk. Careful screening, and matching of surrogate mothers and commissioning parents, are important steps in that direction. Further legislation may also be necessary.

In cases of full surrogacy, where the fetus is not genetically related to the surrogate mother, there appears to be some doubt as to who is the legal mother, and this question will need to be settled. In view of the importance of birth in determining the status of the child, a good solution might be if the question were decided in favour of the surrogate mother, and the child were adopted by the commissioning parents.

Once it is accepted that surrogacy is unlikely to cause any serious harm, the idea that it could be used for social rather than medical reasons should lose much of the horror and condemnation with which it tends to be associated. As mentioned before, the fact that one may not approve of a practice cannot be a reason for wishing to have it outlawed.

A comparison with wet nursing shows up certain similarities, not least because it highlights the way in which fashion, prejudice, and moral attitudes dictate what are the perceived duties of motherhood. During most of the sixteenth century, condemnation of women who employed a wet-nurse to suckle their babies was minimal. As shown by Valerie Fildes, in *Breasts, Bottles and Babies* (1988), during the seventeenth century Puritan theologians in particular devoted sermons and popular tracts to the evils of non-breastfeeding mothers, and they were joined by philosophers and physicians; but this had little discernible effect on the wealthy. Indeed, wealthy mothers who chose to breastfeed their babies were sufficiently exceptional to attract comment, often adverse, from relatives, friends, and a wider social circle.

None of the preceding remarks are intended to be seen as advocating either wet-nursing or surrogacy. What does seem important is that discussions on surrogacy, as on other aspects of reproductive biology, should be put on a more rational basis, and that codes of practice should be regulated by professional bodies, and not by the criminal law.

Future Possibilities

This essay began with a citation from a book on how parents could select the sex of their offspring. Although published in the eighteenth century, the idea was by no means new. It may sound surprising therefore that the problem of *sex selection* before birth has still not been solved, nor is it likely that it will be solved for natural conceptions in the foreseeable future.

What is possible already is to detect the chromosomal sex of a fetus either by amniocentesis or, at an earlier stage of development, by sampling of chorionic villi; and if the fetus is of the unwanted sex, it could be aborted. This procedure is currently adopted in families in which male but not female children have a 50 per cent chance of being afflicted by a serious disease, such as muscular dystrophy.

However, the sex of the fetus will be known in numerous situations of antenatal diagnosis other than for sex-linked diseases, and it now seems that some women seek abortions merely because they are dissatisfied with the sex of the fetus. Some centres therefore decline to disclose the sex of the fetus unless the obstetrician specifically requests otherwise.

Do mothers have a right to select the sex of their babies? At the present stage of scientific development, it is surely sad that a healthy human fetus should be destroyed merely because it is not of the sex the mother prefers. It is an excellent rule not to destroy any living organism without good cause, and this applies particularly to a potential human being. Whether it is a potential son or daughter hardly constitutes good cause for the termination of a pregnancy, and in our society requests to do so must be deemed frivolous. It is to be hoped that education will counteract these requests which are in total opposition to the idea of sexual equality, and in addition seek to use medical and nursing resources which are required to combat disease.

The situation would of course be different if a method eventually became available whereby the sex of the offspring could be selected at conception. This possibility, although not yet on the horizon of scientific advances, is already being proclaimed as a new scourge of humankind. But it need not be so. In Western countries, parents are likely to want about equal numbers of sons and daughters. In a developing country, like India, a preference for sons would be

131

expected to lead initially to a reduction in the birth rate, which would be to the country's advantage; and before long, the more far-sighted parents will realise that in order to have grandchildren, they should select not sons, who may not be able to find wives, but daughters, who will be sought after, and be able to enter into advantageous marriages.

The term *"cloning"* refers to a method of asexual reproduction, such as grafting of varieties of apples, whereby all offspring are exact genetic replicas of the parent stock. In animals, the term is also used for the technique of inactivating the nucleus of an egg and replacing it with the nucleus of a body cell. Each nucleus of an egg or sperm cell has a unique genetic constitution, but the nuclei of the many millions of body cells of an individual all have the same or similar genetic constitution. In theory, therefore, the method could allow one to produce many millions of new individuals with identical genetical constitutions.

In practice a few frogs have been produced by killing the egg nucleus by ultraviolet irradiation, and replacing it with the nucleus from a cell of the gut of a tadpole. No frogs developed if nuclei from adult frogs were placed into the egg. In mammals, no transplantation of an adult nucleus into an egg has yet been successful. The idea of cloning in this sense belongs to science fiction, and may never become a reality.

The principal fears engendered by what has been called the revolution in reproduction are created by ignorance; and as George Corner, who helped to lay the foundations for the new reproductive technology, foresaw, lack of understanding leads to fears, inhibitions and blind taboos. This applies particularly to an understanding of the biological principles underlying the reproductive process. For instance, much of the fear about scientists playing God and creating children can be dispelled if we consider that in the process of *in vitro* fertilization, the scientist allows the sperm to meet the egg in the laboratory instead of the Fallopian tube, which is blocked. The process of conception as such is not affected, and the scientist no more "creates" a baby than does the obstetrician who performs a Caesarean section, an operation which has saved the lives of countless mothers and babies in situations where birth could not take place by the natural route.

In addition to obtaining a better understanding of the biological

132

basis underlying reproduction, we also need more knowledge to evaluate reproductive customs in the cultural environment in which they happen. Studying the history of marriage customs may show that some of today's reproductive practices may not be as revolutionary as they are sometimes made out to be.

What is most needed is rational dialogue based on a liberal education.

Economics of Freedom

MAURICE PESTON

The purpose of this essay is to consider how economic forces limit the freedom of action of individuals and of whole societies. The point is also made that economic progress in the sense of an ability to produce more and make people more affluent is conducive to freedom in a wider sense. But it is as well for me to state at the outset that I am not one of those who believe that providing more consumer goods can make up for limitations on political freedom, or that lack of freedom of expression or freedom of movement can, for the most part, be justified by making people better off in a material sense. As far as I am concerned, these political freedoms are of primary importance. They will usually be enhanced by economic progress and by the more equitable division of society's riches, but if better economic performance could only be reached by a diminution of parliamentary democracy I would choose the latter over the former.

I would actually go further. The freedom of expression and action that is integral to the political process is of wide application. It is no more acceptable to suppress it within the business organisation than outside it. The facts that private enterprise in its operations is anti-democratic, and that advancement in the ranks of management is usually regarded as incompatible with support for the Labour Party, are no less totalitarian and no more acceptable than the corresponding criteria in East Europe.

It is also necessary to interpret "conducive to" in another sense. Being freed of the constraints imposed by sheer poverty is clearly desirable. But it is also worth noting that affluence may impose its own restraints. If the intrinsic need for goods is actually increased by their acquisition, it is a commonplace to remark that the rich may also be enslaved by material possessions. Nonetheless, it may readily be agreed that it is better to be rich and miserable that poor and depressed.

Since before the time of Adam Smith political economists have strongly emphasised economic freedom in their analysis and evaluation of the economy. The ideal of the classical economists and most of their followers in what might be called the British empirical tradition was the "system of economic freedom". They used it as a yardstick to measure the performance of actual economic systems; as a way of judging policy and making policy recommendations.

Although some of them were philosophers, their approach to freedom in their economic writings was pragmatic and common-sensical. This does not mean at all that such people as Smith or Mill were ignorant of the conceptual difficulties surrounding the concept of freedom; but rather that they did not allow them to impede the more practical study of actual economic problems.

Apart from being long-lived, this concern with freedom is characteristic of all sorts of economists who are otherwise in profound disagreement. Thus, Keynes must surely be placed in the classical liberal tradition, and his essays on the subject are models of their kind. The Austrians, of whom Hayek is an exemplar, differ profoundly from the Keynesians on macroeconomics, but they too would wish to be regarded as liberals much in the British sense. (Where the Austrians differ from Keynes and the British generally is in their lack of commonsense and their distaste for the *ad hoc*. It may also be necessary for me to add that "Austrian" does not refer to a middle European nation but to a group of economists chiefly to be found in the U.S. and occasionally in the U.K.) It may also be noted of Marx that, despite the totalitarianism that has been preached and imposed in his name, he too was no mean exponent of liberal causes against the oppressive regimes of his day.

The economist's concern with freedom is multi-faceted. As every student knows, it starts with freedom of choice on the part of the consumer to select which bundle of goods and services he wishes. The same student also is aware that the consumer is constrained by his income and the prices of the goods. What matters, however, is that the choice is made according to consumer preferences.

The student is also aware that the consumer is a wage earner. The analysis of freedom of choice is then extended to job selection, hours of work, and, in more advanced analysis, to choice of training. The restraints here are the nature of the jobs available, their remuneration, and the suitability of the wage earner to take them up. It is a mistake to assume that the labour market is the same as the

135

goods market. They differ in key respects, but what is important in the present context is the extent to which freedom of choice occurs. The point may be generalised to consider other markets, notably those concerned with the acquisition and sale of assets.

In the system of economic freedom in addition to households and workers are firms. These are free to hire labour and other factors of production, and to produce and sell goods and services. The firms themselves are also available for sale as can be seen most emphatically in the merger mania of 1986–87. Such freedom of private enterprise is at least as important in the British liberal tradition as freedom of consumer choice. Moreover, it is as well to emphasise that it is a freedom to start new enterprises as much as to operate existing ones.

I have already made the point that the internal operations of the firm are rather a good example of a possible conflict between freedom and economic efficiency. Essentially, workers at all levels subject themselves to the discipline imposed by other workers and management. Otherwise processes of production would be a good deal less efficient. Although management is in large part rule bound, it is also arbitrary on occasions. Increased worker control of their own working lives is regarded as a threat to management, and, it is suggested, would be costly, because it would reduce the division of labour. Nonetheless, those who argue that freedom is absolute must explain why that does not apply within the firm. To say that the worker chooses that state of affairs voluntarily will not do, since it appears that a great many people are content within a totalitarian environment. The tacit acceptance of life in East Europe does not make those regimes more attractive. Of course, workers can change firms, but that is to move from one authoritarian environment to another. They can set up their own firms, if they can raise the necessary capital. But that merely serves to emphasise the conflict on occasion between apparent freedom and economic welfare.

The individual firm as an enclave of arbitrary power is also to be seen as a place where the greater freedom of one group is obtained at the expense of less freedom for others. Very few protagonists believe that such freedom should be unfettered. Most people recognise that the ad hoc decision-making of management is akin to that of governments. They do not then go on for the most part to advocate the democratisation of firms. Instead they argue the case for rules and procedures, frequently backed by legislation, as the best means of worker protection. Legislation to deal with racial and sexual discrimination in hiring and promotion, to encourage equal pay, and to eliminate unfair dismissal is characteristic of most advanced industrialised countries. There can be no doubt that it limits the freedom of management to do as it wishes. The case for it is partly that it enhances the freedom of others; but it is also based on the proposition that certain kinds of unfettered economic power are undesirable.

Freedom on the production and sales side is interrelated with freedom on the consumption and purchase side. In particular, the circular flow phenomenon must be noted. Workers are hired by firms to produce goods and services using capital assets. They are paid wages to purchase the output, the difference between the value of output and wage income being profits.

Classical economists believed that a system of this kind would work satisfactorily, to put it no higher. Their main criterion of what is satisfactory is, to paraphrase Smith's dictum, that the end of all economic activity is consumer welfare. But they were aware of its imperfections, and also of the fact that it contained to some degree the seeds of its own destruction. Its freedom was limited; some people's freedom conflicted with that of others; and there were always forces at work trying to limit individual freedom. It was also apparent that when the economy, as exemplified (say) by Victorian Britain, was examined in terms of actual outcomes, it left a good deal to be desired. On the one hand, some people clearly did better than others; on the other hand, the system lacked a capacity to respond to kinds of moral precepts that some philosophers and moral leaders deemed to be important. Although Disraeli cannot be placed in the classical liberal tradition, he was clearly aware in *Sybil* of how freedom for some (e.g. the landowners) destroyed the lives of others, notably the agricultural labourers.

The classical economists were aware that the system of economic freedom, even in its most extreme form of laissez-faire, had to build on some degree of constraint, and depended on an appropriate legal and governmental system. Many of them realised that the system to survive required active intervention by the government, especially to mitigate its worst feature, poverty. They disliked intervention *per se*, and disagreed about its necessary extent, but they were optimistic that one way or other the system could be saved and was worth saving.

Other economists, often starting in the same tradition, were more pessimistic. They felt that something more radical was required, and even went so far as to say that the freedom of laissez-faire was a mockery. Economists and others with these views founded the British empirical approach to socialism. Many modern liberals also went down this road. In practice they could all be placed in that part of the political spectrum that gave rise to the mixed economy. (Indeed, so could many Conservatives.) The essence of their position was to limit the freedom of some in order to enhance the freedom of others, and to argue that freedom overall was maximised when some freedoms were diminished or even done away with altogether. Anthony Crosland's *Future of Socialism* is seminal in this connection. The best up-to-date statement of this point of view is Roy Hattersley's *Choose Freedom*. Both of these works are of major importance because they show how parliamentary democracy is not merely safeguarded, but enhanced by democratic socialist interventions on behalf of the poor.

To go back to the classical liberals, they believed strongly in the rule of law, and accepted there should be a government with powers to maintain law and order and to protect the nation from belligerent foreigners. Trade depended on an appropriate law of contract and other commercial laws. The central government needed to be responsible for the quality of the currency, and when the banking systems developed, for regulation there too. (It should be mentioned *en passant* that there are classical liberals today, some claiming to be followers of Hayek, who will have none of this, and who are even opponents of parliamentary democracy too!)

The emphasis on law to enable the system of economic freedom to function, which is *ipso facto* a constraint on individual behaviour, is a clear cut example of one of the paradoxes of freedom. But for our purposes the recognition of the case for legal intervention to make the market work can also be seen as the origin of what might be called consumerism. The consumer is free to buy the goods that are available, but he is constrained by the nature of those goods, and the sorts of business behaviour that lie behind their marketing. Goods not fit for their purpose sold by unscrupulous traders, services less than adequate, fraud especially in the financial sector are all facts of the free enterprise economy. While it might be argued in principle that "good" enterprise will drive out "bad", i.e. that *caveat emptor* is the only relevant principle, consumer ignorance is such that legal and governmental restraints are required. The consumer is given rights against the seller, which are enforceable at law. More to the point, consumer rights and protection enforcement agencies with legal powers are set up by the government. These undoubtedly limit the freedom of producers, but they do so to make the freedom of consumers to choose a more meaningful one.

One reason why consumer protection must be based on the enhancement and modification of market forces by the government is that it is in the nature of a public good. Laying down and enforcing standards that protect one consumer protects all. This public good phenomenon is of wide application. It leads to intervention in the spheres of health, the environment, and transport. In all cases its logic is that the choices made by individuals confronted by the usual economic constraints of prices and income lead to inefficient outcomes. Adding to the constraints actually improves what happens, and enlarges the range of choice.

Consumerism may be interpreted in elementary terms as the desirability of firms responding to consumer demands as expressed through the market. This does not mean merely that consumers should be able to buy anything that is available as long as they can afford it. On the positive side, there is the role of firms in inventing and producing new products, and thus widening and enhancing choice. On the negative side, the consumer is not always seen to be the best judge of his own interests. This is exemplified by limitations on the sale of addictive drugs. Furthermore, where the consumer is a dependent, i.e. a child, an invalid, a mentally ill person, responsibilities are placed on others to make correct choices for him. (One of those responsibilities will be, of course, to strive as strongly as possible to reduce the dependence in question.) It must be said of consumerism in this general sense that it is not limited to the private sector. Its role with respect to services which are publicly provided is at least as important. But all consumerism must be placed within the context of spending power. That is the most significant topic to be tackled.

But, before doing that, there are two other topics that must be touched upon. One is of a philosophical nature which needs to be examined, albeit briefly. Why are the actual preferences of consumers and the freedom to exercise them to be the central criterion of economic assessment? It has already been pointed out that the consumers are not always the best judges of their own

139

interests. It can then be added that preferences do not come out of the air, so to speak. They are socially conditioned, sometimes consciously so, whether by the marketing fraternity or by the education system.

Now, it does not follow from such considerations that interference is necessarily justified. A person must surely be free to "go to hell" in his own way. The influence of others, even advertisers, can surely be beneficial. Against this, people who harm themselves are also liable to create problems for others; and for every advertisement that enhances the quality of life there are many for goods and services which damage it (or are at best pure rubbish).

Beyond all that, are preferences themselves not a form of constraint? "A person has to do what a person has to do." Is the exercise of choice according to given preferences an example of free will or determinism? There is, of course, no answer to be given, but the question does have its practical side.

Implicit in everything said so far is what is also discussed explicitly in what follows, namely the emphasis on income as the key constraint, and the justification of help for the poor on the grounds of welfare and freedom. Most of that justification is connected with the assumption that poverty is not the fault of the poor themselves. Circumstances, bad luck, family and personal disadvantages all form part of the case for taking action to improve the lives of the less well off. That is the easy part.

But suppose some of the poor are in that condition as a result of their own actions? Is it valid to discriminate among the elderly between those who could have saved for their old age and those who could not? Is the unemployed worker who, when in a job, earned well to be treated less favourably for supplementary benefit than the person who even in work was only just above the poverty line? More to the point, is the family of one any less meritorious than the other?

Most people, apart from acknowledging the intellectual difficulty here, would not place great stress on the freedom to be poor. But some would. In a sense, the latter are arguing that a person who makes a choice which eventually creates economic difficulties for himself could have chosen differently. He could in a curious way have chosen to have different preferences! Thus, some people (not the present writer) would say that no case can be made for limiting the economic freedom of others to spend as they choose in order to protect them from the adverse consequences of their actions.

140

This leads on to a second class of considerations concerning the context of free choice.

A good deal of the theory of economic freedom is based on the notion of the consumer as an isolated individual. He interacts with other consumers via the market mechanism, but that is all. Now, this may be a valid abstraction for some analytical purposes. It is not a suitable assumption for all. We have emphasised that the consumer is part of society, and is socialised, so to speak. His preferences are neither arbitrary nor genetically determined. He is not typically a hermit who does not wish to communicate with others. Quite the contrary, most of what he does and wishes to do is predicated on the existence of other people. Moreover, his relationships with them are not linked to the operation of the market mechanism.

Economists have invented another class of concepts to deal with these areas of activity. They refer to external economies and diseconomies of production and consumption. They mean by this the activities of households and firms that directly impinge on the wellbeing and profitability of other households and firms, rather than operating indirectly *via* markets and prices. The fundamental theorem of this part of welfare economics is that in the presence of externalities consumer freedom of choice does not maximise economic welfare. Welfare may be raised by the government using taxes and subsidies appropriately. It may be raised by groups of households and firms combining to act jointly. But it may also be raised by legislative action and other government activity which limit certain choices by households and firms and encourage other ones.

Typical examples are as follows:

(i)   A chemicals firm sends its effluent into a local river thus ruining the water for a trout farm;
(ii) A power station uses dirty fuel thus raising the laundering costs of local housewives;
(iii) One household plays a "ghetto blaster" on a picnic thus disturbing the peace and quiet of the countryside for other households.

All of these are relevant to our present discussion as examples of external diseconomies. When they are large enough and impinge sufficiently on the political process they may be dealt with by taxing those who create them, or by barring the activities altogether. It is interesting to note that economists typically support the tax method; but it is the regulatory one that is more favoured in the U.K. What they illustrate, extremely clearly, however, is the "choice of freedoms" problem. Firms complain that the regulatory environment is so stringent that costs are needlessly raised, ultimately to the disadvantage of consumers. Environmental groups take the reverse position; the power of firms to avoid the rules imperils consumer health and welfare.

Of course, since decisions in this area are taken through the political system, the relevant issues will sometimes be in doubt. Indeed, it may pay one side or both in the political arena to obscure the issues on purpose. A typical example at the present day concerns nuclear power, and possible background radiation from nuclear power stations. To the extent that such stations add significantly to background radiation, they are an external diseconomy. This may be avoided by building conventional power stations (not without their external disbenefits), or by siting nuclear stations totally away from human population, or by shielding nuclear stations even more. All of these alternatives may involve costs. We then have the question of whether the electricity generating board (representing, it is to be hoped, the interests of consumers at large) are to have their freedom reduced for the sake of a local population. But in the debate that has taken place what also happens is that neither side can agree on the most elementary facts. While the existence of extra background radiation might be thought to be subject to objective scientific investigation, the two sides read the evidence in opposite ways. Equally, in the more problematic area of costs, economists and other experts confronted with the same data do not come to a unanimous conclusion on which method of power generation is the cheaper.

The main conclusions we come to are two. One is that the conflict of freedoms problem will always be with us. The simple proposition, always choose more freedom over less, is, despite its apparent merits, of little help. Second, looking back over the past history of regulation of the environment, it is not the case that it has harmed the community at large or put the liberty of the subject in peril. The proposition of the radical right that citizens of London have been enslaved because they now live in a smokeless zone, only has to be stated to be seen for the preposterous notion it is.

Such examples can be multiplied a thousandfold. But they should not be taken to mean that all regulation is acceptable, or that decent social behaviour without regulation is not desirable when it is possible. All restraints must be scrutinised, just as all liberty must be when it verges on licence. Above all, it should not be inferred that, because economics is based so strongly on consumer choice, it simply becomes the intellectual underpinning for laissez-faire.

At this point, we must go on directly to examine the role of income. It is the key constraint on the individual. He is free to buy what he can afford. In the nineteenth century in this country that meant he was free to starve, and it continues to be true for some people even today. More relevant now, however, is that the income constraint for many individuals means they can spend what they have but they are not free to purchase a collection of goods and services anywhere near the national norm. The economic constraint acts also as a social constraint cutting them off from normal social life. Those who believe that freedom of movement and freedom to change jobs are fundamentals of a free society must note that these are inhibited by poverty. Even in a society which is not obviously totalitarian, poverty may act in practice to limit freedom of thought and expression. The fact that access to books and other sources of information is very much more limited in a totalitarian society should not cause one to ignore the problem as it appears at home, relatively minor as it may seem.

The point holds *a fortiori* about access to a decent education. Those who starve the education system of resources or do not use the available resources as efficiently as possible are both guilty of attacks on freedom as well as other crimes.

The income constraint itself requires further examination. For the individual it derives from his intrinsic ability (including his physical condition), from his education and training (i.e. the human capital invested in him), and from his access to capital in the ordinary sense of the word. Much of this is in turn affected by his family circumstances.

As far as the economy as a whole is concerned, the same principles apply. It is restricted by the available factors of production – capital, labour, and natural resources. It is also restricted by the available technology, essentially the ease with which the factors of production can be transformed into desirable output. In its relationship with the rest of the world it is restricted by the terms of trade, i.e. the prices of goods it sells (exports) compared with what it buys (imports). In the short term individuals and the government have access to overseas sources of funds; thus, a country's current expenditure abroad may exceed its current income from abroad. But in the longer run borrowing has to be repaid with interest so that balance of payments does become a restriction.

Again, just as with the individual, due attention must be paid to quality as well as quantity. A country may be rich, and in that sense have greater freedom of action, more because of the quality of its resources than their sheer abundance. Equally, national poverty will be closely connected with technological backwardness. In both these dimensions the U.K. is in special peril at the present time, and the outlook is even bleaker. A neglect of investment in human capital because of backwardness in training and a failure to take education seriously is also reflected in our being increasingly denied access to the latest technology. Whether the primary causes here are social, political, economic or all three is arguable. What is apparent is that they reduce the range of choice of individuals and the freedom of action of government. While it is true that we are always constrained by the harsh facts of economic reality, there being at any moment some practical limits to what can be produced, the breadth of choice is not uniform. Just as some individuals in a country are less limited in what they can do by lack of access to spending power, so are some countries.

If the argument on the constraint of income is correct, and it surely is, paying a decent level of social security, apart from its correctness on humanitarian grounds, is also justifiable on libertarian grounds. While not denying the primacy of political freedom and the parliamentary process, it would be foolish to ignore that the old person relying on an inadequate state pension is less free than his counterpart on a more than adequate indexed-linked retirement income. The same applies to an unemployed youngster compared with his counterpart in work. To say that we are free from arbitrary police action and the knock on the door in the middle of the night is one very important thing (and even that is less true than once was the case). But we must also ask what are we actually free to do, and it is here that economic limitations are of paramount significance.

This leads to the final empirical question. Most of the twentieth century has been characterised by increased government concern with the welfare of the poor, and the desirability of reducing inequality. This has been fought all the way by most, but not all, adherents of right-wing political views. Moreover, their tune has remained unchanged for a century and a half or more. No matter how low the income tax, it is always too high. No matter how many lives are saved by public health provision, or how much individual existence is improved by a decent public education system, these are always portrayed as threats to the liberty of the subject. Above all, any interventions of this kind are continually predicted to undermine the economic prospects on which they are based. Thus, although the economic theory and the evidence is mostly the other way, these people continue to argue that high rates of tax lead to a loss of economic efficiency. They take a similar view about welfare benefits. The latter is especially curious. If an individual privately organises his affairs so as to make adequate provision for adverse economic contingencies such as unemployment or retirement, this is acceptable. It remains acceptable even if the person concerned is able to do so as a result of inheriting a certain amount of wealth. But if the state does something similar cries go up about interference with freedom coupled with emphasis on the deadweight economic loss allegedly involved. This is so, even when the welfare decisions are taken through a democratic parliamentary system. (In this connection the opposition to democracy of some on the radical right should never be forgotten.)

Despite that, the economic systems of the world have expanded non-stop; and where there have been setbacks, these have been temporary and unconnected with so-called progressive economic policies. It is worth reflecting on post-war British experience. It is now being alleged that many of our more recent troubles are the result of the enhancement of the welfare state at that time. The difficulty with such a view is that the following quarter-century was the longest period of continuous prosperity that this country has ever had. It is also worth noting that, insofar as we failed to strengthen and modernise our industry, this occurred after the change in government in the 1950s. Consumer expenditure was given greater emphasis, regulations were relaxed, and firms were set free. This may have been meritorious, but it is arguable that the alternative of ten more years of investment, greater research and development, and more emphasis on industrial training and education (all of which would have involved continued restraints on some freedom of choice) would have served us better. In addition, the Germans and French in their industrial reconstruction did not neglect the welfare state. It must also be emphasised that a comparison across countries would not show that those who intervene on welfare grounds and limit the freedom of entrepreneurs to do anything they like are poorer on that account or noteworthy for reducing individual freedom in general. This is also the case historically. The British and Swedes are no less free than they were one hundred and fifty years ago. However, it must be remarked that whatever the consequences of the past decade of British government, greater freedom for the individual has not been one of them.

SO SHOULD WE HAVE WRITTEN
CONSTITUTIONAL PROTECTION?

A Bill of Rights for the United Kingdom?

NICOLA LACEY

Anyone thinking about the issue of whether the United Kingdom should adopt a Bill of Rights, giving legal force to a set of fundamental human freedoms, is confronted at the outset with a paradox. The paradox lies in the fact that some of the groups which one would expect to have most to gain from this development – disadvantaged groups such as ethnic and religious minorities and women – seem to place so little faith in it. Perhaps this is because of doubts about the utility of exploiting a legal system which seems generally so effectively to protect the vested interests of those who already hold political power. Indeed, the Labour Party, which champions the cause of minority groups in the political arena, has rejected the idea of a new constitutional settlement entrenching a charter of basic human rights. The position in Britain, of course, contrasts sharply with that in the United States, where, for example, members of the black community have made substantial gains, such as in breaking down racial segregation of public facilities, both by exploiting the legislative process and by claiming their constitutional rights in the courts.

The Bill of Rights debate provides us with an interesting example of both practical and political doubts prevalent in British thinking about the use of legislation to protect liberty. In this paper, I shall argue that we have been too quick to dismiss the advantages which could be gained by the adoption of a Bill of Rights, and indeed that the issues which arise are not ones which divide along party political lines. First of all I shall look at the constitutional arguments which have been put against this type of reform. Then I shall turn to the political facts and attitudes which seem to weigh against a Bill of Rights and indeed against any major reliance on legal procedures as

149

a tool for the protection of the most important interests of human beings in political society. Finally I shall make some suggestions about the ways in which the adoption of a Bill of Rights might be accomplished, and the form which such an enactment might take.

The conventional wisdom of constitutional theory is that the nature of our essentially nineteenth-century constitution, and in particular its principle of the sovereignty of Parliament, rules out the effective adoption of a Bill of Rights. On this view, the central principle of our "unwritten" constitution is that statutes enacted by Parliament are the supreme source of law. Thus all statutes have equal legal force, and we have no conception of a "higher" constitutional law which would be capable of invalidating legislation which is in conflict with it. If a later statute is inconsistent with an earlier one, the later statute takes priority, on the basis that it represents the most recent expression of the democratic will. Thus the law-creating power of Parliament is absolute except in so far as it may not fetter the similar power of its successors, for to do so would be to limit the continuing power of Parliament freely to represent its electors.

This constitutional position leads to two specific well-known difficulties about a Bill of Rights. In the first place, since the Bill would be enshrining principles applicable in any social or economic climate which we can realistically envisage, a natural corollary of having a Bill of Rights would be that it should be entrenched – in other words, that it should not be able to be repealed by a simple majority in Parliament. At the very least, we would probably want it only to be repealable by, say, a two-thirds majority in both the House of Commons and the House of Lords. The traditional response is the familiar dogma: "But Parliament cannot bind its successors." Is this objection fatal? I think not, for two reasons. First of all, it is hard to deny that *in fact* certain pieces of legislation do become entrenched. For example, no one would realistically suggest that our Parliament could today repeal the Statute of Westminster, passed in 1931, which gave independence to our former colonies: any attempt to do so might be valid as a matter of legal theory, but as a matter of political fact it would merely amount to a futile symbolic gesture. But we need not content ourselves with this pragmatic approach. Another, more theoretical argument is that Parliament, although it cannot bind its successors, can redefine what counts as an Act of Parliament for certain purposes. In the

150

A Bill of Rights for the United Kingdom?

Parliament Acts of 1911 and 1949, by reducing the power of the House of Lords to delay or reject certain types of legislation, Parliament made the legislative procedure more simple; why, then could it not make it more difficult to repeal a Bill of Rights? This argument assumes that one of the main ideas underlying the principle that Parliament cannot bind its successors is that it would be contrary to public policy for one Parliament to be able to create a legislative vacuum: in other words, to make it impossible for a future Parliament to enact laws in a certain area however necessary it turned out to be. Merely altering the legislative procedure to require a two-thirds majority would never create such a problem, because if the need for repeal or reform were urgent, as in wartime, such a majority would very likely be attainable. So both practical and legal arguments can overcome the difficulties about entrenchment.

The other difficulty to which the nature of our constitution gives rise is more intractable. This is the implication of the sovereignty doctrine that any piece of entrenched legislation which would invalidate later inconsistent legislation would be anti-democratic: it would be an illicit fettering of the continuing freedom of successive Parliaments as representatives of the voters. To give a realistic answer to this we have to undermine the rigid notion of sovereignty as the linchpin of the constitution. One strategy is to ask whether its defender genuinely regards countries with an entrenched Bill of Rights, such as the United States, as less democratic than the United Kingdom? More seriously, we can point to many major constitutional developments such as the emergence of the whip system and the dominance of the executive and particularly the Cabinet over Parliament, which cast doubt upon whether the simple nineteenth-century model of representative democracy is still an adequate characterisation of political life in the U.K. today. Finally, we can try to unsettle the view that sovereignty is the exclusive foundation of the constitution by appealing to other shared and settled judgments; for example, by asking whether opponents of a Bill of Rights would allow that there is something unconstitutional about Parliament, even by the proper procedures, extending its own life to twenty years during peacetime. If they would, then this must be because there are other constitutional principles of equal importance to the sovereignty principle, which in turn suggests that the departure represented by the adoption of a Bill of Rights may not be so

151

radical as the traditional constitutional theorist would have us believe. These other democratic constitutional principles might include our belief that entrenched minorities should always be protected from being disadvantaged by a prejudiced majority and more generally that certain interests are too precious for their protection to be left to the whims of the majority vote, either intrinsically or in that their realisation is a necessary condition for effective participation in the democractic process. We must not allow rigid adherence to an outdated view of the British constitution to inhibit desirable political developments.

Having established that the technical constitutional arguments against a Bill of Rights are not conclusive, we need to turn to practical and political objections. Why is it that many of the groups which such a Bill seeks to protect have been apathetic or even hostile to the idea? It is certainly true that there is in Britain a fair degree of scepticism, especially among minority groups and pressure groups such as trades unions, about the benefits to be gained by taking individual cases to court: and the 1984 decision of the House of Lords in the G.C.H.Q. case, in which the court upheld the Prime Minister's decision to withdraw the rights of certain civil servants to belong to a trades union on the basis that such membership presented a threat of strike action which could in turn endanger national security, has done nothing to alleviate such scepticism. Doubtless it has partly to do with fears about bias and conservatism in the judiciary. But this cannot be the whole story, because it is by no means only those asserting what might be viewed (mistakenly, I think) as "left-wing" interests, such as freedom from discrimination or freedom to be a member of a union, who have fared badly in the courts. Another example is that of James Malone, who, in the course of his trial on a charge of handling stolen goods – a charge of which he was acquitted – found that his telephone was being tapped by the police on the authority of the Home Secretary. The lack of any established principle of privacy in British law meant that Malone had to fight his case all the way to the European Court of Human Rights, a process which took several years, in order finally to establish in 1984 that there had been a violation of his basic rights.
  Such cases suggest that the reluctance of individuals and groups to appeal to the courts to protect their rights may not be so much to do

with scepticism about the courts themselves as with the bankruptcy of our domestic law when it comes to presenting arguments about fundamental values. The fact that our basic interests are referred to as liberties rather than rights is no accident; what it reflects is that they are regarded as being residual: we have total freedom – except in so far as it is restricted by the law! This was of little comfort to a victim of racial discrimination before the first Race Relations Act in 1965; since the common law enshrined no anti-discrimination principle and since there was no legislation on the subject, the person discriminated against simply had no legal foothold for any argument they might have wished to bring to court. This principle of residual freedom, combined with that of the sovereignty of parliament, has the morally astounding implication that, at a constitutional level, all laws restricting personal freedom are of equal status, whatever their content: the theory of parliamentary sovereignty is barren of any standards which could reflect the distinctions which we want to make between justified and unjustified legislative encroachments on personal freedom. And we must remember that, as the Malone and G.C.H.Q. cases show, however sceptical we may be about the use of court cases as a strategy for the defence of our human rights, the choice we are confronted with is *not* one between having and not having legal regulation in this area. Laws which encroach on our fundamental freedoms, such as the offence of blasphemous libel, successfully invoked against the editor of the magazine *Gay News* in 1979, and the Police and Criminal Evidence Act 1984 which widens the powers conferred on the police to stop, search and arrest, do exist: they will be used against individuals and groups, and those proceeded against have no alternative but to respond in legal terms. What a Bill of Rights could do is to provide us with additional defensive *legal* tools for use in cases such as these.

A more fundamental form of scepticism about the usefulness of a Bill of Rights questions the wisdom of presenting political arguments in terms of individual rights at all. Nor is this scepticism confined to those on the political left. The trenchant criticisms of Jeremy Bentham, the utilitarian thinker and reformer who described natural rights as amounting to nothing more than "nonsense on stilts", reflect real doubts about the ways in which the apparently forceful rhetoric of absolute human rights can disguise the need to make certain crucial and complex political choices. A Bill of Rights cannot resolve conflicts between rights or between rights and

153

important social or collective interests, such as one group's right not to be discriminated against on racial grounds and another's right to express its opinions freely. What is more, difficulties arise about whether all the values which we regard as fundamental can be framed in terms of individual rights; how, for example, can important matters such as the protection of the environment and even the planet, or the maintenance of background social conditions such as order and tolerance which are necessary to the realisation of rights, be expressed within the discourse of human rights itself? Does the claim that some person or set of persons has a right ultimately collapse into the simple assertion that it is right for that particular interest to be protected, and if so, why should we regard the idea of a right as being distinctive and of special weight? And can a Bill of Rights offer not just classical liberals but also socialists protection of the values which they regard as fundamental?

These doubts and problems have to be confronted, but they should not be decisive in our thinking about the Bill of Rights issue. First of all, it would be mistaken to assume that interests framed in terms of rights only protect individuals or traditional liberal values. A right not to be discriminated against, for example, typically protects a group, and individuals as members of that group. More decisively, it is the case that adherence to the sorts of rights enshrined in the European Convention on Human Rights also has important social benefits: it aims to secure public goods such as open debate and political participation, which benefit all political parties. Indeed, the very importance which we attach to respect for human rights may well proceed from a background social and political morality which regards protection of rights as being instrumental to the realisation of certain goods, rather than valuable in itself. Second, however doubtful we may be about the usefulness of putting arguments in the political arena in terms of rights, the same objections do not necessarily apply in the legal forum. The practice of framing legal claims in terms of rights is a familiar and convenient one, associated as it is with particularly strong and conclusive forms of legal argument. Finally, although we cannot expect the Bill of Rights itself to resolve fundamental political, moral and economic conflicts, for example between the principle of free expression and that of freedom from discrimination, which can arise from the publication of racist propaganda, or between free assembly and the public interest in order and safety, which can arise from mass demonstrations, we can expect a Bill of Rights to focus judicial and public attention on the fact that these cases really are about such fundamental conflicts, which have to be faced openly, however difficult they may be.

This question of who should have the responsibility of resolving such conflicts raises what is perhaps a more realistic fear about the adoption of a Bill of Rights. The obvious candidates for resolving conflicts about rights would be the judges, and many opponents of a Bill of Rights have argued that its adoption would result in an unacceptable redistribution of political power in favour of a non-elected, unaccountable and predominantly upper-middle-class judiciary. Here we need to distinguish between two sorts of objections. The first has to do with the constitutional arguments which I have already examined: if the judges were to be the final arbiters of the meaning of a Bill of Rights, on the basis of which they could strike down legislation passed by democratic instititions, would this not fundamentally and unacceptably alter their constitutional position? The second objection has to do with the broad and general provisions set down by most Bills of Rights, in sharp distinction to the detailed drafting characteristic of British statutes. Again, I think that much of the apparent force of these objections has to do with their presenting us with a false dilemma: that of the choice between the judges either having or not having political power in the area of human rights. The judges in this country have always proclaimed their role as the guardians of individual liberty, and despite the limitations of the common law as a source of standards protecting human rights, they have seldom hesitated to play an activist role where they have perceived it to be necessary. They have been able to do this by means of the great power which their discretion in interpreting even detailed statutory provisions gives them in almost every instance. No one reading the discussion in the Press of cases raising rights issues, such as the case challenging a doctor's right to give contraceptive advice or treatment, in the absence of parental consent, to females under the age of 16, initiated by Victoria Gillick and finally decided in 1985, or the G.C.H.Q. case, already mentioned, could possibly come away with the impression that the judges do not already have significant power to determine the extent to which our rights are protected and indeed how they are defined. The traditional constitutional theorist will reply that Parliament's sovereignty means that it can always override a judicial decision which it dislikes; but this is hardly convincing when one considers the practicalities of the situation: Parliament has little time even to scrutinise important legislation introduced by the Government, let alone to act as a watchdog over the courts' activities in the field of human rights. Yet again, political realities should make us dubious about arguments from constitutional theory.

Opponents of a Bill of Rights point to the fact that charters such as the European Convention are framed in very broad terms, which would seem to give even greater leeway to creative judicial interpretation than a traditional British statute. My own view is that this risk is outweighed by the advantages to be gained in providing litigants with a wider range of legal arguments with which to defend their rights, and by the effect this would have in making overt what is often covert in British cases: that they do indeed raise human rights issues. By making more explicit a power which judges already have, we could open up their judgments to a greater degree of public scrutiny: judges may not be directly politically accountable, but it would be naive to suppose either that they are totally insensitive to public opinion or that our present method of selecting judges would necessarily remain unchanged were they to abuse the power which a Bill of Rights would give them. As the significant development of the British constitution over the last century shows, constitutional structures are not static; it would be unduly pessimistic to take the view that our system is incapable of adapting itself to accommodate a change which is desirable on independent grounds.

But why should we need our own Bill of Rights in view of our membership of the E.E.C. and our adherence to the European Convention: is this not a sufficient guarantee of our freedoms, whatever our domestic law may say? The answer has to do with the fact that the amount of E.E.C. law relevant to human rights which is directly applicable in British courts is relatively small. Furthermore, the attitude of the courts to the supremacy of our domestic parliament restricts the use to which they will put European standards. Few courts have been willing to give priority to E.E.C. standards – and they are especially reluctant where the national law is clearly intended to be inconsistent with E.E.C. law and has been passed since our accession to the E.E.C. As for the European Convention, since citizens cannot sue directly in the domestic courts for a breach of the Convention, and since the law maintains that individual litigants must exhaust all their domestic remedies before they may take a case to the European Court of Human Rights at Strasbourg, litigants who have little chance of winning in the U.K. have nevertheless to waste an enormous amount of time and money taking their cases through domestic courts only to find what they already suspected – they have no remedy in national law. This is illustrated by the high proportion of cases taken to the Strasbourg court by U.K. citizens in which our domestic law has been found to violate the European Convention.

How, then, should we in this country go about adopting a Bill of Rights? Clearly the simplest solution would be to incorporate the European Convention into domestic law. The advantages would be that, although the Convention is framed in broad and general terms, our courts have already had some experience of interpreting it, and there exists a substantial body of well-argued case law from the European Court of Human Rights, which would be a useful source of guidance for our judiciary. My own reservation about the European Convention is that it says little about economic and social rights, such as the right to a minimum standard of subsistence whether from employment or social security. It may be a truism that civil and political rights are of little use to a person who lacks food and shelter, but the insight is none the less important for that. In the context of high unemployment and an economic recession, we tend to forget that we are among the world's wealthiest inhabitants. Given this fact, it would be shameful for us to shy away from the problems of trying to reach consensus on a realistic set of basic economic and social rights – including a level of legal aid provision which would ensure real rather than theoretical access to the courts to enforce all our rights. Without some such supplementation of the European Convention, its incorporation would run the risk of amounting to a symbolic rather than a real contribution to the quality of our political arrangements in the U.K. Moreover, as I have already suggested, we should not rule out the possibility that the adoption of a Bill of Rights might give rise to, or best be conceived as part of, a package of wider reforms devoted to reconstructing our constitutional framework in the light of the practical political developments which render traditional constitutional theory both an inaccurate description of and an inadequate prescription for the complex reality of contemporary democratic government.

Do the various arguments I have considered lead us to the view that the adoption of a Bill of Rights for the U.K. would be unconstitutional, impractical, or futile? A clear look at each of the main objectives has shown, I would argue, that they rest either on an unreflective and dogmatic conservatism about the nature of the British constitution, or else on misunderstandings about the nature of the choices to be made. We *do* have law on human rights in this country, but it is unclear, unsystematic and incomplete. In a country with pride in the quality of its legal system this position is nothing short of scandalous, as is well illustrated by the national humiliation which we suffer when our law is found wanting by the European Court of Human Rights. In the political and social context of the twentieth century, the legal system needs a Bill of Rights at its foundation. We should not allow our fears about giving new powers to an already powerful judiciary, powers which would at least be publicly exercised, to consign proposals for valuable constitutional reform to the rubbish bins of Westminster. Of course, given the enormous social inequalities and injustices which exist in this country, it would be unrealistic to expect the mere adoption of a Bill of Rights to solve them all. But it could have an impact in important areas, and the fact that it is not the ultimate key to social justice should not cause us to reject the finite advantages which it offers. Open-minded consideration of the Bill of Rights issues must form an important part of responsible political thinking about the wider programme of constitutional reform which is clearly necessary if we are to reconstruct our constitution in a manner appropriate to twentieth-century political practice. Our ultimate goal, I would argue, should be not only the enforcement of civil rights but the attainment of a situation in which those rights are of equal value to all individuals and groups in society. The pursuit of this goal is the responsibility of the politicians whom we elect, but we should not reject, whether in the name of ideological purity or apathetic conservatism, the real contribution to that ideal which could be made by the adoption of a Bill of Rights.

INTERNATIONAL PERSPECTIVES

Freedom and "Balance":
the Global Media Controversy

ROSEMARY RIGHTER

"Freedom of information" was proclaimed in 1946, in a much-cited resolution of the UN General Assembly, to be "a fundamental human right and ... the touchstone of all the freedoms to which the United Nations is consecrated". Two years later, the Universal Declaration of Human Rights defined this as freedom "to seek, receive and impart information and ideas through any media and regardless of frontiers". A generation later the prime minister of Malaysia, Dr. Mahathir Mohamed, dismissed the free flow of ideas and information as "a myth, a myth invented by the so-called liberal west to serve their own purpose – since they, through their world-wide control of the media stand to benefit most". Malaysia's press, he said, "should not subscribe to that kind of freedom, much less be part of their intellectual hegemony. We should think of what is good for our country and our people as a whole." More subtly, but also more prescriptively, a senior minister in neighbouring Singapore, Sinnathamby Rajaratnam, justified 1986 legislation enabling the government to penalise foreign publications which it found to be "engaging in the domestic politics of Singapore" in these terms: "We see freedom of the press not as the end but as means to an all-embracing end – the integrity and independence of our country; its prosperity; the eradication of anything that would sow seeds of social, racial and religious conflicts."

In an international league-table of respect for civil liberties and the rule of law, both of these governments would be placed at the higher end of the scale. On the political spectrum they would have more in common with liberal democracy than with either the Chile of Pinochet or Bulgaria. Their more enterprising journalists do not, as has happened in pre-Alfonsin Argentina, in Mexico or Nigeria,

161

end up in the cemetery prematurely. Both countries are constantly cited as models of successful integration with the global economy, whatever their difficulties following the recession of the early 1980s.

For leaders of two such relatively liberal, stable, prosperous and self-confident countries to be invoking respectively Western conspiracy and the primacy of *raison d'état* to justify restrictions on the flow of information indicates how thoroughly the inter-governmental debate on the media and their "role" had, by the 1980s, woven itself into the fabric of political discourse. In calling into question the lucid simplicities of the 1940s, this debate – conducted principally through the United Nations and the United Nations Educational, Scientific and Cultural Organisation – had progressed beyond the age-old tussles between liberty and censorship. In the name of the right of states to sovereign independence, governments were indeed seeking to legitimise international regulation of the flow of information and ideas; but they were in addition seeking to establish principles governing the role of information and the duties incumbent on "communicators" which governments, in the national interest, would have the right to enforce. These duties involved not merely abstention, but commitment, opening the way to the concept of a guided, rather than a free, press. This line of argument finds its reflection in Singaporean and Malaysian policy. Once "freedom of the press" becomes only a "means to an all-embracing end" and that end is defined not in terms of individual freedoms but state policy; once journalists are to put first "what is good for the country", it is clear that news is a national resource and truth the "truth" of a society. There is here more than a hint of an *agitprop* function for the media, proposed by politicians who would – in these cases – indignantly reject any consonance between their political philosophies and the doctrines of Lenin.

There was, of course, a further element in Mahathir's propositions which goes beyond the pleadings of *raison d'état* to deny the existence of the right to circulate and receive the news without impediment. The challenge to the "free flow" principle has been presented by many advocates of a New World Information and Communication Order very much in Mahathir's terms: as a campaign against the West's "intellectual hegemony".

The controversy over communication has many dimensions, some apparently pragmatic, others overtly ideological. There is the challenge to freedom of information and the logical corollary, its "free flow": human right, myth, or a right which can only be understood in its collective rather than individual dimension? Linked to this are the competing claims of individual rights and national sovereignty, under which are subsumed the relationship between state and media (and state and citizen), the claims by states to the right to control not only the flow but the content of news, nationally and internationally, and the rights and responsibilities of news organisations and of "communicators". Finally there are the resentments over "imbalance" in international news-flows and the vexed question of cultural integrity. What is important to recognise is that the heart of the debate concerns neither the "dominance" of the Western-based press – however much play is made of this dimension; nor its performance – however heartfelt and sometimes justified the complaints against it may be. The central issue is the legitimacy of the concept of freedom of information.

The second thing to bear in mind is that what has been generally described as an international debate has been neither exactly a debate, nor more than marginally international, in the normal sense which would imply exchanges of views involving all those concerned. It has, in practice, been overwhelmingly inter-governmental – and has thus been in essence an argument about the locus of power. And it has been not so much a debate as a confrontation of views which are irreconcilable. And one of the areas of irreconcilability is whether it is the business of governments to pronounce on these matters, or whether their duties begin and end with the requirement not to infringe on freedom of information, subject to narrowly-defined caveats for the protection of national security or the rights of individuals which would apply to the media as to all citizens.

That governments are incapable of discussing information without seeking to regulate it was demonstrated early in the history of the United Nations. The lesson was only slowly imbibed by Western governments. It was the United States which originally pressed for the inclusion of specific references to the means of communication among Unesco's responsibilities to promote international collaboration in education, science and culture. The main purpose was clear: Unesco was to "recommend such international agreements as may be necessary to promote the free flow of ideas by word and image". But the unguarded optimism of the times permitted certain ambiguities to creep into Unesco's constitution. States committed themselves under it "to develop and increase the means

163

of communication between their peoples", but also "to *employ* [my italics] those means for the purposes of mutual understanding". This theme was later to be developed by the Soviet Union as justifying state intervention in news content and by Soviet and Third World leaders jointly to argue that the media should promote friendly relations between states – and that governments should ensure that they did so.

At the UN, American efforts in the 1940s to strengthen governments' commitment to the "free flow" principle boomeranged. The US gained the resolution cited at the beginning of this chapter, but governments, thus encouraged to give the subject their attention, opened up a Pandora's box of counter-proposals – for codes of ethics for the media, for rights of reply for states and for legislation to prevent "false or distorted reports likely to injure friendly relations between States". A sub-commission of the UN Commission on Human Rights was set up, with strong American support, in 1946 to examine the human rights implications of freedom of information. By 1949 it had been empowered by governments on the UN Economic and Social Council to study, among other matters, journalists' obligations, responsibilities and professional standards, the problems involved in dissemination of information and the problem of "false news". Forceful lobbying by alarmed Western editors and press groups, particularly in Britain, persuaded London and Washington to backtrack before too much damage was done, and they succeeded in 1952 in getting the UN General Assembly to dissolve the sub-commission. These early, essentially East–West controversies were reactivated and transformed in the early 1970s by two developments. The first was the telecommunications revolution, the second the development of a Third World campaign, in the context of decolonisation, to assert the rights of states to "information sovereignty". Both were seized on by Unesco, which had in the interim concentrated its activities on facilitating exchanges of information and operating a modest programme of training and technical assistance to develop Third World communications infrastructures, to assert the need for positive policies on communication.

With the launching of Telstar, the first communications satellite, in the early 1960s, a world without frontiers suddenly presented itself. It galvanised both the Soviet Union and René Maheu, then Unesco's director-general, for different reasons. For Maheu, this "monumental advance" suggested a wholly new and ambitious role for Unesco: to see that the means of communication now opening up were properly used. For the Soviet Union, it represented a threat to be countered. In 1972, the USSR tabled at the UN a draft convention governing the use of satellites for direct broadcasting which required that nothing be broadcast without the express consent of the receiving country and that all material should be excluded "publicising ideas of war, militarism, nazism, national and racial hatred ... immoral or instigating in nature or ... otherwise aimed at interfering in the domestic affairs or foreign policy of other states". At Unesco in the same year, a declaration on Direct Satellite Broadcasting was agreed against American, British, Canadian and West German opposition requiring states to "reach or promote" prior agreements on DBS transmissions. Simultaneously, through Byelorussia, the Soviet Union embarked on a campaign at Unesco to obtain agreement on "fundamental principles governing the use of the mass media in strengthening peace and ... combating war propaganda, racism and hatred" – intended to justify its jamming of foreign broadcasts to the Eastern bloc. Negotiations on this issue, which ran from 1970 to 1978, were to place Unesco in the centre of the burgeoning confrontation on the propriety of state regulation of information.

Unesco had already, in the 1960s, stepped onto this dangerous ground in the context of cultural policies. Its long-planned world conference on culture, in Venice in 1970, offered a foretaste of the logical contortions to come, producing a resolution which read: "While respecting the freedom of artists, States will ensure that the media of mass communication are not employed to propagate material which is subversive of agreed values". This either suggests that the artist can produce what he likes, but that the state ensures that unsightly flowers blush unseen by the general public; or that he is "free" only within the context of "agreed values". The state is judge of "subversive" potential. And it prefigures Unesco's pre-occupation with regulating the media.

Maheu proceeded, at Unesco's General Conference that year, to obtain authorisation from governments to embark on a programme of assisting them to draw up comprehensive policies for mass communication. What this might involve was made clear in his long-term plan for the organisation presented to the conference, in which he wrote:

LL—L   165

Liberty and Legislation

The time has come to embark on a line of development which will give priority to the *content* of communication, rather than to the *techniques* for communicating it, upon which work until now has tended to be focussed. Freedom of information, the progress of communications techniques, and the development of communication media are all attended by a corresponding responsibility as regards the use made thereof.

The new communciations programme on which Unesco now embarked was intended by Maheu to complete "the process which, beginning with educational planning twelve years ago" would provide states with new tools for "comprehensive planning for total development".

There is nothing sinister about the idea that governments should evolve policies for the development of communications infra-structures – or that Unesco should assist them (assuming the requisite skills) to do so. But the whole burden of Maheu's grand design was to involve governments in the message, not the medium, to encourage them to ensure that journalists, as part of the "process" which began with teachers, were assimilated to the national development plan.

Thus, before the non-aligned movement turned its attention to communications, Unesco embarked on a deliberate policy of encouraging governments to concern themselves with the content of information. By 1976, in its working papers for the first inter-continental conference on communications policy – for Latin American ministers, in Costa Rica – Unesco was advising them that it would be "desirable ... to determine the rights to and limitations of the international use of certain media" and, domestically, to "define as far as possible the obligations of communication".

It struck a responsive chord. The 1973 summit of the non-aligned in Algiers, which elaborated the main elements of Third World demands for a New International Economic Order and an accom-panying programme of action, also took the first, modest, steps by a Third World political gathering in the communications field. The agreements reached at Algiers focused on collective self-reliance: to lower mutual postal and telecommunications tariffs, to build up national media and to improve communications circuits "inherited from the colonial past" in order to enable countries to exchange news about their "achievements". But the communiqué prefigured

166

a larger goal: to transform not only the flows but the content of news. "The activities of imperialism", the 75 governments represented at Algiers declared, "also cover the cultural and sociological fields", imposing "cultural alienation and imported civilisation" which must be countered by a "repersonalisation by constant and determined recourse to the people's own social and cultural values which define it as a sovereign people". As President Houari Boumedienne reminded his guests, "Decolonisation begins with the decolonisation of the mind".

Insofar as "repersonalisation" was to be effected by strengthening national media and cultural programmes, this was an uncontroversial and indeed overdue recognition of the need to reduce dependence on external sources, and the desirability of creating a more multi-dimensional international flow of information. Presented as a revolt against Western domination of international information flows, Third World demands for a "new world information order" – formally initiated at the next non-aligned summit, in Colombo in 1976 – attracted considerable sympathy. Despite the existence, even then, of more than a hundred national news agencies, the preponderance of the major international news organisations in global news-flows was not in doubt. There was a certain logic in the argument that the necessary corollary of Third World demands for a New International Economic Order was the assertion of cultural sovereignty, and that the development of national media was, as the Colombo summit stated, "an integral part of the overall struggle for political, economic and social independence". There was also enough justice in claims by Third World governments that their affairs were poorly and sparsely reported to make a strong case for assistance in building up their own means of communication.

"Repersonalisation" implied, however, more than national efforts at self-reliance in the information field. The campaign for a "new order" attacked not only the dominance of the Western-based media, but the model of a free press which, however imperfectly, it represented. Internationally, apologists for the "new order" justified regulation on the ground that the "free flow" principle had enabled the Western-based international media to impose Western cultural perspectives, political views and market philosophies, serving the interests of a destructively inegalitarian global system. The principle itself was therefore suspect, to be rejected in favour of "balance". Nationally, news should be treated as a resource through which governments mobilised the masses behind development goals and fostered national unity. In the name of freedom and cultural pluralism, governments claimed "the right", in the formulation of a non-aligned meeting in Tunis in 1976, "to exercise full sovereignty over information, both that concerning its day-to-day realities and that diffused to its people".

A "non-aligned" paper prepared for Unesco in 1978 by Tunisia's permanent representative, with the help of experts provided by Unesco from Cuba, Vietnam and East Germany, spelt out the implications. Communications should be recognised by the inter-national community as "a social goal and a cultural product and not as a material commodity". To enable each nation to "choose its information in accordance with its own realities and requirements", states should have power to regulate "the collection, processing and transmission of news and data across frontiers ... to ensure respect for the dignity of communities and nations". States should also have the right "to rectify false or incomplete information appearing in foreign media" and to minimise the risk of such information, "appropriate criteria" should be internationally agreed to ensure that news selection was "truly objective". News-gathering, too, should be subject to control, through "regulation of the right to information by preventing abusive uses of the right of access to information".

The effect would, Third World politicians argued, be to free their media from domination by Western "monopoly", from the distorting lens of commercialism and from alien concepts of news-values. The collective dimension of rights over information was justified by the benefits which would accrue to the community: at the conference convened by Unesco in 1980 in Yaounde to formulate African communications policies, African ministers declared:

> If information organs are systematically used to strengthen national unity, mobilise energies for development and greater participation by popular masses in communication and re-inforce African solidarity and combat all that divides the African continent and prevents it from asserting itself in all its dignity, this will be a means of liberation and an expression of our peoples' freedom.

Information becomes a tool of national policy; the link between governing and governed works from the top down; and journalists are expected not merely, in the words of a 1946 UN resolution, "to seek the facts without prejudice and to spread knowledge without malicious intent", but to promote national myths and necessary international fictions – "solidarity", continental harmony and collective "dignity" – all in the name of freedom. It follows that such a valuable commodity should be subject to international regulation governing its import, export, and basic design and safety features.

It also follows that similar regulation should govern "cultural" material – above all, the television features and series which, exported primarily from the United States with Britain and France next in the league, glimmer on small screens under corrugated iron roofs from Rio de Janeiro to Manila, and which in volume vastly outweigh the diet of "alien" news. This is where the "repersonalisation" idea of the Algiers summit finds advocates well outside government circles, among educated élites, themselves with international access to books, films and video-cassettes, concerned to protect "national" culture. Local producers, they argue with justice, can hardly hope to compete with soap-operas offered at a fraction of production prices. Exposure to the diet available instils the values of a consumerist society, raises expectations far beyond the society's means to meet them and fosters escapism rather than a sense of community. The evident popularity of such material merely aggravates the sense of injury. The Unesco declaration on satellite broadcasting, while it claimed *inter alia* to aim at promoting "the spread of greater cultural exchanges", laid down as a "guiding principle" "the right of all countries and people to preserve their cultures". Nothing in the complex communications debate has more eloquently presented the paradox of controlled freedom.

It is not to make light of the understandable concern with maintaining a distinctive cultural identity and vitality, particularly in countries which will never have the means to rival the production facilities of the West, to say that there is nothing particularly "alien" or indeed Western about escapism, or to argue that concern for cultural identity may mask rather less altruistic preoccupations with thought control. In addition, with the notable exception of some Latin American countries, the governments whose spokesmen pour forth speeches attacking cultural pollution might reasonably direct their ire at the buying departments of their state-controlled television networks.

The options for many developing countries, which have invested in television without considering how to fill their programme hours, are considerable. They can cut the transmission periods; they can devote more of their small programming budgets to low-cost documentaries done outside the studio; they can put their top talent, rather than their least competent people, into their buying departments to search out the vast range of intellectually stimulating material which is available worldwide alongside *Dallas*. Nobody forces television companies, public or private, to purchase a slush diet. The fact, as distinct from the international rhetoric, is that some governments recognise the utility of keeping people happy and at home with liberal helpings of just the "escapist" entertainment of which they complain; and some inhibit their creative artists to the point where the best are unable or unwilling to produce for the national market. In a 1986 debate on Islam and Islamic values on the French television show "Droit de Réponse", an Algerian deliveryman in the invited audience embarrassed the show's orthodox liberals with an impassioned statement to the effect that cultural nationalism in Algeria, aggravated by Islamicisation, had driven its brightest talent to publish in France – and with good reason, since their work could not even be obtained in the country's public libraries.

National efforts to right this state of affairs have rarely prospered through the imposition of controls. In Indonesia in the late 1970s, national television was heavily weighted to evening diets of sermons (with equal time for the different religions), folk dances and other suitably autarkic material. I watched television with a family in a Jakarta *kampung* one evening; the mother's comments were caustic. Had nobody in the government, she asked, thought that everybody worked long hours and wanted to relax at nights? "Do they not understand about the right to laugh?" It is not, among all the "new rights" advocated by Third World governments, on the list. But in India and Hong Kong, extraordinarily successful film industries have flourished in the absence of controls, producing culturally "authentic" (and wildly escapist) entertainment – and internationally acclaimed films as well.

The "cultural imperialism" argument operates at two levels. Internationally, it represents countries as helpless, passive recipients – whereas in reality news-flows are often tightly controlled and the degrees of literacy, language skills and purchasing power of the poor

170

majority circumscribe their access to "alien" cultural products. Nationally, assumptions about the gullibility and unsophistication of the poor – however belied by their proven skills in inventing livelihoods and finding shelter – are made by élites who consider themselves unpolluted by a richer diet of the material which they claim should be denied to the masses.

Its principal effect is to lend added moral gloss to the debate over control of communications flows. The notion of "relevance" acquires more force when directed at re-runs of "Peyton Place" rather than information. The arguments that Western entertainment programmes exacerbate social divisions, accelerate urban migration and lure the country's talent to the West may be overdone, but have a grain of truth. But the heart of the problem remains that governments tend to take much less seriously the cultivation of "self-reliance" than the panacea of control. And for some at least, the defence of "cultural sovereignty" was less concerned to nurture a national flowering of talent than to assert the propriety of regulation – and to call into question the concepts of individual liberty which stood in opposition to such regulation, by tarring them with "imperialist" connotations.

The dilemma for Western governments, as these ideas translated themselves at Unesco and then at the UN itself into demands for the acknowledgement of sovereign rights over information flows, was that they could not let go by default an issue which they did not believe governments should be discussing. Freedom of information – the free exchange of ideas and knowledge within and between societies – was, they believed, central to the exercise of individual rights which the United Nations had been intended to promote and was, indeed, Unesco's principal *raison d'être*. At the same time, the very act of arguing over the proper role of the media, over news-values and news-content, constituted in itself an unacceptable degree of state intervention.

Diplomats are in addition conditioned to seek out the tolerable middle ground, ill-adapted to deal with circumstances in which there is none. There was no meeting place between those who, for all the perennial tensions between governments and the media in the most liberal democracy, accepted free media as guardians of individual liberties against the abuse of power and those who argued that they should be mobilised by the state, however laudable the purpose. All the arguments about "balance" could not obscure the

171

gulf between a "free flow" and a flow subjected to regulation to ensure that information had been selected according to "appropriate criteria" and respected "the dignity of communities and nations". The demand for a new information order to supplant the "free flow" impressed on Western governments more than any other issue in the gathering North–South confrontation of the 1970s the collectivist pressures on human rights; that it was launched in the name of plurality and freedom only underscored the extent to which "freedom" was being reinterpreted by the governments which formed the voting majority in international forums.

At the same time, the desirability of a richer and more diverse flow of information and cultural material was unquestionable, and the fact that the right to freedom of information had been most conspicuously – and profitably – exercised in the industrialised democracies laid Western governments open, in defending the "free flow" principle, to the charge of protecting vested interests.

The "cultural imperialism" thesis had sufficient resonance, particularly among Western Europeans sensitive themselves to the might of the US communications industry, to nuance their response to Third World attacks on the "free flow". Jack Lang, as French minister of culture, launched a public attack on American "cultural imperialism" at a Unesco conference in 1982 and accused the US of advocating "the freedom of the fox in the barnyard". Good politics, certainly, but also an expression of socialist solidarity tinged with a certain degree of resentment against Anglo-Saxon pre-eminence.

There was in addition a half-acceptance among Western liberals of the claim that the media were resources which governments in the throes of nation-building could hardly be expected not to seek to mobilise – just as there was support for the notion that desperately poor and institutionally fragile societies could not "afford" democracy. Paternalism of this kind easily acquired respectability through reference to cultural pluralism – the more so since there was no denying that a free press was free, within the bounds of the law, to act irresponsibly, even if it was also true that a controlled press, by definition, could not act responsibly.

The merit of the campaign for a new information order was that, in demanding international acceptance of guidelines for the media, it caused the major international news organisations to scrutinise their performance; and forced Western governments to abandon tacit assumptions about double standards and defend the

172

proposition that freedoms were indivisible against Third World dismissals of them as Western "myths". They did so hesitantly and diffidently at first, embarrassed to find themselves negotiating on issues which they did not believe belonged on inter-governmental agendas. Essentially, they sought to make the best of it by assuring Third World spokemen that their "aspirations" were understood and promising Western assistance to develop their communications infrastructures in return for a truce on the ideological front.

The arguments for this kind of "damage-limitation" were both theoretical and pragmatic: the West should be sensitive to the genuine grievances reflected in the demands for sovereignty over information and culture; and failure to negotiate "reasonable language" would also result in resolutions which, while they had no legal force, could be voted through against Western objections and then cited by governments to justify curbs on both domestic and international media. The trouble was that the coalition of Eastern bloc and Third World governments which had formed had ambitions which would not lightly be relinquished in exchange for a few journalism training courses and grants to expand national news-agencies.

These initially surfaced in the long confrontation over the Byelo-russian declaration on the media referred to earlier. In the name of a number of unimpeachable goals such as the promotion of peace and the fight against racism and apartheid, this sought to impose duties on the media and to require governments to use their powers to ensure that they conformed. The final compromise was a declaration which left the basic issues unresolved: on the one hand, the Declaration adopted at Unesco in 1978 emphasised diversity of news sources and rights of access to information and confirmed freedom of information as a human right; on the other, it set a precedent for governments to pronounce on the functions of the media and the content of information. That the Soviet Union interpreted it as a victory was demonstrated by its subsequent insistence on follow-up conferences to review the media's "contribution ... to strengthening peace and international understanding, to the promotion of human rights and to countering racialism, apartheid and incitement to war". That the Third World viewed the outcome as handing over a promissary note to establish the ground-rules which would establish "a new, more just and more effective world information and communication order", the "aspirations"

173

for which were now acknowledged by the West, was proved by the next Unesco conference, at Belgrade in October 1980.

The irony was that many Western governments approached the Belgrade conference in the comfortable belief that the controversy was essentially over. Most had committed themselves, the previous April, to a Unesco programme for the "development of communication" and believed that a tacit bargain had been struck whereby, in exchange for practical cooperation, Third World governments would not insist on spelling out what they wished to do with their new media, and would refrain from pressing for international rules governing the role of the media in relation to the state. They were principally troubled by a report of sixteen experts under the chairmanship of the Nobel and Lenin peace prize winner Sean MacBride, commissioned by Unesco to consider world communications problems. The report (largely the work of a Unesco secretariat team) had come out in vigorous support of the principle of free reporting, but was more ambivalent as to practice.

Very much in the spirit of the Venice resolution on the artist cited earlier, the report – written in impenetrable prose perhaps reflecting its intellectual confusion – suggested that journalists should be free but should also understand that they existed to promote friendly relations between states, foster cultural identity, enhance the dignity of nations and peoples, respect national sovereignty and support just causes such as disarmament and liberation movements. Governments, it said, should formulate communications policies "linked to overall social, cultural, economic and political goals". And communications should be seen as "an instrument for creating awareness of national priorities". (All this was neatly encapsulated, six years later, by Zaire's minister of information, Ramazani Baya, who told the National Union of Journalists that they should be "steeped in the ideals of the Party ... and aware of their responsibility to lead the masses to adhere to the general will" – and reflected in the considered opinion of Unesco's director-general, Amadou Mahtar M'Bow, that the media were vehicles for "the large-scale mobilisation of the forces essential for the chosen goals" of their societies.) The report also called for "effective legal measures" to require media "transnationals ... to comply with specific criteria and conditions defined by national legislation and development policies".

The poor quality of the report was less important than the

regulatory implications of its recommendations – with their explicit encouragement of Unesco's involvement, as an intergovernmental body, with news content and standard-setting. A small group of Third World delegations, led by Iraq, Cuba, Tunisia and Venezuela, proceeded at Belgrade to seek to rectify the major area of reticence in the MacBride report. The commissioners had drawn back from defining a New World Information and Communication Order. Venezuela demanded the preparation of a declaration by Unesco which would establish the principles for a "NWICO", and by the end of the conference the West – visibly unprepared for this renewed ideological confrontation – had agreed to a set of "considerations" on which a new order might be "based". These were described by the British delegation as "equivocal", notably in their omission of "such fundamental principles as the right to freedom of thought, opinion and expression, the free circulation of information and ideas, freedom from censorship and arbitrary government control". The significance of the resolution was however larger than its wording: it established the principle that a new order might be capable of definition, and that it was proper for governments to establish guidelines for the press.

The Belgrade conference also assigned to Unesco a central role in communications policy (reversing, in effect, agreements thirty years earlier that Unesco should confine itself to facilitating the "free flow" of information). Its assistant director-general for culture and communications reported to the UN that autumn that Unesco was now ready to move ahead with a "multi-faceted" communications strategy, "conceptual, standard-setting and operational", addressing "the fundamental and basic changes necessary to either the structures of communication *or its content*" (italics added). In February 1981, it convened a meeting of "organisations of working journalists" for the apparently innocuous purpose of discussing measures for journalists' "protection".

For this meeting, which was – until official protests compelled a last-minute change of policy – closed to reporters and also to professional organisations such as the International Press Institute and the Inter-American Press Association on the grounds that these were "publishers' associations" – Unesco commissioned a working paper from Professor Pierre Gaborit, a member of the International Association of Democratic Lawyers and consultant to the Prague-based International Organisation of Journalists. This proposed the

175

creation, under Unesco's auspices, of an international commission to ensure journalists' protection. It was in due course to include governments, in recognition of the fact that "account should be taken of the legitimate concern of States to preserve their sovereignty in the process of ensuring the regulation of journalists". The commission would register journalists' names and communicate them to governments, issue cards to journalists on dangerous missions, start work on an international code of ethics and act as a world press council to ensure that journalists conformed with "generally accepted" rules of professional conduct and thus merited protection. The possibility of procedures for withdrawing their cards in case of infringement was canvassed. Had editors from the so-called "proprietors' associations" not objected, the commission would have been established.

In the ensuing furore, Unesco disclaimed any intent of licensing or regulating the media. M'Bow himself sought six years later in an interview with *Jeune Afrique* to present Unesco's role as responsive, almost passive:

> the journalists wanted certain actions taken on their behalf. The proprietors disagreed with them. We acted as intermediary. Some journalists wanted Uneseco to go further along this road, but we refused. So when you say Unesco wanted to license journalists, I say that it is false.

Yet Unesco's own history of the protection issue dates Unesco's involvement to a statement by M'Bow during Unesco's 1976 General Conference in Nairobi which explicitly linked "freedom and responsibility" with "protection". "The various considerations on the right to communicate," he said then,

> lead quite naturally to the posing of the whole question of the responsibilities of information personnel vis-à-vis society, both as individuals and as groups possessing considerable powers. In this connection, our Organisation should contribute to the gradual establishment of a common professional deontology, by helping its Member States to define the rights and duties of information personnel.

Unesco's 1979/80 programme, drafted by the secretariat, duly proposed "the improvement of professional standards and status and protection of journalists" and a meeting to examine "ways of protecting journalists ... so that they can carry out their duties with complete objectivity". The supposed confrontation between proprietors and journalists was an *ex post facto* invention. Far from "refusing" to take matters further after 1981, Unesco continued until 1985 to finance and encourage meetings, in active cooperation with the International Organisation of Journalists, on press codes and the "protection" issue. In that year, journalists' organisations agreed to entrust their protection to the politically neutral International Committee of the Red Cross.

Few of Unesco's attempts to foster, in the words of its 1984/85 draft programme, "improved understanding of the relationship between the notions of 'freedom' and 'responsibility' of communicators" and of the "gradual formulation of communication law" attracted such unfortunate publicity. The regulatory bias of its activities was masked by language suggesting openness. Who could object to words like "access ... participation ... democratisation ... the right to communicate", or to plans for "securing the contribution" of the media to sexual equality, or "strengthening the role of the media in solving the major world problems"? Even if participation justified public management of the media, the right to communicate had a collective dimension which opened the way to giving governments an international right of reply, and states were invited to "secure" the media's contribution to desirable goals.

Positively interventionist programmes could always be dressed in the garb of neutrality. "Some assert", M'Bow told Unesco's Executive Board in 1982,

> that information is an invaluable means of keeping power under control and containing its abuses, or even a fully-fledged counter-force. Others hold the view that information should serve the interests of the state and of the development of society by helping to preserve the stability and unity of socio-economic systems. It is not Unesco's business to take sides on this issue.

Unesco's medium-term plan, which the Board was then discussing, stated firmly that "the international community [governments] cannot ignore the problem of the content of ... messages" transmitted internationally, and argued that since "information has become a key development resource ... efforts should be devoted first and foremost to harnessing this new power".

Leaving aside the possibility of an inter-governmental organisation concerning itself with the *content* of messages and encouraging governments to "integrate" media policies with "general development objectives" and "the framework of an international development strategy and of the new international economic order" without "taking sides", Unesco had not been intended by its founders to take a "neutral" view. Its mandate was to encourage the free exchange of knowledge and to recommend international agreements only where "necessary to promote the free flow of ideas by word and image". Its purpose was to persuade governments to refrain from restricting that freedom, not to invite them to draw up "norms applicable, at both national and international levels, to information and communication" within the context of overall state policies for development or any other purpose.

Western governments, throughout the long campaign for a new order, have attempted to square the circle, by accepting the concept while trying to rid it of its regulatory connotations by insisting that it should be seen as "an evolving and continuing process". For diplomats at home with fine print, this somewhat sybilline formula serves as protective bulwark against prescriptive definition, although the direction of the "evolution" is obviously open to interpretation. By the time the US, at the United Nations Committee on Information in 1987, was seeking unsuccessfully to have the issue dropped from its agenda by arguing that the whole concept was "alien to us" because "the word 'order' connotes political and economic systems inherently opposed to freedom of opinion and expression", it was thoroughly embedded in all UN debate on information.

It is tempting to argue that UN debates do not mirror the external world, where journalists go about their business mercifully oblivious to the Unesco declaration enjoining them to contribute to harmony between states, and where government censors are primarily concerned, as ever, to obliterate the embarrassing truth. Resolutions do not bind governments. Evidence, however, accumulates that these debates do put ideas into governments' heads. A meeting in Jakarta in 1984 of the hundred-plus non-aligned governments – more than 60 represented by information ministers – agreed to implement policies to ensure that information supported development and national priorities and respected the principle of non-interference in each other's internal affairs. They issued a "Jakarta Appeal to the Mass Media" calling on them "to eschew tendentious reporting in all its manifestations and to desist from propagating materials which directly or indirectly may prove detrimental or prejudicial to the interest of any member country of the Non-Aligned Movement". And they agreed, in a nice example of the requirements of objectivity under a new information order, to encourage their media "to use, whenever the word 'Israel' is to be cited, instead the 'racist Zionist regime', taking into account the freedom of the press".

A common feature of such meetings is the synonymity in ministerial minds of news and government information services. Nobody would deny the role of the latter, whether it is to circulate information on AIDS in Britain or to promote campaigns for breast-feeding or social forestry in India. But they are distinct entities, and citizens have the right to suspect, when an Indian diplomat defines news (as one did, under Indira Gandhi's state of emergency) as "everything which is true, pleasant and beneficial", that they are being denied the right to learn what they can of the world without the interference of their masters. A free press can present a distasteful spectacle, particularly when it is fiercely commercial. Charles Dickens, himself a journalist, was horrified by the variety he found blooming in the United States in the first half of the nineteenth century. He found it "a frightful engine" and warned that "while, with ribald slander for its only stock in trade, it is the standard literature of an enormous class ... so long must its odium be on the country's head, and so long must the evil it works be plainly visible". He would undoubtedly have been equally appalled by the entrapment tactics used some 150 years later by the *News of the World* to persuade a British politician to pay off a prostitute for the delectation of its readers. Many critics of the press – in the West as in the Third World – worry about its power, and argue that the market system spawns editors (and proprietors) who select news in terms of what will sell more of the *Daily Beast*, who pander to the public's curiosity to the neglect of the higher ground of the public interest, and who dwell on the sensational or salacious.

Those in the West who worry about the power of the press are free to permit themselves, for much of the time at least, the luxury of forgetting that real power lies in the withholding, not the spreading of information. Once the concept of a "guided press" gains respectability, even where the overt ambition is to ensure quality and

179

responsibility and to avoid the excesses of the yellow press, the question becomes who decides what is socially desirable. The Indian government would be unlikely to find that banner headlines on the blinding of "suspected criminals" by the police were "pleasant and beneficial".

Scrutiny of the media is healthy – in a climate of freedom. The kind of scrutiny to which the media tend to be subjected in its absence is not: Freedom House's necessarily incomplete catalogue for 1986 (incomplete because based on verified cases) included 22 journalists killed, 178 imprisoned, 214 harrassed, 40 newspapers and radio stations banned and others bombed, raided or taken over by the state. The rejection of freedom of information as a "Western value", its free flow as a "myth" or (again in M'Bow's words) as a form of "cultural aggression" may be dressed in the language of pluralism. But the trend has been to create national monopolies in its name. George Ayittey, a Ghanaian economist, had the courage in 1987 to document the situation in black Africa in an article in *The Times* which explicitly invited Western media and publics to give them as much attention as they gave to censorship in South Africa. With the exceptions – notably – of Senegal and Botswana, he wrote,

> the press throughout black Africa is under strict government control and serves only the interests of those in power. The least deviation from the "revolutionary path", the slightest allusion to ministerial corruption or the expression of a timidly dissenting opinion brings harsh reprisals ... True freedom never came to Africa. Its people wanted independence from colonial rule, not to be ruled by another set of aliens or black neo-colonialists.

The effect of repression was not, he pointed out, the development of the media, "responsible" or otherwise: "in the 1960s there were more than 300 daily newspapers in Africa; now there are fewer than 140; and nine countries have no newspapers at all." Ayittey's article should be read in conjunction with the Yaounde Declaration.

The most disturbing consequence of the UN debates on freedom of information may, however, lie not in the repressive legislation they have appeared to legitimise from Surinam to Singapore, nor in the mounting pressures on Third World journalists to act as vehicles for mobilising the masses, but in the impoverishment and stereotyping of discussion at a time when it is clear that, however extensively information (or the lack of it) shapes today's world, it will shape it even more comprehensively tomorrow.

Restrictive legislation threatens to cut the developing world out of the communications revolution even more surely than lack of finance, without ensuring for the powers that be the protective carapace which they claim in the name of "information sovereignty" and a new order. The real new order, in the view of Arthur Clarke, the Sri Lankan futurologist, is an "unstoppable tide" in which

> Electronic cultural imperialism will sweep away much that is good, as well as much that is bad. Yet it will only accelerate changes which were in any case inevitable; and on the credit side, the new media will preserve for future generations the customs, performing arts and ceremonies of our time, in a way that was never possible in any earlier age.

It is enormously disruptive – of British stockbrokers' lunches, interrupted forever by the Big Bang, of established customs, barbaric or enlightened. But the trend is essentially democratic. For Clarke, it opened up an encouraging perspective: the end of the closed society. "The debate about the Free Flow of Information which has been going on for so many years", he told the United Nations on World Communications Day, 1983,

> will soon be settled – by engineers, not politicians ... No government will be able to conceal, at least for very long, evidence of crimes or atrocities – even from its own people. The very existence of new information channels, operating in real-time and across all frontiers, will be a powerful influence for civilised behaviour. If you are arranging a massacre, it will be useless to shoot the cameraman who has so inconveniently appeared on the scene. His pictures will already be safe in the studio five thousand miles away; and his final image may hang you.

For Third World reporters lacking typewriters and telephones, this is a distant prospect, however; and the governments which frame the laws which further handicap them persist in acting as if it were not true. UN debates remain stuck in the deep groove of "balance" versus "freedom". By the mid-1980s, Unesco's acute institutional crisis had had a temporarily dampening effect on inter-governmental confrontation – with even the Soviet Union (perhaps influenced by *Glasnost*, but more probably by its desire to see the return of the United States to Unesco) suggesting that "it is necessary to withdraw confrontation from the cooperation sphere". Only Unesco's programmes seemed stuck in amber, maintaining their emphasis on content – and conduct.

But at the United Nations, inter-governmental committees – generally comprising relatively junior diplomats whose ignorance of the issues was matched by their tenacious attachment to the litany of the NWICO – continued to press for its "establishment". At a meeting between members of the Committee on Information and journalists from both Western and developing countries in March 1987, Mihailo Saranovic, director of the Yugoslav news agency Tanjug, attempted to convince its members of the futility of further discussion. It was one thing, he said, to press for a New International Economic Order, which "involves strict and precise obligations and rules"; but a new information order "will be the achievement of each country, through democratic processes which challenge censorship, self-censorship or manipulation". Almost no professional journalists, he complained, had been involved in this "interminable debate; but they, not governments, not Unesco, not the UN, should have the decisive word". As to the imbalance in news-flows, in the first place the situation had changed greatly in 15 years; the non-aligned news agency pool was circulating 3,000 items a day, more than any single agency was technically able to digest: its problems were equipment and poor standards, not the absence of binding norms. In the second place, he said,

> I am against mathematical equality and balance. It makes no sense: Japanese statistics show that worldwide, only 7% of the information circulated is published. All news is merchandise; what matters is equality of quality, and only the better products should find customers on the world market.

He appealed to them to cooperate in raising quality, "in the clear understanding that better informed public opinion is the route to international understanding, and the only route".

If Saranovic was greeted with considerable hostility by Third World committee members, this was partly because discussing the politics of communication is more entertaining than sticking to the Committee's original remit to review the performance of the UN's department of public information. But there are deeper reasons to suppose that governments will be reluctant to relinquish the assault on freedom of information.

The call for a new information order provides a powerful cement of solidarity among governments of completely different political persuasions and largely incompatible economic interests – particularly valuable at a time when debt and economic collapse place severe stresses on Third World cohesion as a bargaining entity in international forums. Domestically, the concept of a guided press has more rather than less attraction in times of acute crisis; and that concept, to be workable, requires constraints on international information flows. And above and beyond that, the questioning of freedom of information as an individual human right forms part of the questioning of "Western" values which has been a prominent feature of the search for a Third World "identity". In one sense, given the vast variety of the countries which compose the developing world, the concept of a common identity is nonsense; but it has been a remarkably tenacious feature of the past quarter century. Nationally and as a group, developing countries are still, with the exception of a self-confident few, groping for the expression of a collective consciousness; and in the information age, it is not surprising that they should take the view that it is through the media that consciousness grows.

The question is whether Unesco, for so long part of the problem, could recover from the doldrums of ideological confrontation to become part of the cure. Its original mission, to promote the free flow of ideas, remains no less relevant than it was in 1945. The enormous powers which UN secretariats have to set the agenda – both in their programmes of work and in the terms in which they propose discussion – could enable it to relay the tracks of debate, since governments tend to follow rather than initiate. The verbal commitment of Professor Federico Mayor, elected to succeed M'Bow in 1987, to "a free and uninhibited flow" of information, could point that way. Developments in the Soviet Union in the late 1980s provided a window of opportunity: Unesco was unlikely fatally to alienate one of its most powerful member states by beginning, as the Soviet delegate had suggested, "a search for the most efficient solutions" within the bounds of agreed purposes. That it might go further, to the point of actively promoting freedom of information, is perhaps too much to hope. But it could do much to make the control of information a source of embarrassment rather than pride.

183

Freedom and the Breakdown
of International Order

PIERRE DE SENARCLENS

Freedom is a metaphysical puzzle which philosophers have always sought to unravel. However, from the vantage point of the social sciences, freedom does not exist in itself. Instead it is defined within a political context by which it is endowed with meaning and purpose. Every society requires institutions, customs or laws which tend to enforce a specific order. Therefore, at least in its elementary forms, freedom cannot be dissociated from the political framework perpetuating that order. In other words, the relationship between freedom and politics amounts to determination. Indeed freedom is made up of elements which assert themselves through the conceptualization and the implementation of authority relationships and of social relations. Admittedly, the scope of freedom goes far beyond the area of politics. However, it is within political limits that the foundations of liberty are laid.

Though freedom is politically grounded, its relationship with politics is not unambiguous. The main goal of politics is not to implement liberty, but rather to balance collective aspirations and needs. This is achieved by organising the authority relationships and social relations necessary for the preservation of order and security. Furthermore the concept of freedom does not just assert itself. It is an integral part of values and strategies which emerge together or in a loose-rank ordering. Its links with the ideals of equality, justice or security are highly problematic. Hence the need for liberty may conflict with other social values which are just as strongly upheld. Alternatively it may clash with the constraints without which the order necessary for its implementation cannot be preserved.

Its requirements, often construed as absolutes, are somewhat contradictory. Their fulfilment in practice is always impeded by conflicts between political values and interests. Since the concept of freedom is closely bound up with politics, its contents and its objectives change as society evolves. So do the means which must be applied to comply with its prerequisites. The definition of its nature and of the conditions on which it depends fluctuates over time and from one school of thought to another.

Freedom is an important component of the systems of mythical and ideological references which legitimate authority relationships and the social order. This makes its relations with politics all the more complex. Indeed politics cannot be dissociated from the myths and the ideologies which chart its path. In the West, the concept of freedom is rooted in a cultural heritage derived from the conjunction of Greek philosophy and the Judaeo-Christian tradition. This legacy took shape through a series of historical processes, with the Renaissance, the Reformation and the age of Enlightenment as salient points. Even before it acquired a political content freedom imposed itself as a spiritual requirement. It was expressed in pleas for religious toleration and in the acceptance of unbelief. It has been posited rightly that freedom of conscience, as it developed in the seventeenth century, was invented in Europe. This view of liberty asserted itself in the first splits of Christian civilization. It opened the way to the secularization of Western society, to the detachment of politics from religion and even from morals, and to the development of individualism.

By reinterpreting natural law, such seventeenth-century thinkers as Grotius, Pufendorf and Locke came to separate law from theology. Thus they initiated the trend towards the secularization of politics which is a central component of Western freedom. Liberty has been inseparable, ever since, from the secularized cultural values which brought in their wake a range of institutional changes. It is these values which challenged Western man to free himself from the constraints of Providence and those of Nature and to take charge of his own fate. This version of freedom is predicated on the secularization of political and social relationships. It is inseparable from rationalism, individualism, egalitarianism, and from the values and aspirations on which the ideological archetypes of the Judaeo-Christian tradition rest.

Since the eighteenth century, ideologies have taken over from religious belief systems as bases for political and social organization

185

and as the eschatological horizon of history. They have tended to imbue the idea of liberty with sacredness. This has extended to the institutional schemes related to freedom. Our understanding of liberty is also permeated with the myths of Western political culture. Their archetype consists in the ideas of equality, of justice, of reason, of happiness, of progress. It is expressed by idealizing certain historical events invested with a symbolic meaning, such as the Glorious Revolution, American Independence, Bastille Day etc. Since the end of the eighteenth century, the idea of freedom is closely linked with the concept of nation-state. This state has been a confluent of the institutional and political structures derived from the *Ancien Régime* and of the political ideologies of the Revolution.

Henceforth political freedom was achieved through popular sovereignty asserted within a national framework. The concept of nation gradually became a focus for the collective sentiments which rationalism tended to turn away from the Church. Even if they sever their links with the religions in which they originate, the network of myths and symbols associated with nationhood retain an illusory and sacred dimension. Hence they cannot be reduced to a contingent political dimension. Ideologies define the scope of tolerance in political and social matters. Freedom is obviously at stake in these conflicts. This is why the myth of liberty, when translated into politics, is pregnant with every form of despotism. Thus the assertion of freedom by French revolutionaries ended by providing an alibi for tyranny. Nevertheless it underpins most systems of political legitimacy in the nineteenth century and even now.

Freedom is intimately connected in contemporary ideologies with a set of values which are difficult to rank-order and whose patterning gives rise to political conflicts. Antagonisms focus also on the means needed to implement the desired objectives, i.e. to promote freedom and its concomitants. Towards the end of the eighteenth century, a broad consensus seemed to emerge, particularly among philosophers, to base freedom upon legality. The political order was to rest on a constitution and on laws capable of promoting the institutional prerequisites for freedom. Constitutions and laws were to give liberty a certain immunity from political fluctuations. The American and French revolutions in the eighteenth century asserted the primacy of law. This principle was to ensure equality, justice and democracy as prerequisites for freedom. At the time, law was also expected to determine the social conditions on which freedom must rest, especially the limits of political power and the foundation of social co-existence.

However law cannot supersede politics. It can only tend to guide in a predictable direction. It can neither overcome conflicts of interests nor stop the natural drift of power towards arbitrariness and violence. Any power is bound to turn the law into an instrument dedicated to the pursuit of its own designs. This is why the English liberals, to whom Montesquieu and his followers in continental Europe were indebted, stressed the need for checks and balances. The objective was to provide the institutional structures on which freedom rests. Liberals also granted an important part to cultural factors in order to preserve and develop the preconditions for freedom. In this perspective, freedom presupposes mores favourable to tolerance, and a socio-political climate predicated on moderation. Thus, to eighteenth-century philosophers education became the main way of developing rationality as a prerequisite for the rule of liberty. It is also significant that the French Revolution produced a wealth of educational programmes intended to play a prominent role in implementing ideals of freedom.

Since liberty cannot be dissociated either from history or from politics, it has been conceptualized in different ways over time and according to dominant ideologies. During the nineteenth century, socialist movements, without really challenging the classical view of freedom, provided many new ideas about the means of its implementation. Civil and political liberties are devoid of substance unless material resources are provided for making them operational. Hence freedom entails the material means required to promote individual or collective autonomy. It implies a continuing change of economic and social structures aimed at an egalitarian sharing of wealth, so that all may participate fully in the assets of national sovereignty. In the twentieth century, a new grasp of freedom was achieved, thanks to the discovery of the unconscious psychic structures which underpin individual and/or collective autonomy.

After the end of the Second World War, the Universal Declaration of Human Rights, adopted by the General Assembly of the United Nations, summarized the dominant view of freedom in Western democratic societies. This Declaration adds to a legal definition of freedom a number of far-reaching political, economic, social and cultural principles. In fact, they are among the most progressive within Western political thought. A new liberal utopia is thus expressed in legal terms. Reacting against the fascist experiments which convulsed the world, the authors of this Declaration asserted a view of freedom which agreed in the main with that already accepted towards the end of the eighteenth century.

From the ideological viewpoint, the immediate post-war period was a kind of restoration. Thus the Declaration begins by defining freedom by reference to classical civil and political rights. It covers therefore the protection of individual integrity and autonomy, i.e. the right not to undergo torture or arbitrary arrest, the right to express one's beliefs, to participate in associations and in the public affairs of one's country etc. This outlook on individual freedom sets limits to the authority of the government and to that of society. The individualist bias of the Declaration is obvious: all its articles are coherent and systematic in referring to a notion of society founded on the predominance of the individual.

Admittedly the individualism of the Declaration is tempered to a great extent by the concept of equality and of distributive justice. Freedom is closely connected to a political goal, namely to the provision of a minimum standard of economic and social security for all citizens. The range of material and cultural freedoms defined in the Declaration goes far beyond the requirements of classical liberalism. The ideals of social democracy are explicitly and coherently integrated therein. Political and social ideas which have become accepted in European socialist and liberal circles from the end of the nineteenth century onwards are also expressed in the Declaration. Thus its design is impregnated with a neo-liberalism on which the depression of the 1930s had a great impact. This school of thought inspired the experiment of the New Deal. It emerged in Britain during the war with the Beveridge reports and in continental Europe in the political programmes of the Resistance movements. In the aftermath of the war it stimulated the economic and social experiments of most Western countries and culminated in the evolution of what came to be known as the Welfare State. The Universal Declaration amounts therefore to a kind of normative summary of the experiments conducted in most Western countries after World War Two. It overlapped in more than one respect with the kind of ideological consensus which prevailed at the time and focused on the political tenets of social democracy.

Society must give to every individual a social security cover, provide him with work which he can carry out under "just and favourable conditions" and protect him against unemployment. It must ensure for him and his family "an existence worthy of human dignity, grant him the right to rest and leisure, and secure for him a standard of living adequate for the health and well-being of himself and his family, including food, clothing, housing, and medical care and necessary social services". Nonetheless the economic, social and cultural rights stated in the Declaration are exclusively targeted upon enhancing the potential and the advantages of the individual. By individual is meant an independent person, endowed with specific needs and aspirations which cannot be reduced to the collective requirements and wishes of society.

As has already been suggested, freedom is both determined and delineated by the political order. The model of liberty proclaimed by the United Nations is asserted within a political universe whose nature may have remained the same, but whose scope and socio-economic bases have changed. Since the Second World War, the political order has remained dependent upon national institutions, legislation and policies. Yet it has depended more than ever upon the conditions prevailing in international society as a whole. Almost everywhere this has been a dominant factor. Freedom is therefore necessarily dependent upon the international political order.

The implementation of freedom, as it is interpreted in the Declaration of Human Rights, requires an order whose structure is complex. Three closely interlinked components are at stake: (1) the Welfare State; (2) an international order founded upon a liberal economy and upon the rule of law; (3) a worldwide socio-cultural model which requires the development of values, aspirations and needs deeply rooted in the liberal civilization to be developed.

(1) The Welfare State

As in the past, freedom entails the existence of the rule of law. It requires a democratic government. "The will of the people shall be the basis of the authority of government." "Everyone has the right to take part in the government of his country." It is also predicated upon the separation of power, and especially upon the independence of the judiciary. Though the Declaration is not explicitly

189

committed to any economic system, the rights it proclaims, and the right to property ownership in particular, are bound up with an intrinsically liberal world view.

This plan for freedom does not only enshrine a classical democratic system, based on the rule of law and the separation of power. It relies also on the introduction of a wide network encompassing economic, social and cultural institutions. This progressive approach to liberty necessarily endows the political authorities with an increasingly important role in implementing its prerequisites. From this vantage point, the government becomes the main promoter of freedom. The state has a calling to intervene in all areas of social life. It becomes a decisive instrument for social growth and for the distribution of welfare benefits. Freedom is guaranteed from then on by governmental legislation as much as by the official economic, social and cultural policies aimed at its implementation.

As in the eighteenth century, education plays a considerable role in the implementation of the rights and freedoms set out as political and social ideals. In particular, it is to help promote the individualist and egalitarian design which underpins them. Its outcome must be "the fulfilment of the human personality". In other words, education is to help achieve the happiness of the individual which is the target of this neo-liberal programme. In practice, this outlook entails the organization of educational and cultural systems conducive to personality development in childhood and adolescence. As a corollary, psycho-educational institutions must be set up to track down the causes of psychological disorders. Therefore public and private networks intended to help personality development have to proliferate.

The demands addressed to the Welfare State have ambivalent effects for freedom. The safety and welfare that citizens expect their government to provide necessitate a more elaborate administrative and political machinery. Indeed, as individuals rely on the government and on public institutions to promote liberty, state powers are considerably enhanced. Consequently, threats to individual autonomy are generated. Yet, in the practice of democracies, power structures which delineate the scope and conditions of freedom remain widely diverse. In addition to the traditional institutions of representative democracy, there is a complex network of public and private interests and of pressure groups, whose interplay tends to protect individual liberty.

2. The International Order

Freedom is no longer secured only by democratic laws and institutions within a national context. It is also dependent upon an international order capable of preserving peace, security and the prerequisites for economic, social and cultural progress. It presupposes a wide scheme of international cooperation on the world scale, covering the areas of politics and economics, society and culture. This scheme is a logical corollary of the structural transformation undergone by international society.

In the Western world, fascist regimes and war helped undermine the concept of the nation state and, above all, the nationalist ideology on which that particular political system rests. The nature of modern weaponry, the increased exchanges between countries and the unprecedented expansion of communications tend to confirm that order and security, as prerequisites for freedom, must be sought in the whole of international society. These trends impose new frontiers on politics. As a rule, the aspirations and needs posited by neo-liberalism require a transcending of the confines of the nation-state. It is generally accepted that the scope of national sovereignty, in the traditional sense, should shrink since its main attributes (e.g. military security, economics, ecology) are profoundly affected by international cooperation or by decisions made by a few great powers.

International cooperation becomes therefore a necessity if the foundations of peace and the terms of material prosperity needed to preserve world order are to be ensured. To this end different types of complementary institutions are required. International law plays a basic part in promoting this order. So do the organizations intended to implement world or regional cooperation in the political, economic, social and cultural fields. For the designers of this international system, order must rest on the principle of free trade. Hence it presupposes financial and commercial institutions capable of supporting a stable and coherent monetary system. They must also be able to further the liberalization of transactions in goods, services and foreign exchange. This is the target of the Bretton Woods institutions, set up and developed alongside rather than within the system of the United Nations. It is also that of the regional organizations, which appeared mainly in the wake of the Marshall Plan.

191

3. The Universal Socio-Cultural Model

This neo-liberal design was indissociable from a universalist socio-cultural model. The Universal Declaration asserts more or less explicitly the ideal of a universal man whose needs, aspirations, collective representations, economic, political, social and cultural views are supposed to be the same everywhere. The ideal of universal man is that of the individual in control of his thoughts, of his spiritual commitments and of his acts, which emerged in Europe from the Renaissance and the Reformation onwards. In this anthropological perspective, man is a rational being, imbued with individualism, pursuing freedom and – perhaps even more – equality. He is a citizen within a state, a property owner, a worker, with a concern for his own interests and his material welfare.

The socio-cultural model suggested by the Declaration is the characteristic man of industrial and urban civilization. He is autonomous, somewhat hedonistic, seeking to improve his material position. He puts his trust in science and technology; in mankind's unlimited ability to dominate nature and to prevail over the traditional and the sacred; in the future and in progress. The concept of progress subsumes those of economic growth, of change and of modernization. It emerges as the mobilizing myth of international society and is asserted as the immutable law of world history. The authors of the United Nations sytem were thus faithful to the legacy of the Enlightenment. They linked the world order to economic, social and cultural progress, i.e. to the development of societal conditions reflecting Western aspirations and needs.

The neo-liberal ideology which underpins this notion of human rights assumes that the aspirations and needs it proclaims are universal. It makes the same assumption about the order it posits. From this vantage point, any developments conforming to its intrinsic logic are equated with progress and the growth of rationality. The importance attached to universalizing this cultural pattern was shown by the creation of Unesco in 1945. "Since wars begin in the minds of men", education, science and culture are expected to produce the prerequisites for a new world order. In this order peace would be guaranteed, as would respect for the rights of man. Such an idealistic approach posits that conflicts are the product of "mutual lack of understanding". In principle, the fact and the worth of cultural diversity may be accepted. Yet, basically, the conviction remains that freedom is conditional upon the diffusion of a cultural model rooted in liberal rationalism. Another aspect of this liberal utopia was represented, somewhat later, by the concepts of development and modernization. They provided the rationale for the first programmes of technical assistance to "backward" countries.

With the advent of the United Nations, freedom becomes a myth underpinning the principles intended to legitimate the world order. As always, liberty is a complex notion, whose political functions are somewhat contradictory. First of all, it belongs to the array of principles which aim at legitimizing the political order introduced by the Western powers. Since universal freedom is expressed by reference to a legalistic utopia, this may have enhanced such a conservative function. By advancing an individualistic interpretation of human rights and of their implementation, Western countries resisted the legal conceptualization of collective aspirations which are more obviously political. Thus, when international covenants were being negotiated, they tended to object to the right of peoples to self-determination.

The ideological outlook built into the Universal Declaration of Human Rights is consonant with the preservation of Western hegemony. The Western countries which invoke them aim not only at resisting totalitarianism, but also at promoting their own economic and political structures. They impose their own terms of comparison. Rationalism and individualism of the neo-liberal type and the socio-economic structures associated with them entail their own norms and constraints.

It is no accident that the Declaration coexisted in time with the propagation in international society, particularly through the United Nations, of the twin concepts "development/under-development", which come to be inseparable from the dichotomies modernity/tradition or advanced societies/backward societies. A novel legitimation for relationships of political, economic and cultural dependence between the Western world and the new states on the world scene may be derived from these ideological concepts. So-called "developed" countries, by universalizing their modes of economic, political, social and cultural organization, impose unattainable objectives on countries which are less or differently

193

advanced. These standards become the criteria by which international society assesses any collective endeavour. To emulate the values and achievements of dominant societies is construed as a prerequisite for progress. Thus under-development is defined by reference to the laws of development evidenced by the world powers. In order to achieve development, the countries of the so-called Third World must follow endlessly the trajectory of a history which is not within their grasp.

Yet, because it is grounded in the myths of liberty, progress, equality and reason, the neo-liberal ideology is also subversive of all established political structures. As the utopia it conjures up makes the existing international order unacceptable, it provides an inspiration to political movements which challenge these structures. This function has been enhanced by the association established between liberty and the new myths, i.e. development and modernization.

It has been rightly pointed out that "the rights of man" embody a sort of built-in contradiction which is difficult to overcome. The ideal targets posited cannot be reached immediately and imply therefore the performance of change. Yet they are predicated on a juridical order which is, by definition, resistant to change. Thus the freedom asserted by the Declaration encourages constant challenges to the established order. By corollary, it prompts controversy about the legal system designed to protect human rights. These are posited as a wide set of absolute values. Hence they tend to blur and undermine the political necessity to harmonize contradictory short-term interests.

While it is presented as a universal model of institutions and culture, liberal industrial civilization expresses the design of a minority in international society. Of course, the ideals of liberty, justice, human dignity and solidarity stated in the Declaration and upheld by international institutions are not the prerogative of Western civilization. Yet the myths and the ideological, political and social concepts of neo-liberal thought inherent in this text and in the charters of these organizations are obviously the product of Western history. They are inextricably bound up with an ideological outlook, with political institutions, with economic, social and cultural structures anchored in the industrial civilization whose essence is capitalist and liberal. It is by reference to them that human rights are expressed and articulated.

As a matter of fact, when in 1948 the General Assembly of the

United Nations adopted the Declaration, international society had lost any common purpose. The Cold War was disrupting the alliance from which the setting up of the United Nations as a system had derived. The universalist endeavour of the West was undermined thereby and the tenuous institutional framework was paralysed. This is why the countries within the Soviet sphere of influence refused to give their formal assent to the Declaration in the General Assembly. For those states imbued with Marxist philosophy, it was impossible to endorse a set of principles enshrining liberal values and institutions. Despite their formal allegiance to freedom and to democracy, socialist states do not accept the worth of representative institutions. They invoke a fuller interpretation of liberty by refusing to separate the state from civil society. They tirelessly advocate an overlap between individual and collective rights, as if the implementation of the latter always brought about more freedom and greater political rights. They uphold the state's complete responsibility for outlining and operationizing human rights. The universalism to which they refer should extend the socialist revolution on a world scale.

Moreover, colonialism and/or the sequels of Western political domination endured simultaneously in most parts of international society. Admittedly the majority of dependent countries seemed attracted at the time by some aspects of the dominant liberal programme. During the struggles for decolonization, independence movements took over several *leitmotifs* of the political discourse prevailing in the United Nations. They posited the creation of a nation-state as the goal of their fight for independence. Therefore they aimed at promoting a political regime which would conform to the national state structures evolved in Europe during the nineteenth century. Their aspirations and claims pertained to an ideological framework which inspired or justified this form of political organization. They expressed the intention to achieve the same type of economic and social development. Thus the main concepts of Western political culture seemed to become universal – apparently without any obstacles. The myth of liberal individualism was transported to the level of nations and states, which are said to be fully equal and sovereign. Everywhere the ruling elites invoked freedom, human rights, and peoples' rights and national sovereignty.

In reality, as political independence followed decolonization, the new rulers could not establish governmental and administrative structures capable of meeting the political, economic and social challenges of nation-building. Politically, the pattern of the nation-state, with its trend towards centralization, was not always suited to the conditions of countries freed from the colonial yoke. Whether in its liberal or in its Marxist version, the doctrine of national sovereignty rests on the postulate of majority rule. Hence its relationship with the problem of minorities has always been ambiguous. In newly independent countries, the process of decolonization often culminated in the constitution of states lacking the institutional attributes of governmental authority, as well as the characteristics of nationhood. Among these, the collective will to share a common destiny was missing.

In theory, the doctrines of national sovereignty or peoples' rights are inseparable from democratic structures which enable the collective will of individuals to be expressed. But how is this will to be recognized when the setting up and the effective operation of representative institutions are hampered by illiteracy, dire poverty and cultural traditions? National sovereignty is predicated upon economic and social development. Yet the new states generally failed to possess the basic prerequisites of economic development, as imposed by the dominant structures of international society. How is one to reconcile the exigencies of development with the political instability inherent in pluralist regimes?

Thus the United Nations helped disseminate in many parts of the world views of freedom requiring economic structures, cultural reference systems and institutions which newly independent countries as a rule lacked. Their creation entailed an ideological mobilization which contradicted in many respects the main pre-conditions of democratic freedom, based on the individual. Whereas in Western countries the provision of welfare states tends to compensate for the symptoms of *anomie* generated by the development of industrial civilization, another response to the onset of modernity is provided in newly independent countries by nationalism, which is often associated with religious movements. While the Welfare State is legitimated by the defence of individual freedoms, nationalism or religion assert collective endeavours.

The widening of the international scene, effected by decolonization, highlights its cultural diversity. The secular, rationalist and individualist interpretation of freedom outlined in the Declaration

196

appears to be the standard product of a particular cultural area. Though their influence or their hegemony affect more parts of the world, the myths and the history underlying this outlook remain particularist.

In many cultural systems, freedom does not refer to power or to the attributes and needs of the individual. Instead it is focused on the attributes of the family, the kinship group, the caste or other types of community organization which define social statuses and hierarchies. In some instances, communal values, needs and aspirations, traditionally reproduced over centuries, predominate over everything else. The very concept of the individual is unknown, for the social order does not allow any space for the conceptualization of personal life. Furthermore, authority relationships differ widely from one socio-cultural system to another. As a rule, the democratic type of authority relationships, derived from individualist and egalitarian myths, are not anchored in non-Western socio-cultural traditions. In many African, Asian and Latin American societies, the relation of the individual to authority and the whole range of social hierarchies rest on assumptions other than the liberal model.

In the aftermath of decolonization, it becomes apparent that freedom is differently conceptualized in various cultures or political regimes. Above all, it becomes obvious that the conditions of implementation are construed in the context of economic, social and political circumstances very different from those prevailing in the Western world. Therefore the political model suggested by the United Nations, the type of legitimacy prescribed, the type of social relations and the economic system implied are far from universal. As they expand, the concepts of neo-liberalism rooted in Western history are reinterpreted. They are reshaped to fit cultural codes and historical contexts which are widely different from those in which they originated. The political vocabulary remains the same, the institutional forms similar. Yet the nature of the socio-political phenomena they cover are often almost unrelated to the principles and the structures they are meant to represent. These semantic distortions result in an ideological and political blur which is downright harmful to the defence of freedom. While invoking the rights of peoples, national sovereignty, justice, liberty, and development, the governments of many countries actually impose autocratic arbitrariness. Such systems tend to dominate all aspects of social life.

More than ever, the political order which determines the nature and scope of freedom is now shaped by transnational factors. Throughout the world the main components of peace, of material welfare, of individual and collective autonomy derive from circumstances which transcend the confines of the nation-state. This growing interdependence of societies is most obvious in the fields of security, economy and ecology. It is effected by the irresistible expansion of industrial civilization on a world-wide scale. This process generates a growing homogeneity of material needs and aspirations on the international scale. It also results in the increasing uniformity of the production systems catering for these needs and aspirations. An ever tighter and ever faster network of communications is yet another outcome.

Despite this material development and the growing interdependence it promotes, the institutional foundations of the international community, needed to protect rights and freedoms, are bitterly contested. Yet the elements of a new international order have not emerged clearly; nor has a political programme capable of compensating for the deficiencies of the present system.

In the West, the Welfare State, which has been the great provider of freedom, is increasingly challenged. Its achievements rested on growth and prosperity. It fits in badly with the recession and seems unable to halt unemployment. Its utopian inspiration is on the wane. There is an increasing disenchantment about its social ambitions and about the areas of freedom it endeavoured to offer. After the decline of organized religions, we are witnessing the decay of the belief systems which took over from them. Traditional modes of legitimation seem to have been undermined, while no new "alternative" frames of ideological reference are available. In the advanced capitalist societies, the development of the consumer society contributes no doubt to the decline of ideologies. So does the professionalization of political life generated by the expansion of the Welfare State. These socio-political phenomena may even undermine the myths and symbols on which the hold of ideologies over politics rested. At any rate both myths and symbols have lost some of their power to inspire. More than ever liberty is equated with happiness, i.e. with the right to enjoy the material benefits afforded by modern societies. However, it is no longer conceptualized by reference to its basic relations with politics.

In other regions of international society, national structures have had difficulties taking root. This is partly due to processes of marginalization or social destructuration brought about by the expansion of industrial civilization and by transnational production and consumption patterns. In the Middle East, as well as in several areas of Asia and Africa, violent clashes between ethnic and religious communities challenge the model of the nation-state introduced after decolonization. In many parts of the world, especially in Africa, the state tends to collapse. It is crushed by ethnic conflicts, by the disintegration of modes of production, by social and economic polarization, or by the impact of natural calamities. The governments of the new states tend to owe their legitimacy to national independence in the wake of decolonization rather than to real freedoms conferred on their societies.

Under the guise of normative categories and of political structures borrowed from liberal democracy, new types of legality have emerged which are in fact antagonistic to the principles of democratic legitimacy. The religious dimension of community organization becomes more and more blatant. It is opposed in the main to the secular principles on which the Western concept of freedom is founded.

In international law and organizations, a new trend has emerged which may well challenge some normative and institutional bases of freedom. Admittedly the protection of basic rights and liberties remains a concern in the world. It is backed by a strong body of public opinion and supported by a range of non-governmental organizations with a truly universalist calling. On the other hand, the growing heterogeneity of international society has reduced the coherence and the authority of international law and of the organizations in the United Nations system.

In the 1960s decolonization seemed to favour a democratization of international law. The representatives of newly independent states could from then on participate actively in the elaboration and development of this normative system – a prerequisite for the world order necessary to freedom. However, since the governments established after decolonization have not always been democratic, their participation in the evolution of international law has had no real meaning for protecting freedom. Hardly any agreement exists any more on the sources of international law, on the content of its basic principles, on the interpretation of norms which should regulate international society and on the legal and political requirements deriving from them.

International law has become a hybrid system; it is hardly feasible to identify its regulatory principles. This normative crisis is obvious in the area of human rights and peoples' rights. No consensus prevails on the basic principles regulating them and on the hierarchy of governmental obligations deriving therefrom. The representative of the Islamic Republic of Iran explained recently to the General Assembly that his country accepted no other legal tradition than Islamic law. Thus all conventions, declarations and resolutions incompatible with Islam were invalid, as far as his government was concerned. In particular, he condemned the secular outlook from which the Universal Declaration of Human Rights derived.

This normative crisis is also evidenced by the growing inability of states to agree in some basic spheres of international law. Thus the categories of subjects of international law, the mechanisms for the peaceful settlement of conflicts, the means of implementing the law and the regulation of international economic relations remain undefined.

The Western world may occasionally reiterate its attachment to the principles on which the international system has rested since World War Two and which enshrine its interpretation of freedom. However, it no longer accepts the responsibilities and the sacrifices needed actually to implement such standards on a worldwide scale. In politics, the super-powers, and particularly the United States which seemed most concerned after the Second World War to imbue the principles of international law with authority, adopt attitudes unrelated to these norms. This contradiction is obvious in their relationships with developing countries. The notion of a new economic order based on the principle of international solidarity is clearly on the wane in the Western countries. The values of internationalism seem to be receding everywhere, in favour of local or regional concerns.

It remains possible, of course, to move and to mobilize public opinion in the West for a short spell, by revealing the tragedies which strike other parts of the world. This humanitarian sensibility is accentuated by the individualism prevalent in Western societies. Sporadic help is available for people living in dramatic circumstances which affront elementary ethics and sensitivity. Yet public opinion and governments are not prepared to define a policy of assistance or economic strategies which would effectively challenge economic and political power relations between the countries of the North and those of the South. At any rate, any programmes which would reduce the benefits accruing from existing prosperity in Western societies are rejected. In a similar vein, there is an obvious and widespread increase in the interest accorded to human rights. However, this is not so much a concern for their legal prerequisites or their political, economic and social underpinnings. It focuses rather on a humanitarian message of the individualistic kind. From this vantage point, the fashion of human rights, like the spread of pacifism, corresponds to an illusion, very common in the West, about the end of politics, about a utopian society in which law or "the management of things" would allegedly replace politics altogether. This type of attitude is favourable to a reduction in major political and social confrontations and to the relative peace of the post-war period. But it does not further the understanding of what is at stake in mutual dependence and of the prerequisites for a form of international order. It cannot be dissociated from the conservative trends which prevail in Western societies when they are faced with some structural problems of international relations, e.g. migrations and refugees.

This normative crisis is also experienced within international organizations. Significantly, the General Assembly of the United Nations was unable to agree, during the solemn celebration of the Organization's fortieth anniversary, on a simple declaration reaffirming its member-states' commitment to the principles of the Charter. Yet the text of this reassertion had been prepared over a period of eighteen months. It is evident that the representatives of the states which make up international society can no longer endorse, even formally, the few basic principles which should underpin the utopia of an international community.

The troubles of Unesco are merely a specific expression of a crisis which affects the whole system. It is indicative of the decay in the cultural frame of reference which presided over its creation. If all cultures have the same intrinsic worth, as Unesco states, it is no longer possible to define a few landmarks necessary to the programmes of such an institution. In particular, the criteria of progress or development which are prerequisites for its activities are in jeopardy.

The economic and financial institutions of the Bretton Woods system seem to resist this disintegration of multilateralism. They even seem more capable of constraining the economic and political strategies of the poorer states. However, this growing impact is founded exclusively on sheer economic power. It is linked with transnational economic forces, mainly those of the multinational companies. These are to a great extent beyond the control of states or international institutions. Economic and political power is no longer founded upon an authority derived from an order held to be legitimate. The monetary system has collapsed. The Western powers, and the United States in particular, show hardly any respect for the elementary principles intended to guide the development of an international economic system. The crisis of indebtedness is one of the manifestations of this situation.

No contrast is posited here between an idealized version of the order the Western powers attempted to establish after Second World War and the present disorder in international relations. As has been stated, the neo-liberal design of the United Nations was never fully acknowledged by the Marxist-Leninist states. Nor was it endorsed by the movements and the countries which struggled against Western hegemony to gain political independence, even though their challenges implied a tribute to the order they rejected. It should also be recognized that international society is so hetero-geneous by nature as to tend towards disorder or even anarchy.

However, one might wonder whether contemporary disorders amount to an anarchy which threatens the endurance of the elementary bases on which liberal societies rest. Such unrest in the world of today is evidenced by the increasing economic and social polarization in international society, by conflicts and the refugees they uproot, by unleashed ethnic and religious fanaticism, by an escalating and irrational arms race, by a terrorism which thrives on poverty or oppression and on the disintegration of international norms. There is no freedom in the state of nature. The tragedy of Lebanon illustrates this everlasting truth very aptly. That strife-torn country represents now something bigger than a small society divided by religions, ideologies, ethnic conflicts, and the ambitions of close and distant neighbours. It is the harbinger of a much greater tragedy which threatens an international society losing the institutional foundations of the order necessary to its development and to the preservation of its basic freedoms.

THE FUTURE OF THE PROGRESSIVE CONSENSUS?

THE NATURE OF THE PHILOSOPHY OF
SCIENCES

Freedom, Liberalism
and Subversion

KEITH GRAHAM

You don't have to be a Marxist to believe that ideas often lag behind reality and are dependent on it for further development. Freedom, or liberty, is a case in point. Progressive liberals argue the case for various specific freedoms, pertaining to seat-belt legislation, artistic expression, religious practice, or whatever it might be. They necessarily do so by explicit or implicit reference to a particular *conception* of freedom: a particular definition, a theory showing why liberty as so defined is something to be cherished and valued, and a theory enabling them to move from these relatively abstract thoughts to the kind of concrete arrangements which they sponsor in the name of freedom. Yet that conception, I suggest, is essentially nineteenth-century, a product of the thinking of an era at some considerable distance from our own. So far as the actual underlying philosophical conception of liberty is concerned, calls for a return to Victorian values are unnecessary. We have never left them behind.

Now to describe a piece of theoretical luggage as originating in a given era is not yet to say whether is is acceptable or not. New does not necessarily mean better, nor old worse. On the other hand, conditions of life in the late part of the twentieth century are vastly different from those in the nineteenth, and this may be quite enough to give rise to the suspicion that if the anchor for a cluster of views about contemporary liberties really is a conception from that earlier time, then some new theoretical construction work needs to be undertaken.

In this paper I shall argue that liberals' underlying philosophical conception of liberty suffered from chronic deficiencies at all times, as well as being more obviously inadequate in modern conditions. Moreover, this is a problem which must be taken seriously by

205

liberals. The philosophical underpinning for liberal views on particular issues is not a mere optional extra, an heirloom to be taken down and dusted off on special occasions. Liberals have a special commitment to *arguing* for ideals, rather than imposing them on people, and if there is no initial agreement concerning concrete social arrangements, then it is necessary to trace these concrete commitments back to their source in some more general principles. They need to carry out this work of intellectual justification because there are alternative ways of viewing the world which place some value other than freedom, as conceived by liberalism, at the centre of things. If we tend to forget that there is this need, perhaps it is because we live in the midst of a liberal culture where it is too easy to ask for confirmation of our own under-examined prejudices by like-minded people. In any case, liberals face opposition not just from illiberal forms of society elsewhere in the world but increasingly from within. It is therefore necessary for them to give a philosophical defence of their views.

In the next section I identify the philosophical conception of liberty which underpins so much liberal thought, and indicate its connexion with concrete arrangements. In the third section I point out some of the difficulties facing that conception, both in general and in contemporary conditions. In the fourth section, I consider the political institutions sanctioned by liberalism and indicate their shortcomings. In the final section I place the theoretical issues discussed in the wider context of global politics. Throughout, I emphasise that more far-reaching thinking, and more far-reaching action, is called for to remedy the defects which I hope to identify than anything which would normally be contemplated within a conventional liberal framework of political theory.

We can, in fact, be very precise about identifying the Victorian origins of the liberal conception of liberty. The single most important source is John Stuart Mill's *Essay on Liberty*. In what must be one of the most frequently cited passages in the history of liberal political thought, he asserts that the sole end for which mankind are warranted, individually or collectively, in interfering with the behaviour of one of their number is for self-protection. No such warrant is provided by paternalistic considerations (the conviction that interference against the will of the agent will be for his or her own good) or by what one might term purely moralistic considerations (the conviction that what the agent is doing is morally undesirable even if not actually harmful). This basic idea, that people have a right to be left alone unless they threaten to harm others, has been elaborated in our own century by many theorists, Isaiah Berlin and F.A. Hayek being amongst the most influential both intellectually and politically.

What are the main components in the approach being adopted here? First, the definition of liberty is the negative one which equates liberty precisely with not being interfered with, rather than, say, an alternative definition which might equate liberty with what one has the capacity and opportunity to do. The two definitions are not equivalent, and what liberties someone is taken to have will differ, depending on which definition is used. So, for example, it may be that no one is preventing me from dining at the Ritz, but because of a lack of money I am unable to do so. In that case, I have a liberty according to the liberal, negative definition which I lack according to the alternative definition. This is a consequence which is generally explicitly acknowledged to follow by liberal theorists. The liberty they are concerned with consists in the absence of legal impediments to engaging in given courses of action, and, correspondingly, the presence of legal constraints on others who attempt to obstruct one's engagement in those actions.

Associated with this definition of liberty is a particular image of the nature of the creatures for whom liberty is important. We are seen as autonomous, rational individuals, capable of formulating conceptions of the world we live in and our own principles about what is right and wrong, and capable of acting in accordance with these principles. For such creatures a peculiar appropriateness is felt to attach to extending to them the kind of liberty specified, and a particularly deep kind of insult is implied in cutting across their own plans of life. Being left alone to govern ourselves, except where we choose courses which would obstruct others in governing themselves, is at the heart of the liberal aspiration, and this has its source in properties which we are all thought equally to possess, purely by virtue of being the kind of creatures we are.

What then emerges is the idea that such creatures live their lives in two spheres, as it were. There is the private sphere – not private in the sense of being hidden from other people, but in the sense of being an area where I am not harming others and where I am therefore justified in erecting Keep Out notices, to protect myself from unwelcome interference. And there is the public sphere, where my decisions and actions as an autonomous agent do threaten to impinge on others, and so do threaten harm, and so stand as susceptible to legitimate interference from others in the interests of self-protection.

This general and relatively abstract conception of freedom then explains some of the preoccupations of liberals at a more tangible level of social policy and political arrangement, as well as the interesting blend of publicity and privacy on which they place a premium. The premium placed on publicity is attested to in the laudable insistence on the importance of civil liberties. If we are capable of making our own choices of what sort of life to lead, and if it is important that we should be free to do so (subject to the proviso of not harming others in the process), then it is appropriate that social conditions should be so arranged as to facilitate that process. An essential feature of making rational decisions is that one should be sensitive to suggestions, criticisms, and so on from elsewhere. But then if this is to be achieved, it will be appropriate that there should be a free flow of information, that people should be free to associate together to work for particular ends, or to argue against ends which they see as undesirable. This therefore leads to a natural concern with freedom of speech and assembly, liberty of thought and conscience, and the like. It explains the premium placed on such provisions as those embodied in the First Amendment to the United States Constitution, and on the Freedom of Information Act passed by the US Congress in 1966 and strengthened in 1974.

On the other hand, privacy is valued. In Britain, the decriminalisation of homosexual activity between adults in private is an obvious example, following some years after the influential report of the Wolfenden Committee, which had recommended such a step after taking the conspicuously Millian view that 'there must remain a realm of private morality and immorality which is, in brief and crude terms, not the law's business'. This illustrates that earlier principle I referred to, according to which behaviour which may be thought immoral, but is nevertheless not harmful, merits no uninvited interference. The less successful campaigns in Britain against fluoridation of the public water supply and car seat-belt legislation illustrate the other principle mentioned, that of resistance to paternalistic intervention, and the liberal underpinning available in their support: provisions of this sort may be to our advantage, but it was argued that *imposing* them on mature adults involved a failure to acknowledge their independent status as rational creatures and was for that reason unacceptably insulting to them.

Of course, the route through from abstract philosophical principles to concrete social legislation is a hazardous one. It is often far from obvious what commitments follow from subscription to a liberal stance on freedom, and therefore derivatively it is sometimes unclear whether a disagreement over social legislation reflects differing views on what the liberal stance requires, or on the contrary a confrontation between a liberal and some other stance. In that connexion, we might note the fact that homosexuality in any circumstances continues to be illegal in many US states; that Britain has no Freedom of Information Act, and does have an Official Secrets Act whose second section is particularly draconian with regard to what it allows in the way of a free flow of information; and that opposition to the availability of pornography has brought some sections of feminism into alliance with self-appointed custodians of morality.

The liberal conception of what human beings are like, and what sort of treatment they are entitled to, has much to recommend it. It has served as an important counter to the sort of view which regards individual human beings as just so much expendable material. The fact remains, however, that no modern organised society is run according to the liberal principles described. Massive interference in people's lives, in circumstances where they threaten no direct harm to others, is seen as a perfectly normal occurrence. Much of this interference emanates from the state, a fact to which we shall return.

Now the explanation for this failure of modern society to conform to liberal principles may be that a set of good ideas has simply not been taken up in a systematic way. But the suspicion may arise that this is no accident, that the principles themselves may be flawed in ways which make them unsuitable for adoption in our lives. There is no shortage of possibilities to back up this suspicion. I mention three: the first two are well-recognised, the third is generally not so well-noticed though I believe that in the end it is of considerable importance.

First, take the idea of harm, which is central to liberal principles. There are very simple and straightforward cases which anyone

209

would recognise as involving harm – for example, where physical or material damage is caused to someone. But as we move away from these, matters cease to be so clear-cut. Do I harm someone if I do something which affects them in a way they do not want? Or will that depend on whether what they want is actually good for them? Should we perhaps restrict harm to those cases where we adversely affect someone's *interests*, regardless of what their own actual desires are? Does giving offence to someone count as harming them? That is a particularly important question to raise in connexion with freedom of expression, and in answering it we must take care to ensure that we do not commit ourselves to a principle which gives some results we approve of only to give others we find unacceptable. For example, a liberal might favour race relations legislation which made the giving of offence an infringement of the law, on the grounds that this embodied the principle that causing harm licenses intervention; but the same liberal might not be so happy at the prospect of, say, criminalising the literature of a sexual minority because others were sufficiently sensitive or bigoted to find it offensive. A further difficult question is whether harm necessarily involves positive acts of damage, or whether I can harm someone by *not* doing something. If I do nothing, someone starves: am I then harming them?

Now it may be that all that is required for answering some of these questions is a further elaboration of the liberal position. But the last question, about whether inaction can constitute harm, is especially important, and even if it can be dealt with satisfactorily, it will in a moment bring us to the second general difficulty which we should notice. There is a temptation to say that inaction *can* constitute harm, and if we do so this would certainly provide us with a justification of some of the widespread state intervention in people's lives which I mentioned. Taxes are imposed on me, and I may complain that this is not justified on liberal principles because I am not harming anyone. If it is true that my inaction may constitute harm, then my plea will be based on a falsehood, and a liberal justification for intervention is available. But notice what happens if we take this line. The liberal view rests on the idea that human life can be divided into two spheres: one where we affect other people and one where we do not. But it is difficult to see how this distinction can be maintained if we allow that even my inaction can adversely affect others in a way which deserves to be called harming them. It

210

will then be exceedingly hard for me to justify erecting Keep Out notices in *any* area of my life, because whatever I am doing, it will always be possible to redescribe it as failing to do something which would benefit someone else.

That fact alone may cause a liberal to retract the original concession, and insist that inaction cannot count as harming. But really this case is just a specific instance of a more general point which is not so easily dealt with. The second general difficulty then consists simply in this: human life, above the most trivial actions, is characterised by massive and complex human *inter*action and interpenetration. Even if all I do is sit in a room and scratch my head, it requires tremendously sophisticated coordination amongst large numbers of people before there is any room there for me to sit in: production, marketing and distribution of bricks, timber, metals, plastics, and so on. I depend on their cooperation. If I want to do anything more adventurous, the implication of large numbers of other people in my plans is even more obvious. But in that case, more or less anything I do will involve and affect an indefinite number of other people. This brings with it the possibility of their being *adversely* affected and therefore harmed. And from this it follows that I cannot, in advance, mark out significant areas of my life and say that they affect only myself. The liberal picture has made us all out to be Robinson Crusoes, neglecting to notice the army of Man Fridays on whom we depend and whose lives we affect (and, of course, at other times we may well take on the Man Friday role ourselves in relation to someone else). The liberal's two spheres cannot, after all, be kept distinct.

Beneath this point there is a third. So far, we have looked at some reasons why the conception of autonomous individuals and the circumstances in which they find themselves will need modification. But we have looked only at *individuals* in relation with each other. It is also essential to realise that this does not exhaust the social world. There are also various *collective* bodies, of which individuals are merely constituents. There are, for example, governments, cabinets, committees, housing associations, tenants' rights associations, and the like. In contexts like these, I do not act as an individual; I act precisely as a constituent, a component in something more complex than an individual. This introduces a whole new dimension of complication into the issue of liberty. I have to define my behaviour in relation to collective bodies both from the outside and from the inside, as it were: that is, both when I am a part of such a body and when I am merely affecting or being affected by it, just as I might in relation to another individual. Here, questions of harm will re-surface. Whether or not the harm it is possible to do to a collective body is analogous to that done to individuals, it is certainly possible for such a body to harm *me*.

Now so far, these are points which the liberal conception of liberty needs to take account of in more or less any realistically imaginable circumstances of human life. But they lead on to difficulties which crop up particularly for our own immediate historical location. Take, for example, the issue of freedom of expression, which I have argued is an appropriately central one for liberal theory, given the notion of the autonomous, rational agent with which it works. Even for Mill this was a problematic issue, one on which he found it impossible to sustain a consistent position. On the one hand, he held that if his arguments were correct there ought to exist the fullest liberty to express any doctrine, however immoral it might be considered. On the other hand, he placed a very similar qualification on freedom of expression to that placed on freedom of action: it should cease when it constitutes instigation to some mischievous act. In other words, the criterion of threat of harm to others is re-invoked in this context.

It is instructive to notice the examples Mill uses in support of this. There ought, he suggests, to be freedom to express the opinion that corn-dealers are starvers of the poor, or that property is theft, if this is circulated through the press; but the case changes if that view is expressed orally or handed out in a placard to an angry mob at the house of a corn-dealer. What puts Mill at such a distance from our own circumstances is this. He wrote before the era of mass circulation newspapers and other media of mass communication. Thus he is able to use the newspaper case as a paradigm of innocuous communication, and the addressing of a crowd as the paradigm of potential harm.

Today this could be very nearly reversed. Face-to-face communication under the elements has long since ceased to be the main channel of propaganda for any political organisation well-supported or well-funded enough to come in out of the rain, and placards would now be handed out to people who had already been subjected to an enormous volume of communication, and a compli-

cated process of conditioning, via daily newspapers and omni-
present television and radio channels which reach into their
dwellings in a way in which nothing did in Victorian England. Under
the race relations legislation in Britain which curtails freedom of
expression the total number of prosecutions has been relatively
small, but such prosecutions as there have been have predominantly
concerned newspapers or similar types of publication. And if Mill
wanted a contemporary example of potential harm resulting from
expression, he might do worse than cite such activities as those of the
Sun newspaper, read by millions of people every day, which in
January 1986 carried a headline referring to an "Arab pig". When
the Press Council ruled that this was intemperate, abusive and
insulting (though not, curiously, racist), the newspaper carried a
cartoon suggesting that pigs would object to being called Arabs.

My point here is not just that circumstances are now vastly
different, important though that is. It is that they are different in a
way which reflects on the liberal theoretical position. For instance,
it might be said that what has changed since Mill's day is that there
are now immensely powerful and influential press barons like
Rupert Murdoch, who are in a much more powerful position than
anyone ever was who handed out placards. This is true, of course,
and no doubt a cause for concern. But it misses the deeper point.
Murdoch does not write, set, print and deliver the *Sun*. He is
dependent on a vast, complicated organisation to do that. Hence, if
we want a proper causal understanding of a process which has a
result we may find undesirable, then we must recognise the role of a
collective, corporate body in producing it before we move on to any
condemnation or remedy. We have to move away from a simple
personalising of the issue which is encouraged by the individualism
of the liberal position.

Compare the distance between Mill's time and our own when it
comes to the question of the state. The state of the late twentieth
century reaches into every corner of our lives. It has a decisive
influence in such matters as how and where we are born, what sort of
houses we live in and what we may do to them, how we educate our
children, what sort of medical treatment we receive and how we are
disposed of when dead. And where there is influence, there
necessarily comes with it the possibility of harm. Mill pays no
particular attention to this potential source of threat: he talks of his

theory as governing the relations between the individual and "society", but he had no theory of the state as such because in the nineteenth century there was far less of a state to have a theory of.

But there is also a second omission in his theory. He offers a criterion for determining when intervention in people's lives is justified. If this is to govern actual social dealings, however, the further question must be answered *who is to decide* that the criterion has been met. What agency actually applies the theory? In our own day it is the state once again which is a major factor here in deciding where intervention in social dealings is appropriate (though whether it does so by reference to the simple criterion of harm is far less obvious). It was, for example, the state which, via the office of the Director of Public Prosecutions, decided that no intervention was called for in the case of the *Sun* cartoon mentioned above; and it was the state which, via the office of the Attorney-General, forbade a private prosecution of the newspaper under the 1936 Public Order Act. Generally speaking, we may say that the government of the day and the various arms of the legal process will be highly influential in the matter. Once again, we are in effect talking about relatively complicated corporate bodies, and the image of one human being crossing the path of another is an inadequate and potentially misleading one for enhancing our understanding of actual social intercourse.

In this section I have made a number of points about the liberal conception of liberty in general and also in the context of our own historical situation. Some of these points will be familiar. It is worth making them not simply in order to show that that conception has its own problems, but also to bring home the fact that our thinking is not completed merely by calling attention to these weaknesses. Something then has to be done about them: we have to elaborate an improved conception of liberty or replace it with something different altogether. That is not a job to be accomplished in one paragraph, or indeed one paper. But by way of general indication, I should suggest that we need a conception which, if such a thing is possible, preserves the moral importance of the individual whilst taking into account the complications to do with human interaction and collective bodies which I have mentioned. It would depart from the liberal conception in rejecting the equation of freedom with being left alone, since it would recognise the extent to which the positive efforts of others can make a difference to the repertoire of activities open to a rational agent; it would also depart from it in stressing the need for substantial provision rather than merely legal or formal means to the achievement of ends, if what is to be valued is a rational agent's actually acting in certain ways. In short, it would be a great deal more sensitive to the various complexities of the total social context in which rational agents find themselves than the liberal conception. It would be in important respects a post-liberal conception of freedom. How far the construction of such a conception is a prerequisite of any justifiable challenge to the concrete institutions of liberal society is a question now to be touched on.

At this stage liberals might object that they do not fail to take account of the considerations I have called attention to. On the contrary, they might say, they do pay heed to the existence of the state. The history of liberalism in practice, it might be argued, is precisely the history of attempts to preserve the domain of the individual to the greatest possible extent against the encroachments of collective bodies, and to engage in the delicate task of carefully delineating the legitimate relations which may obtain between individual and state. What, after all, are those reforming measures earlier mentioned if not that?

Notice the practical political context in which these reforming efforts take place. At the heart of our system is parliamentary democracy: the periodical election of a government in circumstances in which groups of individuals are legally entitled to form political parties, for the purpose of attempting to win sufficient of the popular vote to gain access to political power for a limited period. What candidates compete against each other for is a position of vastly greater legislative control than those who elect them. Even within the privileged group of elected representatives, the degree of control which this position confers will vary widely, from that of a backbench opposition MP to that of a government minister. Power at the latter end of the spectrum may be very concentrated indeed: the increased use of the device of statutory instruments in contemporary government illustrates how the power to legislate may be acquired in a way which may even obviate the need for parliamentary debate or proper public knowledge.

No doubt a host of factors will operate to temper the power differentials implicit in this system. Ministers will have to take cognisance of their backbenchers, and all MPs will have to take cognisance of public opinion, because their lease of power is temporary and conditional on renewed support. Arguably, too, it makes a difference to the evaluation of a system of this kind if the voters themselves accept it as legitimate (because they cannot then themselves complain about the unequal power distribution). But none of this will gainsay the result which is integral to this system: it is of its nature to distribute political power in a drastically unequal way. (I speak, of course, of the official constitutional arrangement. If it is said that real political power rests with the civil service, or the IMF, or some other agency not directly accountable to the electorate, the same conclusion will still follow.)

The parliamentary system has many merits, but this ought not to blind us to the degree of antipathy which exists towards it. The idea and the practice of "extra-parliamentary opposition" have become increasingly familiar in the last twenty years, with acts of terrorism as their most repugnant manifestation. Where there is not hostility to parliamentary democracy there is often apathy. In contemporary Britain something of the order of one person in four fails to engage in the act of voting in public elections, the most obvious and minimal engagement required in this system. It is a matter for speculation how far this betokens apathy and how far active hostility, but it certainly ought not to be taken as a sign of contentment. If disaffection on this scale is to be understood, then the deficiencies in the system which evokes it must themselves be understood, and in achieving that task we might do worse than notice the relatively small degree of political control which remains with average citizens in this system, the extent to which decisions which may have major consequences for the way they live their lives are taken without their active participation. That seems a relatively poor concrete realisation of the abstract conception of equal autonomous agents being free to pursue their rationally chosen goals without interference.

There is one particular aspect of the liberal democratic state, itself productive of further inequalities as between autonomous rational agents, which is worth commenting on. The parliamentary system protects itself from attack, as does the wider society which has given rise to it, and to that end it employs a network of coercive forces whose members again stand in vastly superior power relations to those whom they police. The role of surveillance policing in the political sphere is of particular interest, and much has been written about the "chilling effect", the process whereby citizens are deterred from exercising perfectly legal freedoms for fear of interference from state officials. The official role of the Special Branch in Britain is interesting in this connexion. According to the "Home Office Guidelines on the Work of a Special Branch", issued in December 1984, the role of such a branch is to gather information about threats to public order from persons or organisations which may be judged to be subversive to the state, so as to help determine an appropriate level of policing. Subversive activities are defined as those which are intended to undermine or overthrow parliamentary democracy "by political, industrial or violent means".

The juxtaposition of the trio of means – *political*, industrial or violent – is interesting. Violence is incontestably a morally objectionable means (though it is a much more extreme view to take that violence is *never* justifiable); and perhaps industrial means are thought in some way inappropriate for achieving political goals. But why should *political* means be similarly stigmatised as a way of achieving a political goal? It might be replied that what is envisaged here is not just any old political goal, that stigma attaches properly speaking because of the end in view, the overthrow of the parliamentary system. But there is something tendentious in talk of "undermining" or "overthrowing" here. There may be wholly negative and destructive political acts which have nothing more than this as their objective, but there may well be others which have as their objective the replacement of the parliamentary system by political forms thought by the agents in question to be an improvement. Why should the project of attempting to replace that system, by means which are not of themselves objectionable, stand in any bad odour at all?

A liberal might make two different replies to the question: hard-nosed or soft-nosed. The hard-nosed reply would be that what is in question is the cornerstone of liberal society, the very institution which allows citizens the measure of freedom which they have, so that niceties about civil liberties or respect for autonomous agents cannot be allowed as an excuse for failing to protect it against those who would seek to attack and destroy it. The soft-nosed reply would be more concessive. It would emphasise the need for "checks and balances" in the operation of such sensitive agencies as the Special Branch, and the accountability of coercive forces.

Both replies contain something of the truth, though the hard-nosed reply is, in my view, preferable for its more robust realism and

217

awareness of the point at issue. Obviously there can be variations in the degree of freedom which citizens have from the interference and attention of agents of the state in a liberal parliamentary democracy. Adjustments will be possible in settling the appropriate degree and ensuring that it is observed, and it is the strength of the soft-nosed reply to emphasise that. But the adjustments must vary within the limits set by the nature of that system itself. As we saw earlier, no theory about justified intervention in people's lives is complete until it has specified not only what criteria are to be applied to indicate where intervention is justified, but also who is to apply them. The unambiguous answer which modern liberal theory returns to that question is that it is the state and its various agencies which are to have that role. In the circumstances, it is hardly surprising if those who compose those agencies place highest priority on deflecting threats to the agencies themselves, for without them there would be no enforcement of the theoretically postulated criteria for social regulation. Calling individuals to account who have a place in the collective agencies deputed to protect against possible harm may be of importance, but it cannot alter that basic arrangement. (And at its worst it can misleadingly suggest that interference simply results from those individuals overstepping the mark or manifesting a bad character, rather than for the more deeply-rooted structural reasons.)

But if the soft-nosed view fails to appreciate the force of these facts, it does not follow that the hard-nosed view is in the end acceptable. Rather, it emphasises the fact that the acceptability of liberal political institutions becomes problematic by the standards of liberalism itself. The maintenance of a particular system is justified on the grounds that it is necessary for the promotion of liberal principles. But that maintenance may lead unavoidably to incursions into some individuals' lives in ways which fail to accord them a status, as independent autonomous agents, which it is the business of liberal institutions to protect; and it certainly must lead to grossly unequal treatment of different individuals, since there are no entities other than individuals to form the agencies which protect the system.

An alternative to both the hard-nosed and the soft-nosed view would be the fatalist view: that in modern conditions there is no alternative (or no desirable alternative) to the existing parliamentary system, so that there is no good reason to tolerate incur-

218

sions against it by whatever means. One major bad reason for reaching this conclusion will be examined in the final section; in the meantime, there are independent reasons for disputing it. The developments of modern technology have made the dissemination of ideas over a widespread and numerous population much simpler; provided the opportunity for participation in decision-making at a distance; and also brought with them the possibility of reducing working hours markedly, so that proportionately greater time could be devoted to civic affairs. Whether this technology will in fact be used in these beneficial ways is another matter, of course, and it would take very wide, concomitant changes in our social structure before it could do so. But it is one enabling condition, as it were, of a very different set of political institutions, and it would be wholly unimaginative not to notice that it could be called in aid for many different possible relations between representatives, as defined in our present system, and electors. There are many intermediate stages between the total involvement of every citizen in every political decision, which really is impossible in modern society, and the very large degree of freedom from accountability enjoyed by representatives which is inseparable from the present system.

The upshot is that unless we believe that that system is some kind of culmination, impossible to improve on, it is not clear why the project of attempting to replace it, by means which are not of themselves objectionable, should suffer the degree of condemnation which it standardly does.

Finally, we must place liberal political institutions and their underpinning theory in the global context. For most of the twentieth century the main visible alternatives to the various forms of liberal parliamentary democracy have been one-party dictatorships of the Eastern European variety (with occasional phases of fascist dictatorship offering an even less appealing prospect). It seems to me unquestionable that liberal systems are vastly preferable to these, and none of the criticisms made of liberal theory and practice in this paper should be taken to indicate otherwise. In a world where the available alternative is brutal and oppressive regimes, openly committed to crushing any opposition, it has been relatively easy for liberalism to retain its plausibility. Moreover, in those concrete respects in which I have suggested liberalism is deficient – the widely diverging degrees of political freedom which it assigns to differently-

219

placed citizens – it has been especially impervious to criticism. For in those respects it and its main rival coincide. Whatever may be the differences between them, they both endorse the concentration of effective political power in relatively few hands. And where systems which are in other respects so different agree in some fundamental feature like this, it is very easy to conclude that that fundamental feature is inescapable, that this is a matter in which there are no other options.

In effect, what I have argued is that we ought not to be restricted by the implicit standard of comparison in use here. The system of concrete institutions ought not to be judged solely by reference to actually existing alternatives (though that is one relevant and important standard of comparison). There is also a set of underlying principles to which the institutions may or may not conform. Judged by those considerations, liberalism does not fare so well.

Imagine now two contrasting reactions to this suggestion. It might be objected that people's attention can be caught only by tangible, concrete alternatives to what they are surrounded by, so that abstract criticisms of liberalism must remain relatively ineffective. On the other hand, it might be objected that people may if anything be too impressed by mere abstract possibilities, and that this may encourage unthinking attacks on existing institutions which, with all their imperfections, have much to recommend them; and the consequence may then be that in the resulting vacuum something infinitely worse is brought into being by people of good will who do not have a sufficiently clear idea of what they want. This may give rise to the suspicion that we are caught in a kind of vicious circle here. Either we cannot escape from the limitations of a liberal system, or else we cannot escape to anything better.

There is some validity, it seems to me, in each of these reactions. I am not in a position – no one is – to point to or even give a general specification of a whole set of institutions, distinct from those of liberal parliamentary democracy, which are a better realisation of the liberal ideal in so far as that ideal is defensible, or a realisation of a different ideal in so far as it is not. And there is no doubt that unbridled attacks on that system in present circumstances are disastrous. But the vicious circle is not quite complete. It might be possible, in circumscribed areas, to *exemplify* relations qualitatively different from those afforded in the liberal institutions of society at large, and in such a way as to engage people's attention.

The most obvious and salient arena for such exemplification is that of a political movement itself. It might aspire to the introduction of new political structures and institutions into the wider society, with very different relations between rulers and ruled from those currently visible. It might then explore relevant alternative possibilities in its own internal organisation. We are already aware of a whole range of options here from our knowledge of committees. A committee may be appointed by a larger body to discharge tasks not convenient for the larger body itself. The committee may be given *carte blanche*, or general instructions, or a set of definitive options to choose from; the larger body may review the committee's decisions and retain the power to reverse or nullify them; and it may operate sanctions of varying degrees of severity, including dismissal, against a committee whose decisions it disapproves of. This already indicates that there is an entire range of theoretical possibilities between the total involvement of every person in every decision, on the one hand, which is as impossible for a political movement as for a large-scale modern society, and the degree of licence which characterises the role of representatives in contemporary liberal systems, on the other.

A political movement with the unconventional aim of challenging liberal institutions could then attempt to run its own affairs in accordance with principles lying somewhere in this range. It could serve as a model for illustrating possibilities of ordinary human beings exerting an influence over matters of concern to them, without having to rely on others to take on vastly superior positions of power, and it could foster in microcosm practices which would become infinitely more valuable if introduced into the wider society. Or at least it could try to do so. If it failed, then little damage would be done in the meantime to the wider political fabric. But if it succeeded, then this is one way in which practice might run ahead of theory, and the result might be a conception, and eventually a social system, which combined the appropriate form of respect for individual freedom with an appropriate recognition of individuals' place as constituents in overall collectives.

To make a suggestion of this kind, however, is to call for a political tradition which does not exist. Conventional political parties, by their nature, do not challenge the system in which they compete for power. Other political movements, largely influenced by Leninist theory and practice, challenge it by means of a pernicious doctrine

221

which sanctions a self-appointed vanguard to act on behalf of others, without any evidence of a popular mandate. Both types of political organisation reflect, in their own internal organisation, the wider political values which they subscribe to. An alternative tradition to both of these would have to be *created*, and it would certainly not come into being without conscious efforts to create it, any more than the political system that it might prefigure, which afforded ordinary citizens appreciably greater involvement in political decision-making than the parliamentary system. But that, at any rate, is the direction in which we might choose to persuade our fellow human beings to head. Unfortunately, in doing so we run the risk of becoming subversives according to the official criteria of our liberal society.

Notes on Contributors

John Alderson, CBE, QPM, LL.D, D.Litt, Barrister at Law. Visiting Professor of Police Studies, the University of Strathclyde; formerly Chief Constable of Devon and Cornwall.

Bernard Crick is Professor Emeritus of Politics of Birkbeck College, London, author of the best selling *In Defence of Politics* and *George Orwell: A Life*. He has recently written *Socialism* (Open University Press) and a pamphlet with David Blunkett, MP, *The Labour Party's Aims and Values: an unofficial statement* (Spokesman). He lives in Scotland and is chairman of the *Political Quarterly*.

James Ferman has been Director of the British Board of Film Classification since 1975, prior to which he was for 17 years a television director.

Larry Gostin is Executive Director, American Society of Law & Medicine; Associate Director, Harvard University/World Health Organization Collaborative Centre on Health Legislation. He has written the standard text on mental health law, *Mental Health Services: Law and Practice* (Shaw & Sons). He has also edited *Civil Liberties in Conflict* (Routledge).

Keith Graham was born in Smethwick and educated at the Universities of London and Oxford. He now teaches philosophy at the University of Bristol. He has published widely in the philosophy of language and social and political theory. His most recent book, *The Battle of Democracy*, was published by Wheatsheaf Press in the UK and Barnes & Noble in the USA. He is currently working on a book about Marx.

Nicola Lacey is Fellow and Tutor in Law at New College, Oxford, where she teaches Criminal Law and Justice, Legal Theory and Public Law. She was formerly Lecturer in Law at University

College, London. She is the author of a forthcoming book, *State Punishment: Political Principles and Community Values*, and has published several articles on criminal justice and constitutional theory.

Sir Norman Lindop was Chairman of the Home Office Data Protection Committee, whose Report formed the basis for the discussions which led eventually to the 1984 Data Protection Act. He was at the time Director of Hatfield Polytechnic, an institution which he led from 1966 until 1982, when he became Principal of the British School of Osteopathy. A chemist by profession, he has held posts in industry, the civil service and a number of institutions of higher education.

Ursula Mittwoch is Professor of Genetics at University College London. Her publications include *Sex Chromosomes* (1967) and *Genetics of Sex Differentiation* (1973).

Professor The Lord Peston is Professor of Economics, Queen Mary College, University of London. He is the author of numerous works on economics, economic policy, and education.

Rosemary Righter is a foreign leader writer on *The Times*, and formerly Diplomatic and Development Correspondent of *The Sunday Times* and assistant editor of *The Far Eastern Economic Review*. He books include a history of the International Press Institute, *The Undivided Word* (1976) and *Whose News? Politics, the Press and the Third World* (1978). She is completing a book on the United Nations for publication in 1989.

Pierre de Senarclens is professor of International Relations at the University of Lausanne. He was Director of the Division of Human Rights and Peace at Unesco from 1980 to 1983. He is author of *Le mouvement "Esprit" 1932–41. Essai critique*, L'Age d'homme, 1974; *L'impérialisme*, PUF, 1980; *Yalta*, PUF, 1984; *La crise des Nations Unies*, PUF, 1988.